Constituting Communities

Constituting Communities

Political Solutions to Cultural Conflict

Edited by

Per Mouritsen
Associate Professor of Political Science
University of Aarhus, Denmark

and

Knud Erik Jørgensen
Professor of European Integration
University of Aarhus, Denmark

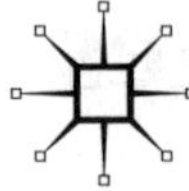

Editorial matter, selection and preface © Per Mouritsen and Knud Erik Jørgensen 2008 All other chapters © the respective authors 2008

All rights reserved. No reproduction, copy or transmission of this publication may be made without written permission.

No paragraph of this publication may be reproduced, copied or transmitted save with written permission or in accordance with the provisions of the Copyright, Designs and Patents Act 1988, or under the terms of any licence permitting limited copying issued by the Copyright Licensing Agency, 90 Tottenham Court Road, London W1T 4LP.

Any person who does any unauthorised act in relation to this publication may be liable to criminal prosecution and civil claims for damages.

The authors have asserted their rights to be identified as the authors of this work in accordance with the Copyright, Designs and Patents Act 1988.

First published 2008 by
PALGRAVE MACMILLAN
Houndmills, Basingstoke, Hampshire RG21 6XS and
175 Fifth Avenue, New York, N.Y. 10010
Companies and representatives throughout the world

PALGRAVE MACMILLAN is the global academic imprint of the Palgrave Macmillan division of St. Martin's Press, LLC and of Palgrave Macmillan Ltd. Macmillan® is a registered trademark in the United States, United Kingdom and other countries. Palgrave is a registered trademark in the European Union and other countries.

ISBN-13: 978–1–4039–9743–2   hardback
ISBN-10: 1–4039–9743–8   hardback

This book is printed on paper suitable for recycling and made from fully managed and sustained forest sources.

A catalogue record for this book is available from the British Library.

Library of Congress Cataloging-in-Publication Data

Constituting communities : political solutions to cultural conflict /
    edited by Per Mouritsen and Knud Erik Jørgensen.
        p. cm.
    Includes bibliographical references and index.
    ISBN 1–4039–9743–8 (alk. paper)
    1. Minorities—Europe.   2. Muslims—Europe.   3. Minorities—Canada.
    4. Civil society—Europe.   5. Nationalism—Europe.   6.
    Citizenship—Europe.   7. Europe—Ethnic relations—Political
    aspects.   8. Culture conflict—Political aspects—Europe.   I.
    Mouritsen, Per.   II. Jørgensen, Knud Erik.
    JC312.C68 2008
    323.14—dc22

2007052971

10   9   8   7   6   5   4   3   2   1
17   16   15   14   13   12   11   10   09   08

Printed and bound in Great Britain by
CPI Antony Rowe, Chippenham and Eastbourne

Contents

Acknowledgements

The original impetus to this volume came from an interdisciplinary research project, *Communities and the Meeting of Culture*, which was financed by the Danish research councils for the humanities and social sciences in 2000–3, and a series of international conferences, jointly organized with the Danish Network of Political Theory, in 2003–4, also financed by these bodies. The editors would like to express their gratitude for this financial support on behalf of the research group.

Chapter 8, by Bellamy and Castiglione, is a revised and extended version of an article, 'Per la storia del pensiero gioridico moderno', originally published in *Quaderni Fiorentini* 31(1): 349–80, 2002. We thank the editor for allowing us to use the material.

Thanks are also due to Ulla Veronica Willner and Annette B. Andersen for their expert secretarial assistance in preparing the manuscript and of course to Gemma d'Arcy Hughes and Alison Howson at Palgrave Macmillan.

Preface

It has long been commonplace in political theory as well as public debate that the challenge of cultural diversity should be solved by political means. 'Political' here denotes a bewildering variety of ways of transcending, dissolving, accommodating, laundering – or controlling – culture. Most of the time, however, it involves some form of understanding that the way we constitute modern communities, where people of different creeds and ethnic origins live together, cannot be old-style assimilation into or dominance by a complacently self-perpetuating *Kulturnation*. It must somehow be thinner, more liberal, more formal and more civic. And the dealings of its inhabitants correspondingly must be those of citizens, rather than ethnic blood brethren, co-believers or sharers of cultural heritage. However, that culture calls for politics is only the beginning of a discussion, which must address the essential contestability, not only of culture and cultural pluralism, but also of the very distinction between culture and politics. In particular, it must ponder the forms of politicizations of culture that come with the distinction itself.

Some academic literature and much public commentary represent cultures as neatly compartmentalized groups and immutable portable identities. Often such conceptions, trading on a variety of ancient dichotomies, mirror equally neat notions of a sphere of politics, which is seen as peculiarly autonomous, detached, neutral and indeed cleansed of culture. In the realm of culture lives are led, needs are met and belongings are experienced, while politics lies elsewhere. But this does not sit well with the real world's controversies over the very representation of what is cultural and political, which abound in discussions about secularism and religion, in distinctions between 'culture' as such and 'political culture', in contrasts between 'our culture and their culture', in fierce debates over which forms of particularity are too conspicuous, immature or unreasonable to be represented, let alone accommodated, in a public realm, and in notions of more or less thin and universalistic conceptions of citizenship practice and (constitutional) patriotism as opposed to nationally particular traditions. In and through these representations we construct anew the parameters of inside and outside in political communities.

Depending on these problem framings, the meeting and mediation of cultures becomes conceptualized differently – and real or imagined cultural conflicts do so too. The idea of this book is to focus on different ideas, to be found in theoretical discourse as well as political-administrative practice, of insisting or implying that these different problems of cultural pluralism and conceptualizations of cultural conflict can only be adequately addressed through a variety of political means. The latter, here, may refer to political institutions, spheres, modes of interaction, roles, languages of justification or emotive/identitary frames of belonging. Political solutions imply transcending culture, taking out of culture, negotiating culture, domesticating culture – or creating security against culture. It implies formality, universalism, incomprehensiveness, thinness, mediation, differentiation, but also administrative processes, legalization and control.

While the flavours of political solutions to cultural conflicts vary inside diverse vocabularies of modern political cosmology, cultural pluralism poses two main challenges to democratic states. *Legitimacy* concerns the lack of fair accommodation of what liberal philosophers call reasonable pluralism – the fact that the practices, values and forms of life directly or indirectly supported by almost any state are those of ethnic majorities. Or, to some authors, it concerns the possible right of states to be partial to the needs and wishes of these majorities as bearers of authentic, original national identities. However, this book is mainly concerned with such issues as they pertain to the second problem, of *political integration*, i.e. of facilitating unity, solidarity and the willingness to share the burdens of taxpayers and citizens with specific groups of compatriots, inside certain territorial boundaries, and affirming some form of allegiance to, or identification with, a state and community. Are certain forms of culture positively detrimental to such integration and solidarity? To what extent must political communities be perceived as culture-neutral to command the allegiance of citizens? Does political integration in fact require the maintenance or creation of a specific national identity? Is the solution instead some form of *political* culture beyond the formal and legal community of equal rights? And to what extent is such a political culture – and the values, practices and perhaps common memories it contains – itself necessarily 'particular'? Through which means may one or the other common culture be legitimately created? Finally, could it be that political integration first of all presupposes the accommodation of cultural diversity through forms of multicultural recognition, differentiated citizenship or associational pluralism, and what could this mean in a supranational context? Or could such measures spell the death of a common political community?

This dual problematic is aggravated in familiar ways by developments which challenge Ernest Gelner's well-known idea of national homogenization as a functional necessity of modern, differentiated states. First, globalization challenges otherwise comfortable, monocultural national hegemonies; and growing migrant populations across the world are increasingly unsusceptible to the heavy-handed assimilation processes of the past as a price for equal citizenship. Secondly, whereas states used to be the sole containers and mediators of pluralism, European integration has introduced a new level where states become players trying to advance their (national) cultures inside an emerging new polity, inside which, moreover, the very nature of political solutions to cultural diversity are part of the conflicts between constituent and constituting states which make up the 'ever closer union'. That Europe is not *only* a higher federal level, but also a complex reality of conflicting, multilevel and overlapping spheres of jurisdiction only adds further controversy to what political solutions to cultural difference could possibly imply, in terms of identities, political culture, citizenship roles, constitutional content and forms of democratic governance.

This book, written by political theorists, sociologists, political scientists and scholars of migration studies and international relations, examines these and other challenges related to political responses to cultural diversity.

Notes on the Contributors

Ricard Zapata Barrero is an Associate Professor of Political Science at the University Pompeu Fabra, Barcelona. His main lines of research deal with contemporary problems of liberal democracy in contexts of cultural diversity, especially the relationship between democracy, citizenship and immigration. His selected works include: *Multiculturalidad e immigración* (ed. Síntesis, 2004), *Multiculturalism, Muslims and Citizenship: A European Approach* (Routledge, 2006) (co-edited with T. Modood and A. Triandafyllidou), (ed.) *Conceptos Políticos en el contexto español* (ed. Síntesis, 2007), (ed.) *Immigració i autogovern* (ed. Proa, 2007), (eds.) *Discursos sobre la immigración en España* (Ediciones Cidob, 2007, co-edited with T. Van Dijk), *Fundamentos de los discursos políticos sobre la immigración* (forthcoming, 2008). He is currently working on different lines of research: the link between two types of cultural pluralisms: immigration and national minorities, the political theory of borders, the regional Euro-mediterranean politics of immigration, the political discourses on immigration.

Richard Bellamy is a Professor of Political Science at University College, London. He was Academic Director of the European Consortium for Political Research from 2002 to 2006. His research covers European social and political theory since 1750, particularly in relation to citizenship, constitutionalism, democracy and liberalism. He has published extensively and directed many research projects in the field of normative European Union studies. His books include *Making European Citizens* (with D. Castiglione and J. Shaw) (Palgrave, 2006), *Liberalism and Pluralism* (Routledge, 1999), and *Lineages of European Citizenship: Rights, Belonging and Participation in Eleven Nation States* (with D. Castiglione and E. Santoro) (Palgrave 2004).

Dario Castiglione is a Reader in Political Theory at University of Exeter. His main research interests are the history of political thought, theories of democracy and civil society, and European constitutionalism. His recent publications comprise co-edited volumes: *Making European Citizens* (with R. Bellamy and J. Shaw) (Palgrave, 2006), *The Language Question in Europe and Diverse Societies* (with C. Longman) (Hart, 2007); and *Constitutional Politics in the EU* (with J. Shonlau, E. Lombardo, M. Aziz, C. Longman, Perez-Zolorzano) (Palgrave, 2007).

Tine Damsholt is an Associate Professor of Ethnology at the University of Copenhagen. Her primary research areas are political cultures, nationalism and patriotism in modern Europe. She is currently working on citizenship ceremonies in Western countries. She is author of *Fædrelandskærlighed og borgerdyd* [Patriotism and Civic Virtue] (Tusculanum Press, 2000), and a forthcoming monograph entitled *Doing Citizenship – Citizenship Ceremonies between the Sacred and the Secular*.

Bülent Diken is a senior lecturer in the Department of Sociology, Lancaster University. He has published extensively in social theory. His books include *Strangers, Ambivalence and Social Theory* (Ashgate, 1998), *The Culture of Exception – Sociology Facing the Camp* (with C. B. Laustsen) (Routledge, 2005) and *Sociology Through the Projector* (Routledge, 2007).

Klaus Eder is Professor of Comparative Macro-sociology at Humboldt University, Berlin. He has written numerous articles on sociological theory, the public sphere, symbolic power, citizenship and social movements. He recently co-edited *Collective Memory and European Identity. The Effects of Integration and Enlargement* (with W. Spohn) (Ashgate, 2005) and *European Citizenship between National Legacies and Postnational Projects* (with B. Giesen) (Oxford University Press, 2001). He is co-author of *Collective Identities in Action. A Sociological Approach to Ethnicity* (with B. Giesen, O. Schmidtke and D. Tambini) (Ashgate, 2001).

John Erik Fossum is a Professor of Political Science at the ARENA Centre for European Studies and Adjunct Professor at the University of Bergen. He is co-architect and substitute coordinator of the EU 6th framework programme RECON, co-edits the Routledge Series on Democratising Europe and has published widely on the EU and Canada within the areas of deliberative democracy, constitutionalism, identity and citizenship.

Jan Ifversen is an Associate Professor of History at the Department of European Studies, University of Aarhus. His research comprises political theory, culture theory and conceptual history. His publications include 'Europe and European Culture: A Conceptual Analysis' (in *European Societies*, 2004) and 'The Crisis of European Civilization: an Inter-war Diagnosis' (in *Globalization and Civilizations*, ed. M. Mozzafari, Routledge, 2002).

Knud Erik Jørgensen is Jean Monnet Professor and Professor of European Integration at the University of Aarhus. His research field is international – especially European – relations, on which he has published many articles and book chapters. He chairs the ECPR Standing Group of the European Union. Recently he edited the *Handbook of European Union*

Politics (with M. Pollack and B. Rosamond) (Sage Publications, 2007) and *International Relations in Europe* (with T. B. Knudsen) (Routledge, 2006).

Carsten Bagge Laustsen is an Associate Professor of Political Science, University of Aarhus. His research is in religion and security, terrorism, social theory and political theory. Recent publications include *The Culture of Exception. Sociology Facing the Camp* (Routledge, 2005) and *Sociology through the Projector* (Routledge, 2007) (both with Bülent Diken).

John W. Maynor is an Assistant Professor of Political Science at Middle Tennessee State University. His field of research is contemporary political philosophy and the history of political thought, especially civic republican theory. He is the author of *Republicanism in the Modern World* (Polity Press, Cambridge, 2003) and editor of a forthcoming book on Phillip Pettit's work, *Republicanism and Political Theory* (with C. Laborde) (Blackwell).

Per Mouritsen is director of the Centre for University Studies in Journalism and Associate Professor of Political Science at the University of Aarhus. His research interests are political theory, migration studies and the history of ideas. He is partner in the EU 6th framework programme, EMILE. His work includes 'What's the Civil in Civil Society? Robert Putnam, Italy, and the Republican Tradition' (*Political Studies,* 2003), 'Four Models of Republican Liberty and Self-Government' (in I. Honohan and J. Jennings, *Republican Theory, Republican Practice,* Routledge, 2004) and 'The Particular Universalism of a Nordic Welfare State (in T. Modood et al., *European Challenges to Multicultural Citizenship: A Contextual Approach,* Routledge, 2006).

Ephraim Nimni is Reader at the School of Politics, International Studies and Philosophy at Queen's University, Belfast. His research interests are comparative ethnic conflicts, theories of nationalism and minority rights, and multiculturalism with particular reference to models of national self-determination without separate nation states. He is author of *Multicultural Nationalism* (Routledge, 2008), *National-Cultural Autonomy and its Contemporary Critics,* an edited volume on the work of Karl Renner (Routledge, 2005), and editor of the English translation of Otto Bauer, *The Question of Nationalities and Social Democracy* (University of Minnesota Press, 2001).

Islam Qasem is a Doctoral Candidate of Political and Social Science at the University Pompeu Fabra, Barcelona. He holds an Advanced Degree in Political Science from UPF and a Master's Degree in International Affairs from Columbia University, New York.

Ole Wæver is a Professor of International Relations at the Department of Political Science, University of Copenhagen. His research field is international relations, theories of security and conceptual history. His recent work includes *European Integration and National Identity: The Challenge of the Nordic States* (with L. Hansen) (Routledge, 2001), *Regions and Powers: The Structure of International Security* (with B. Buzan) (Palgrave, 2003), and 'In Defence of Religion: Sacred Referent Objects for Securitization' (with C. B. Laustsen) (*Millennium*, 2000).

1
Political Responses to Cultural Conflict: Reflections on the Ambiguities of the Civic Turn

Per Mouritsen

When, on 30 September 2005, *Jyllands-Posten* published a series of cartoons depicting the Prophet Mohammed it did so in the name of freedom of expression. Muslims and other religious groups, the editors claimed, had to accept that any religious symbol could be the object of satire and ridicule and that such irreverence of religion-taken-seriously was an essential aspect of a secularized public realm. Indeed, mocking religious figures was seen by many as a civic virtue, part of an informal style of Danish anti-authoritarianism, which newcomers had to learn (Rasmussen, 2005). Reactions to the unfolding events, including those of various dictatorial regimes in the Middle East and the plight of the cartoonists in hiding, opened deep divisions across traditional ideological lines, on which principles were involved (freedom of speech, blasphemy, religious tolerance/recognition, press responsibility, public civility) and what their meanings were.

When a large majority of the French parliament in February 2004 passed a law prohibiting the wearing of visible religious symbols in state schools a different idea of secularism was implied. The wearing of headscarves by Muslim girls was framed by various commentators as a matter of either religious freedom or female autonomy/oppression (Laborde, 2006). Yet, retreat from *laïcité* (secularism, the secular state) also connoted an unwillingness on the part of some French to accord equality to *citoyens* who identified with their republic whatever their private inclinations. In other countries, notably the US and Britain, religious headwear is less controversial and associated with quite different conceptions of religion, pluralism and public sphere – each incidentally understanding itself as a manifestation of 'secularism' (Levinson, 1997; Modood and Kastoryano, 2006).

In Germany, moves away from the traditional *ius sanguinis* naturalization policy to accommodate the large population of German-born Turks without citizenship reflect a political contest between two types of republicanism, where one (liberal egalitarian) sees citizenship as facilitating integration, while the other (statist communitarian) sees it as a reward bestowed only on those who have successfully achieved it (Faist and Triadafilopoulos, 2006). With extensive powers vested in the *Verfassungsschutz* institution to monitor minority associations and to screen or block 'Islamist' applicants suspected of terrorist sympathies, including groups who explicitly recognize the constitution yet work with 'subtle means', the growth in naturalizations in Germany whereby Turks in particular 'are increasingly becoming citizens who fight for their rights and seek to establish them by democratic means' has brought with it a form of 'moral panic' (Schiffauer, 2006: 6, 98). *Ius soli* comes at a price. In Germany, historically, citizenship was essentially a legal category, associated with a political culture of passivity (Turner, 1990). Allowing immigrants to acquire this status has invested it with a new civic pathos, which has also securitized it. The French tradition assumes any child born in the republic to be willing and capable of becoming a good citizen. In Germany lowering the citizenship threshold has necessitated defining which values and competences characterize a truly democratic citizen, and screening out intruders who do not possess them.

The move towards political solutions

These incidents have several features in common. First, they indicate a turn in Western political culture to what this book calls *political solutions to cultural conflict*. In Western Europe cultural conflict signifies religious conflict, with Islam as the all but inevitable Other (Modood et al., 2006). Western societies are converging on ostensibly civic understandings of national communities, although clearly, as the examples show, 'civic' carries diverse connotations and consequences in different places. Governments certainly still wish to privilege majority heritage and traditions, and migration pressure continues to fuel political concessions to the New Right (Hedetoft, 1999). However, with the human rights revolution, urbanization and cultural globalization, the idea of a powerful *kultur*-nationalism as gatekeeper and integrator, an old-fashioned assimilation style is clearly on the wane. The dominant rhetorical style counter-poses 'political' to 'cultural', 'universal' to 'particularistic' values and principles, the latter to be kept at a distance in the private realm and the former standing for more modern, rational, 'thinner' types of solidarity.

Secondly, in this opposition, cultural and religious identities are strongly politicized and presented as problems, indeed as security problems

(Wæver, this volume). Western majorities, on the other hand, are associated with modernity, rationality and universal values. Multiculturalism has an increasingly poor press and is equated with anti-liberalism and relativism, and above all the danger of social and political disintegration.

Hence, thirdly, while recognizing that a plural modern community must be conceptualized as thin, political and universal, Western societies are also increasingly concerned with *who and what we can see ourselves to be* as a community, to have sufficient commitment, loyalty and willingness to pay taxes to strangers. French concepts of integration and social cohesion which have taken some flak at home are spreading to Germany, Denmark, The Netherlands and even Great Britain (Goodhart, 2004) and fitted into new discursive contexts. What cohesion really means is far from clear. The idea of a *Leitkultur* still begs the question of what type and degree of cultural sameness is required. National identity concerns, moreover, are tied to – or confused with – ideas of specific civic competences, and both are conceptualized in contrast, on the one hand, to traditional nationalism assumed left behind and, on the other, minority parallel societies.

Theoretically, these movements constitute a play of conceptualizations within three different conceptions of politics and of politics as responses to 'culture', the first two of which have been traced by the conceptual historian Kari Palonen (2006). One is a conception of politics as a legally delineated *sphere*. Here, political denotes constitutional protections, rights and immunities, which are taken out of public contestation, thereby defining legitimate forms of human interaction and the exercise of power. Secondly, a political community or identity denotes a form of *communality and belonging* which is specifically civic as opposed to ethnic or cultural. Thirdly, politics refers to an activity and its concomitant competences and virtues.

All this appears to lower the normative threshold of political community. It seems easier to affirm abstract liberal principles and values than to conform to an entire way of life. It is easier to identify with a polity than to share a nation that was in place before one's arrival. Acting as a citizen is less taxing than sharing all of life's communal dimensions. The contributors to this volume agree, at some level, that old-style nationalist-assimilatory versions of these thresholds are a thing of the past, and that the modern community must in some sense be political. In a moment we shall look at some of these responses at the level of theory. Before we do so, we shall note the reasons why the political turn is a quite demanding one.

Politics as (political) culture

The turn to politics-as-response-to-culture is itself an indication of culture, or, we may say, a culturalization of politics. This means a number of things, which correspond to different connotations of the term culture. In the final section of this introduction it is argued that the turn to politics needs to be analysed as a form of a new civic nationalism, which is implicated in various types of unacknowledged particularism. At this stage the different if related point is that the movement is towards treating politics increasingly *as* culture, or to what may be termed *political or civic culture*.

The connotation of culture here is not the romantic or anthropological one of particular identity, but the earlier Enlightenment association with *Bildung*, civility and civilization. Culture concerns the progress and perfectibility of norms, identities and practices in relation to communal life and political affairs. Political or civic culture is liberal or universal culture. Moreover, each of the three moves towards this type of high political Culture (with a capital 'C') at the same time constitutes culture (anthropological 'cultural culture', with a small 'c') as an obstacle and form of backwardness.

First, political values and norms are not mere legal rules to which private individuals must comply. They must be positively internalized. We must carry the constitution in our hearts and show the world that we do so in citizenship ceremonies or naturalization tests. We must let these principles override private or cultural inclinations, let the latter become shaped and coloured by the former, stand up for them and transmit them as a heritage to new generations and newcomers. We must also actively identify with institutions and compatriots and maintain a modernist sense of community, which again overrides any group commitment. Finally, the modern polity requires that we act, and become socialized into acting, as citizens. In short, we cannot simply be private selves with private pursuits; we must be members of a culture of citizenship.

To each aspect of politics-as-culture (values/principles, identity, virtuous activity) correspond assumptions of traditional minority culture, which mirror traditional anthropology and early relativistic multiculturalism. Commentators (e.g. Phillips, 2007) increasingly note how discourses of multiculturalism, favourable as well as unfavourable, present cultures as essential vessels of meaning, exaggerating their stability, absence of internal conflict and comprehensively explicable content. Culture as cause of human action is similarly overstated and independent reflection by its carriers overlooked. Essentializing minority culture generally entails politicization of such culture. While pluralism is seen as inevitable and legitimate *per se*, it requires discipline and drawing of lines in the sand. Minority culture becomes problem-culture, imbued with risk and uncertainty, in need of modification and fixing, but also difficult to modify or fix. The need to place constitutional principles above culture and unlearn parts of the latter gets stressed in connection with practices which are seen to militate against these principles in specific national contexts (e.g. freedom of speech = acceptance of religious mockery; secularism = absence of religious symbols in public space). In similar fashion virtues of tolerance or civic deliberation are framed as an escape from traditions, which are inherently incompatible with such practices.

Citizenship discourse – four vocabularies of political responses to culture

In Western political discourse the three elements of political culture – affirming and internalizing values and principles, sharing overarching identities and learning democratic civic virtues – are also stable elements in a very influential turn towards *citizenship* as a progressive idiom (e.g. Favell, 2001). This discourse has been employed differently in diverse national contexts, to address different problems, of passive citizenship/subjecthood (Australia), regional disintegration or federal legacy (Spain, Italy, Germany) or lack of constitutionalism (UK). In countries like Australia, citizenship discourse is in principle aimed at newcomers and residents alike – e.g. encouraging resident British nationals to adopt Australian citizenship. In Europe, however, the vocabulary of citizenship is mainly employed as a response to problems of migration, its proponents often overlooking that strong citizenship ideals, whatever flavour and ideological pedigree, is far from fully established among the old majority population.

At one level this looks like a political theory movement from liberalism (rights and constitutionalism) towards republicanism (participation and civic virtue) and back to communitarianism (identity and belonging). In fact, each of these three political responses to culture, which correspond to conventional analytical dimensions of citizenship (Eder and Giesen, 2001), takes place *inside* broad traditions of theorizing pluralism, each of which conceptualizes the predicament of speaking politics to culture in different ways. An entire range of positions – liberal, republican, communitarian and multicultural to use convenient labels – are all pushed towards *political* restatements.

They are political, first, in the sense of accepting relatively less common ground ('thinness') among members of a community, and further conceptualizing this ground as above and beyond comprehensive ethical universes ('formality'). Another way of putting it is that political theorists these days are all liberal, even if they are liberal republicans, liberal communitarians or liberal multiculturalists. But they are also political in the second sense that the spheres, practices and identities of proper thinness and formality become invested with a strong civicness. Whatever else they are, the communities of moderns are citizens' communities (Schnapper, 2001). Thinness thickens when each vocabulary encounters cultural pluralism as a condition for citizens to endure, navigate or transcend – e.g. in tolerance, deliberation, agonal contestation, self-critical interpretation of one's own national tradition or intercultural dialogue.

Moreover, each register of political community and cultural pluralism links to real-life discourses. The following sections sketch the main vocabularies of political solutions to cultural conflict, including some of their shortcomings and ambiguities.

Liberalism and constitutional patriotism

A liberal register of politics involves the separation of a public and a private sphere, which constitutes one as a space of debate on common affairs and another as a protected realm of individual rights. Disagreement remains on the comprehensiveness of the latter, notoriously between egalitarians and libertarians. To liberals culture refers to private particularism, and cultural pluralism, more or less benign (Rosenblum, 1994), is a function of the individual pursuit of universes of value which spring from group memberships in civil society. Because pluralism of life projects is inevitable – indeed cherished and encouraged – the only reasonable conception of political community is a scheme of 'the right' as opposed to 'the good' (Rawls, 1993).

Liberal problems with culture, above all religion, have several aspects. One concerns practices which fall outside the bounds of liberal tolerance, because they are oppressive or are themselves intolerant. Another concerns values and beliefs which are held too uncompromisingly and *unreflectively*, thus jeopardizing an autonomous life, which is either valuable for its own sake or politically important as underpinning the democratic reasoning of liberal citizens (cf. Rawls, 1993 with Kymlicka, 1995). A third culture problem concerns motivation. To Rawls (1993) a community is stable only if liberal principles can be affirmed from inside diverse comprehensive worldviews – a condition which becomes the more demanding as such principles themselves admit of a measure of reasonable pluralism. But liberals are also challenged from the outside as to whether formal principles can integrate a community in the first place (Taylor, 1989). May, indeed, the lauded irony of self-decentring individuals, while facilitating inclusiveness, jeopardize the types of solidarity that come with personal inconvenience or sacrifice, *a fortiori*, if the favoured political community is a redistributive and participatory one? Is there a trade-off, so that one must accept any collective identity at hand (including nationalism and traditional religion) to have solidarity even where this means compromising on liberal principles?

While such criticism has been voiced by liberal nationalism (below), an influential response has employed the concept of constitutional patriotism. Originally directed against the particularism of traditional nationalism rather than religion (Habermas, 1992), debates over constitutional patriotism, also prominent in this volume (see Nimni, Fossum, Ifversen and Maynor), are complex and growing. They share liberal interpretations of the three turns to citizenship as culture outlined above. Solidarity must derive its legitimacy from (overlapping) consensus on liberal constitutional values. Liberalism is compatible with patriotism in the sense of accepting and maintaining national boundaries, and the direction and constraints of a liberal consensus are compatible with, indeed may be supported by, emotional attachment towards distinct polities, which embody specific traditions or identities. Finally, partaking in this liberal solidarity requires an active citizenship stance in the form of situated political dialogues or processes of self-interpretation of national political cultures.

Important differences exist. Some concern the fit between particularistic cultures, universal principles and motivation. Is motivation done by principles as such, or do principles require a particularistic backing to become effective? If the latter, do principles merely constrain the range of admissible, but necessary emotional attachments, including national and ethnic ones (and how much)? Should they help debunk such identities, or does criticism of identities also involve their re-construction (Føllesdal, 2000; Lacroix, 2002)?

One unexamined ambiguity is whether to regard constitutional patriotism as a normative ideal which should and could unite citizens in a polity, and also inform the citizenship regime of a given country (Fossum, this volume), or more sociologically as a modern, reflective-but-nationally-situated solidarity. Is the issue one of urgently *needing* particularistic identities to have effective motivation, or the rather different one of *accepting* such ties as inevitable, but making them safe for liberalism (Føllesdal, 2000)? Another ambiguity concerns the nature of contextualization. Does particularity denote national *versions* of liberalism so that each people must customize liberalism to its culture circumstances in order to feel bound by it? Are values rendered 'concrete' (rather than 'particularistic') simply by being enshrined in a constitution – an institution, one may note, which is invested with varying degrees of pathos in different countries (Ingram, 1996)? Do liberal values become charged with emotion and identity simply by linkage to institutions, or does history and broader political culture play a role (Markell, 2000; Laborde, 2002)?

Authors who employ the concept often appear to have somewhat unrealistic assumptions about the coherency and authority of constitutional traditions. In any country groups admire different constitutional principles and associated institutions, or press to have existing settlements altered, sometimes by reference to arrangements elsewhere. Some favour Swedish welfare institutions or American checks and balances. Others are alienated by nanny states or democratic impotence. Britain, France and Denmark have never had a real constitutional tradition. Constitutional patriots 'underestimate the level of indeterminacy of liberal-democratic ideals' (Laborde, 2002: 602), also when they acknowledge a reasonable diversity of liberalisms, but assume homogeneous interpretations *inside* countries. Having a thinner set of principles as the core of consensus is no solution, as adversarial politics will build and amend contested settlements way beyond such a core. Citizens, it may be argued, continue to share a political project, not because they identify with all underlying principles, but despite the fact that they do not.

Although the civic turn in Europe may look like a vindication of Habermas's progressive concept and as a relatively unmixed blessing (Müller, 2007), important differences remain between then and now, in Germany and elsewhere. To Habermas – who certainly did not convince all Germans at the time (Rossteutcher, 1997) – the concept was largely formulated as a critique, loosening national and ethnic identities and their associated histories and a way to insert them in a new Europe without borders. In Spain it has been used, still with reference to history, to legitimate a constitutional arrangement of regional autonomies ('multinationalism'), offering an overarching solidarity of citizens and minorities (Nuñez, 2001). In Italy it signified a culture of legality, responsible citizenship and minimal common national purpose in the face of regionalism and secession, and was criticized as such for its impotence (Rusconi, 1993). At stake in these debates was no specific interpretation of principles, but promotion of *Rechtstaat*, citizenship and state responsiveness against nationalism, regionalism and neoliberalism.

By contrast, since the mid-1990s, the solidarity of liberal values has had religious pluralism, above all Islam, as its backdrop. Not self-criticism and progressive politics, but the need to stand firm on 'our liberal values', and to do so in the name of a reconstructed concept of the nation. A recent analysis (Mouritsen, 2006a: 81–3) of Denmark's *Leitkultur* debate exemplifies this. It demonstrates that although politicians who speak of 'common values' assume the high Habermasian ground of equality, democracy and human rights, this does not render the discourse inclusive. Party programmes present these values as embedded in the social fabric of society, as emerging from the past of the Danish people, but also as inaccessible. They are an old, unbreakable and unchangeable *cultural* whole which is difficult for others, particular Muslims, to share. By contrast to a Kantian view, where allegiance arises from *a* functioning cooperation in justice, wherever one may find it (Lacroix, 2002), these universal and non-negotiable values also often come across as intrinsically Danish, even universal *qua* Danish. They invariably get presented as not just uncontested internally, but also as *superior*, due to happy historical and geographical circumstances (freeholder agrarianism, smallness), which less fortunate nations have not enjoyed.

In a similar way, the requirement to affirm a list of political values has become institutionalized as an entry requirement in the naturalization process of many countries, often tied to citizenship declarations, ceremonies and tests which use a range of emotive mechanisms well known from early nation-building, and assuming more or less benign and demanding forms (Damsholt, this volume). The perceived clash between non-negotiable (liberal) secularism and (fundamentalist) religion in the West (Wæver, this volume) highlights similar ambiguities in terms of the questionable status of the universalism it celebrates. Many liberal principles and institutions have non-secular – Christian – origins, and there are almost as many ways of dividing religion and politics as there are national political traditions.

Instrumental liberal neo-nationalism

In the Danish debate, politicians stress that affirming liberal values and learning the country's civic styles does *not* require old-fashioned cultural assimilation (Mouritsen, 2006a: 82). Even so, the offer of a universal citizen identity often slides towards a stratum of 'cultural culture' (i.e. language, heritage, even religion), indicating a competing discourse of integration.

However, this is not generally speaking a traditional communitarian idea, which privileges ethnic culture on independent grounds to do with cultural expression or self-assertion (Miller, 1995: 49–80). The most influential public national identity theory argues that some homogeneity, and its maintenance through education, assimilation and immigration control, is *necessary* and hence legitimate not only to have community, but above all to have a well-functioning *liberal* community, *a fortiori* a redistributive, strongly participative one. The argument, which comes in several versions (Abizadeh, 2002), is that citizens are more likely to have trust – based on common interest, ease of communication or identification – where the life of a nation is characterized by a homogeneous culture. This view, which we may call instrumental liberal neo-nationalism, has its roots in Rousseau and nineteenth-century liberalism. Contemporary versions include Dominique Schnapper (2001) in France and David Miller (1995) in Britain. In public debates the view is tied to a sceptical representation of multiculturalism as implying the existence of parallel societies (Goodhart, 2004).

The conception of politics at stake is liberal in the sense of a distinction between a public realm of collective decisions and a private realm of rights. A separate distinction is made between individual or group-based identities and the shared *public or political* culture and identity of the nation. But whereas liberals would conceptualize the latter as a universal political Culture (the *Bildung* of liberal values and citizenship) in the instrumental national view every nation has *its own* flavour of public culture and sense of nationality, in which political life is embedded. This is not just cultural in the sense of particular or specific but also in the sense of including elements from what liberals see as the non-political sphere of heritage, customs, national identity, even religion; and in regarding the distinction between the levels as difficult to draw. The boundaries of this *more or less thick* public culture are flexible. To Miller, 'a national identity requires that the people who share it should have something in common, a set of characteristics that in the past was often referred to as a "national character", but which I prefer to describe as a common political culture'. The latter in turn

> may be seen as a set of understandings about how a group of people is to conduct life together. This will include political principles such as belief in democracy or the rule of law . . . social norms such as filling in your tax return or queuing as a way of deciding who gets on the bus first. It may also embrace certain cultural ideals, for instance religious beliefs or a commitment to preserve the purity of the national language. (Miller, 1995: 25–6)

While assuming an ethnic core, Miller recognizes that nationality is also constructed. Indeed, his theory is very much about deliberate maintenance and contestation of an artificial common culture. It is Rousseau's world, not Herder's, a form of deliberative assimilation philosophy. Newcomers must learn to appreciate the common culture and relegate much of their own background to the private realm. But as citizens they have a say in making this public culture more inclusive. The virtues of neo-nationalism include dialogue, impartiality and restraint – not old-fashioned custody of the majority tradition's authenticity. Correspondingly, *problematic* (minority) culture is an inherently unreflective, un-transcendable, non-compatible culture and particularly such minority culture which *refuses* to enter the integration dialogue.

Miller's theory has been criticized (Føllesdal, 2000; Abizadeh, 2002). Debates concern the causality of trust and solidarity in social groups and individual minds, whether homogeneity is a sufficient – even a necessary – condition for bringing about either, and if it is, also the requisite type, comprehensiveness and degree of such homogeneity. While lack of solidarity and trust is often associated by political scientists with empirical ethnic heterogeneity (Putnam, 2007), it is less clear that it jeopardizes the possibility of a welfare state (Banting and Kymlicka, 2006). Indeed, Scandinavian welfare state theorists stress institutional path dependencies of functioning and just institutions and the rational appreciation of reciprocity by welfare state citizens (Rothstein, 2005). Such reciprocity, arguably, still requires that others actually exhibit a sufficient work and taxpaying capacity to be partners in a welfare state – a form of 'homogeneity' in terms of citizenship capacity, which new immigrants may not always possess.

Of course, some theorists of ethnicity will maintain that the differences that constitute shared identity are products of boundary maintenance rather than this or that shared cultural trait (Barth, 1969). Accepting a soft constructivism of imagined communities (Anderson, 1983) introduces ambiguity between what a community has learnt to think it has in common and which values or characteristics it actually, empirically, shares. It facilitates a further slide from national public culture to a sense of shared fate or *identity*, which appears to do the work in ethnically and linguistically heterogeneous nations like Switzerland (Miller, 1995: 194–5). At any rate, it is far from clear that attempts at *homogenization* – as in the heyday of nationalism, when peasants were turned into Frenchmen, Italians and Danes – are at all feasible if, as claimed by Bhikhu Parekh, 'a culturally homogeneous society whose members share and mechanically follow an identical body of beliefs and practices is today no more than an anthropological fiction' (Parekh, 1997).

Be that as it may, we may ask how a discourse of integration with this basic argumentative structure – common culture as necessary for distributive and democratic institutions – actually functions politically. Here, several familiar problems emerge. First, there is some distance between a political theory which requires *a* shared public culture and public debates which invariably centre on *our* shared (national) culture. Also, the language of instrumental nationalism is easily conflated with older languages about the moral right of the majority culture to dominate, and with chauvinist assumptions about this culture's superiority (Mouritsen, 2006a). Emphasis on homogeneity and assimilation in its name appears pragmatically opposed to self-criticism and dialogue. Unlike traditional nationalism, which allows space for those who cannot and should not be integrated in the first place, instrumental nationalism raises the stakes considerably by making integration (cultural assimilation) a matter of securing the health or survival of society itself. In this process, by the very nature of discourse, a vocabulary of instrumental homogeneity becomes a flexible, disciplinary tool, which keeps the markers of cultural assimilation vague and undefined (Modood, 1994).

Particularly pertinent is a tendency (also in theory) to confuse the instrumentally required 'shared culture' with the type of political 'Culture' (trust, solidarity, deliberative democracy, willingness to distribute, etc.), which the former is meant to facilitate. This syndrome again relates to the tendency simply to *define* what 'we have in common' in terms of broad political values, treasured institutions and generally agreeable things, such as democracy, the welfare state and tolerance. The equation presumes a binary opposition between two equally essentialized forms of culture: culture 1, civil and progressive culture, which is what 'we' happen to have arrived at around here; and culture 2, which is the backward, uncivil culture, within which 'they' remain caught. This equation has a mystifying effect. If part of the distrust and lack of solidarity between, say, majorities and immigrants has to do with a (real or erroneously believed) lack of certain civic skills or liberal practices, debates should concern *which* practices, attitudes and skills are needed in a democratic society and *whether* they are lacking. What is needed may be neither more shared or common culture as such nor more of 'our' culture, but more *civic* culture, as well as a greater understanding of what this means in a pluralist society.

Openness to newcomers is no doubt a scarce good. In this volume Nimni disputes liberal belief, in particular Habermas's, in a purely civic state-community based on voluntary adherence to liberal values. Contemporary liberals who think a working sense of justice produces effective obligation (Patten, 1996) ignore what nineteenth-century liberals knew – that well-ordered states started as, and remain, nations. Indeed, nowhere is reliance on the nation, or on some functional equivalent of it, more evident than in recent discussions among liberals who accept (against moral cos-mopoltans) bounded societies, but search for ways to deal with dilemmas of moral obligation and moral psychology in the face of immigration (Buchanan and Moore, 2003).

While it is unclear that solidarity requires cultural homogeneity, it does seem plausible that the internal cohesion of modern states requires an identity through time, i.e. a sense of common past, present and future. Moreover, such identities are most likely 'ethnic', at least as predicates of *distinct peoples*. Peoples here have elementary *a priori* emotional ties and effective obligations towards kin – concretely, one's own children and the children of those who are considered members of the people now (Canovan, 2000) – meaning such ties and obligations which do not gen-erally require specific actions, affirmations, attributes or competences to be activated, as is the case with newcomers. The most open society will still have some sense of privileging those who are there already. However, *what*, over and beyond elementary kinship, can constitute the imagined identity *substance* (or competing conceptions of it) of this group – e.g. religion, language, historical narrative, sense of shared fate – and *which* parameters of inclusion of newcomers will operate, are contingent questions.

Republicanism and civic patriotism

A third registry of political solutions to cultural conflict, in some ways a middle path between the former two, is the republican one. Republican theory and discourse stand divided on its central ideas. While all agree on a conception of politics that emphasizes civic virtue, the maintenance of a public sphere and some form of self-government, the requisite virtues and types of activity remain disputed, and quite different theorists, including some that have been discussed (Habermas and Miller), associ-ate themselves with different delineations and readings of the tradition.

In particular, the concept of liberty (Mouritsen, 2005a) divides Aristotelian civic humanist (Pocock, 1975), communitarian (Sandel, 1996), liberal (Dagger, 1997), and neo-Roman readings (Pettit, 1997; Skinner, 1998; Maynor, 2003). The latter regards republican liberty as a common good jointly secured by active citizens, but also a species of negative liberty, whereby citizens enjoy a set of mutual protections and liberties, which are defined and constituted by law, but where the specific content of this liberty is a product of self-government and hence, to some degree, his-torically contingent. In addition, bracketing different readings of the *pathos* of citizenship, civic status is associated also by civic humanists and communitarians with *recognition*, i.e. acknowledgement of contributions towards the common good (Honohan, 2002).

Culture to a modern liberal republican at least (the tradition dates back long before invention of the concept) may be understood as private pursuits, which citizens may legitimately use their liberty *for*. But it may also be harmful particularism. Here, culture divides citizens, creates parochialism or separatism, and takes minds away from the common good. Culture, particularly in a French-Rousseauvian understanding, should be kept *outside* the public realm. Ethnic and religious identities compete with, and detract attention from, equal citizenship. Here, it tends to stand for backwardness, immaturity, lack of civic competence and above all inequalities of inherited tradition. But culture may be allowed *inside* this realm, when utilized as integrating background culture; not Rousseau's peasants' culture but civilization-carrying high culture, associated with Enlightenment rationalism and French language.

Two broad sets of political solutions to cultural conflict, both corresponding to old republican themes (Mouritsen, 2005b) and each picking up a thread from the section on nationalism, may be discerned. One concerns activity and virtue. By participating in common affairs – fighting in wars, serving on juries, deliberating in forums – newcomers earn recognition as citizens and learn to *identify* with common goods that unite individuals whatever their private diversity. Political action also inserts previously excluded voices in the shaping of common liberty. Another solution is patriotism as a *civic* identity, which springs from mnemonic narratives of predicaments, trespasses experienced, agreeements reached and institutions created in the history of liberty in specific communities. Patriotism unites all who contributed in the past with those who, by contributing now and in the future, carve a narrative space for themselves. Unlike nationalism, republican patriotism, because tied to liberty, can be rational and reflective. Indeed, according to Maurizio Viroli, foremost chronicler of republican patriotism, 'love of country' is 'a charitable love of liberty' which 'produces only liberty', whereas 'bigotry, intolerance, and war are the products of another love, that is, love or longing for oneness or uniqueness' (Viroli, 1995: 185).

Each solution has been criticized. Criticism of participation and deliberation is as old as theories about it. To the extent that participation is more than a means to represent interests or control power, it raises questions of how much and when, and suggests functional issues of participation overload and coordination in modern societies. It is difficult to sustain, produces conflict as well as concord, and is biased towards the well-educated and resourceful. As regards patriotism, critics note the difficulty, even if the distinction makes sense in conceptual history, of separating patriotism and nationalism. 'Common liberty', after all, is particular peoples' liberty, of which there may be many interpretations. Struggles for independence and rights even in liberal states are linked to cherished ways of life, traditions fought for (including religions, languages, and ethnic symbols) and culturally bound notions of virtuous practice. Some narratives of liberty exclude old minorities who were on the losing side in wars, as well as newcomers who do not relate to its symbols and components. Insisting on emotion and pathos, moreover, borrows from the logic of nation-building and invites scepticism about the moral psychology of patriotism (Bader, 1999; Mouritsen, 2005b).

Bracketing theory, one may consider the increasing appeal in public discourse to active citizenship and patriotic community identification, including citizenship ceremonies (Damsholt, this volume). What previously served the heavy-handed creation of national citizens in parochial peasant societies comes to mean something different in multicultural societies with Islamic groups. Explicated civic ideals form part of discursive opportunity structures, which immigrants – including Muslims – may exploit, but they do so with difficulty and at the risk of alienation. Contemporary republican citizenship discourse often constructs its virtues in direct opposition to religion, at any rate to religion taken seriously. The continuing *affair de foulard* and ensuing debates in France and elsewhere highlight this. The assumption of secular citizenship – even the pre-citizenship of adolescent education – as a neutral and rational identity forces some individuals to *choose* between citizenship and recognition as good Muslims. The artificial equality of republican citizens is counter-posed to religious hierarchy and the marks of sexual submission. And public autonomy – the ability to deliberate reasonably and independently – is counter-posed to religious authority, symbolized, of course, by the headscarf (Laborde, 2006).

Recently, Denmark introduced a *Declaration of Integration and Active Citizenship in Danish Society*, which an immigrant signs when applying for permanent residence. It contains a 16-point list which newcomers must declare they understand and intend to follow. None of the points are about 'cultural' Danishness. Several stress the importance of being a self-supporting and taxpaying citizen and learning to speak Danish. The declaration begins, innocently enough, 'I shall comply with Danish legislation and protect the Danish Democratic Principles in every respect', but continues on a when-did-you-stop-beating-your-wife track, impressing on immigrants that men and women have equal rights, that women are allowed to participate in politics, that beating one's children or spouse is illegal ('I understand and accept that it is illegal in Denmark to commit actual violence or threaten violence against one's spouse'), as is 'circumcision' of girls and forced marriage, that one must respect the 'Danish values' of sexual equality, freedom of speech and anti-discrimination, that one must report and stand up to terrorism, and that 'active commitment to the Danish society is a precondition for a good life in Denmark *regardless of how long it will last*' (Danish Ministry of Refugee, Immigration and Integration Affairs, 2007; emphasis added).

The purpose of a citizenship declaration, arguably, is as uncertain as that of a civic oath (Bauböck, 2002). Terrorists will hardly be persuaded to mend their ways, nor will they give themselves up by refusing to sign. Immigrants are asked to confirm something that nationals are never confronted with. Still, oaths and confirmations may be seen as solemn rites of passage, pledges which confirm the value of citizenship. The Danish declaration, however, is both inept and insulting. It fits a political conception of Danish community, but does so in a chauvinistic way. It implies that such values are often not shared by newcomers, and that one cannot assume a willingness to internalize them in a manner that overrides religion.

In a similar vein (discussed by Wæver, this volume), appeals in Western societies to secularism and placing religion below the rule of law politicizes in an exclusivist way the virtue of reasoning and rational dialogue. While such demands make sense in political theory, invoking them as an entry requirement to the public realm, apart from insults and stigma, may even constitute a double standard. To Wæver, it arbitrarily excludes one (religious) form of irrationalism from real-world political dialogue, which in other respects hardly conforms to Habermasian strictures. In a different vein, we noted above that the Cartoon affair highlighted alternative ways of conceiving the required 'civicness' of a Danish public sphere, i.e. promoting irreverent, authority-mocking humour and teaching the religiously sensitive to *put up with being offended* – as an editorial style in a serious national newspaper rather than from the stage of a stand-up comedy show.

Muliculturalism and cultural dialogue

Multiculturalism grew out of criticism of the biases of Western political theory and society, i.e. its *de facto* privileging of the religions, symbols and histories of majority cultures and silencing of minorities. Colour-blindness and neutrality merely masked assimilation, not only in French-style countries where integration into a national high culture was the only passage to full citizenship. Whereas first-generation academic multicultura-lism, borrowing from postmodernism, tried to unmask the universalistic pretensions of liberal or republican values – i.e. 'Western' individualism, rights focus and ideals of neutrality – multiculturalism today is generally speaking set on liberal foundations, as is the majority of claims by Western minorities in the name of multiculturalism – this is a condition of their likelihood of success. Various new and old formulations by Will Kymlicka (1995), Joseph Raz (1994), Rainer Bauböck (1996) and Tariq Modood (2007) emphasize individual rights, internal group constraints and exit possibilities, but also employ in different ways deeper, more culture-sensitive (or identity-status sensitive, e.g. Phillips, 2007) understandings of equal treatment, ranging from subsidies for background cultural struc-tures and group rights to effective anti-discrimination laws and exemption rights to preferential treatment. In different ways individuals here should be recognized as *both* culturally different *and* equal citizens.

Also multiculturalism offers its distinct takes on politics and culture. In a world where heterogeneity is the norm, and where at least some of this heterogeneity consists of individuals who are also members of rela-tively organized and united religious or ethnic communities, politics as a response to cultural conflict may be conceptualized as complex forms of institutionalized power-sharing or constitutional settlements, a Foreign Office-type diplomatic democracy, or – more influentially, and mirrored in the official discourse of self-proclaimed multicultural states – as an ideology of habitual mutual respect and accommodation. Above all, it is a pragmatic feature of the acceptance of multiculturalism that any group recognizes the legitimacy of other groups, the right of all individuals to *their* belonging, and the *prima facie* reasonableness of 'culturalist' framing of needs and claims by other groups than one's own – even such that one is predisposed to dislike.

Correspondingly, problematic culture is culture that does not allow (gradual, gentle) liberal 'laundering' in terms of respect for individual rights (Kymlicka, 1995), and cultural groups characterized by chauvinist particularism ('ours is the only true and right worldview') as opposed to 'operational relativism' ('what is good for us is not good for them'). Problem cultures are also those that (in the eyes of competing groups) masquerade as such – i.e. non-authentic, unstable, poorly integrated cul-tural groups – and which, as a matter of the administrative-political logic of a multicultural society, are difficult to represent and deal with in terms of clearly defined needs and mechanisms of policy.

The main problem of multiculturalism, in theory and practice, is the tendency towards group essentialism (Benhabib, 2002; Phillips, 2007) and employment of old-fashioned island-type ideas of culture (Bauman, 1999). Interest and identity logics, difficult to escape by the young, apostates and internal reformers, are nurtured by the righteous custodians of religious or national tradition, and in turn fuel external stereotyping. Although recipients of multicultural policy are individuals and citizens, whose 'need of culture' (belonging, identity) is recognized, the very logic of multiculturalism is the public negotiation of which *cultures* are worthy in a given society. Arguably, only relatively stable settlement of minority status protects societies from hyper-politicized ethno-corporatist contests over new rights, resources and platforms of power, leaving ordinary poverty with a poor press. On the other hand, normal politics increasingly implies 'culture' as a political coinage among others, allowing entrepreneurs to mobilize group constituencies and frame claims according to the discursive political structures at hand in specific national settings (Koopmans and Statham, 2003).

These problems are increasingly discussed in mainstream multicultural theory. There is more focus on the dialectics of power, stigma and status than on ascribed needs; on the diversity of minorities and types of cultural substance – above all the difference between North American and European conditions; and on the variable national contexts of claims. Moreover, a movement is visible, which brackets the more thorny philosophical questions about what constitutes illiberal practices and forms of life, how much to interfere in private lives to rectify them, and how to balance personal autonomy against perfectionist socialization – and towards concentrating, instead, on 'political' questions of exemption rights, anti-discrimination, community enhancement and public space-sharing in specific communities (Modood et al., 2006).

Theoretically, also, multiculturalism is increasingly going *civic*. One example is Bhikhu Parekh's dialogical multiculturalism (Parekh, 2000; cf. Habermas, 1994; Benhabib, 2002), which models the (re)framing of culture claims in ways that can be accommodated into the conceptual categories of liberal majority society. A theory that recognizes neither unequivocal liberal rights transcendence nor nationalist assimilation is almost predisposed to take this path. However, a backlash is taking place across Europe. Increasingly, the ideal of we-ness *through* cultural dialogue and recognition of difference, claimed by Parekh as well as such diverse writers as Kymlicka, Bauböck and Modood, is presented as succumbing to a reality of isolation and *Verzeuiligung*, which jeopardizes social cohesion and tolerance, as well as the autonomy to exit, criticize and hyphenate identities. It is by no means clear to what extent the existence of 'parallel societies', lack of identification with the national community, let alone fundamentalist sympathies can be blamed on multicultural policies, as opposed to, say, labour market segregation, political marginalization and low education attainment levels of immigrants. Indeed, the shift is very apparent in countries such as Germany, Denmark and France that never really had much multiculturalism at the level of policy. But it is also evident in the subtle realignment in Great Britain from a discourse of multiculturalism to one of integration-with-diversity, paradigmatically exemplified by the Commission for Racial Equality (2007) and its head Trevor Phillips (who succeeded Bhikhu Parekh), who does not so much criticize the various concrete policies in Britain of multicultural space-sharing as the danger that 'our racial or religious identity . . . becomes an obstacle to our belonging to the wider community' or constitutes coercive 'identity wells' for young British Muslims or blacks (Phillips, 2006).

Pluralist republicanism and community beyond the nation

The four vocabularies leave a sense of convergence. Everybody nowadays is a liberal. However, theory and public discourse increasingly demonstrate a *comprehensive* liberalism of deep autonomy and reflection. Moreover, each vocabulary is becoming *civic* in the sense of emphasis on activity, contestation and dialogue. From all perspectives cultural and religious pluralism as well as recalcitrant nationalisms require us to examine our own partialities, to question overly *thick* conceptions of community (but also to conceptualize *thinner* substitutes) and to enter into dialogue with others who share our political space. It requires an ability to live with pluralism and conflict as constitutive of community. Where does this leave us? While the contributors to this volume move in several directions – descriptive, analytical or normative – from different starting points, it makes sense to speak of a clustering of theory around what may be loosely termed a new pluralist republicanism. In traditional republicanism (minority) culture is a civic distraction. But some of the contributors suggest or comment on reworkings of a republican politics – culture nexus, based on a politics of identity contestation and deliberative participation, which reopens cultures, mobilizes reinterpretation and facilitates dialogue.

First, while critical of liberal versions of constitutional patriotism, Ephraim Nimni condones Cecile Laborde's notion of *civic patriotism*, i.e. the idea that national solidarity and sense of belonging require that citizens be familiar with the relevant political culture in the sense of a shared conversational space, 'the malleable frameworks which sustains our political conversations over time' (Laborde, 2002: 609) – even as some participants are critical of aspects of this space. Such ideas arguably correspond to more contextual readings of Habermas (Markell, 2000), also discussed in this volume, which connect both motivation and legitimacy to critical engagement with the past and present of specific communities, embodying principles in national traditions but also rendering such traditions self-reflective – and thus more open to newcomers – because they are carried by groups of individuals including nations who care about and discuss 'who we are and want to be' (Habermas, 1990: 151).

Nimni asserts that attention should still be paid to distinct ethnic/national communities, each with its *separate* mnemonic vocabularies. A conversational space should be facilitated for *all* the distinct ethnic 'cultures of the republic', conceptualized in the form of an *agonal patriotism* giving the right to a created sense of overarching political belonging. Fossum (this volume) compares constitutional patriotism with Charles Taylor's *deep diversity*, the notion that a specific, geographic constellation of differences allows a sense of citizens' solidarity where belonging means different things to different groups. Both discussions re-cast the ancient category of republican patriotism to accommodate, first, the blurred boundaries in the first place between *natio* and *patria*; secondly, that 'a people's liberty' connects to (and will be normatively influenced in turn by) more than one set of historical-particular memories, and thirdly, that modern community requires dialogue between several distinct voices, who conceptualize past and future. Indeed, it is this dialogue, with its constant insertion of new memories and projects, rather than a specific 'identity-outcome', which integrates a community.

Different republican pedigrees, de-emphasizing the identity trail but giving attention to politics as collective self-legislation, are sought in this volume by John Maynor, and Richard Bellamy and Dario Castiglione, who go beyond the nation-state to the level of the European Union. Maynor develops Phillip Pettit's notion of republican non-domination (Pettit, 1997; Maynor, 2003) to facilitate a polity-centred conception of European citizenship, which he argues is more robust than constitutional patriotism, while Bellamy and Castiglione connect a language of participatory citizenship to a context of multi-level governance, characterized by a complex, overlapping pluralism of issues, advocacy groups and jurisdictions. While both approaches may be seen to conceptualize a reconstitution of distinct peoples' liberties, which gradually incorporates new reasonable demands, Maynor remains, at a European level, with a Rousseauvian (or Habermasian) perspective of a unitary polity united in a dialogue about the common good, whereas Bellamy and Castiglione rely on a republicanism of self-constituting, overlapping sovereignties.

Conceptualizing community beyond the state, ultimately in a *cosmopolis*, is a response to refugee flows, work migration and elite mobility. As people in a single life work, study, find partners, have children and incur obligations to institutions, projects and causes in different countries, nation-based citizenship models come under pressure, particularly when tied to comprehensive (social) rights schemes. Hannah Arendt's analysis of citizenship as a geographically bound, legally constituted 'right to have rights' underscores the plight of the superfluous and displaced (Arendt, 1958: 267–302), but also the need for effective supranational entities. States which police their borders also increasingly restrict access to pension schemes and education for citizens returning from abroad, in the process undermining citizenship and certainly the remnants of *jus sanguinis*. Mobile elites, on the other hand, enjoy transnational corporate privileges and services, which crowd out their willingness to pay for national schemes, and leave states without one of the last solidarity-enhancing mechanisms of capitalist modernity (Turner, 2001).

It is not obvious, however, that state-based citizenship and nation-centred loyalties should be given up before the institutional foundations for supranational citizenship, and *its* mechanisms of solidarity and loyalty, have emerged (Laborde, 2002). Even so, we need to customize or reinvent political theory to address the transformation of a nation-state framework in ways that correspond to real-life discourse about supranational and transnational identities (Ifversen, this volume). A divide has opened in theory and public debate between proponents of (nation-) state-centred ideas and those who search for regional or indeed global forms of solidarity. Contributions to this volume fall on both sides of this divide, from Nimni's assertion of the continued relevance of national and ethnic solidarities and Eder's 'realist' sociology of political community foundations to Bellamy's flexible Euro-transnationalism and Laustsen's and Diken's appeal to a Derridean politics of cosmopolitan friendship as the best hope of the displaced and superfluous of today – the transient refugees, the inhabitants of the modern camp.

The civic turn as culturalization of politics

Is the *civic turn*, visible across conceptual registers, a good thing? In real politics the new civics corresponds to discrediting traditional nationalism or the idea, *Leitkultur* or not, that old majorities deserve cultural supremacy. It has even been argued (Joppke, 2003) that the new integration ideologies overlie a structural convergence on universalistic, non-ethnic principles in migration and nationalization law and policy (whatever their harshness).

Whether 'our own kind first' is consistently waning awaits further investigation (Müller, 2007). Be this as it may, the gains of speaking politics to culture remain ambiguous for reasons, which correspond to aspects of *culturalization of politics*, over and above the first meaning of this term – i.e. the notion of a three-fold turn to politics as culture – which we noted in the beginning.

First of all, the charge that multiculturalists see culture as homogeneous and unchanging is just as relevant against other theories, despite variations in the stuff and thinness of communality proposed. They overlook the anthropological commonplaces that real observable systems of beliefs, practices and 'values' are overlapping, fragmented and contested. What is stipulated as *a* culture could be broken down in other ways for other purposes, is often mixed with similarly amorphous entities, and rarely corresponds to boundaries of states or to sharing *ethnies*. This holds for Miller's public culture, with its fallback notion of a shared *identification* in countries like Switzerland as for Maurizio Viroli's patriotism, which implies that citizens of any class, age, region or political affiliation attach the same meaning to the rites of passage of the republic. Even proponents of constitutional patriotism tend to assume homogeneous interpretations of liberal principles *inside* countries.

Of course, some countries are more homogeneous than others. Yet often more diversity exists *inside* countries with strong national identity (e.g. the US) than *between* others with very similar values, which have not prevented historical antagonism (e.g. Denmark or Sweden). Homogeneity in important senses is what we make of it, and the very idea that sameness, of whatever kind, is constitutive of solidarity as such (as a necessary or sufficient condition) may be seriously flawed (Abizadeh, 2002). Yet the notion of a need for cultural or value homogeneity, a *Leitkultur* of sorts, is extremely influential in contemporary political discourse, as are attempts to talk such homogeneity into existence.

In part because the very notion of homogeneity as necessary to integration is so powerful, a second type of culturalization of politics is widespread. Culture here denotes not what a group shares in a behavioural sense, but what is represented in dominating discourse as shared. Whereas all sorts of cultural paraphernalia, from eating habits to humour, enter into the constructions of identity and difference, in terms of an English, German or Danish 'mentality', what is meant here are the specific conceptions of value, belonging and character traits, which become represented as *entry requirements*. Culturalized politics here means representations of who we are and what people like us, or people who want to take part in our community, must share (cf. Wodak et al., 1999).

Because of their demarcating function these representations often become politicized forms of civil religion, markers of collective identity with a sacred, not-to-be-questioned-or-challenged character. Such culturalized political culture is analysed in Damsholt's anthropological discussion of past and present citizenship ceremony practices. From an international relations perspective, Wæver shows its role in securitized constructions of 'secularism' and 'Islam', while Zapato-Barrero and Qasem highlight the different roles of 'Islam' as a (still negative) defining other in the national discourses of France and Spain.

Thirdly, we see a paradoxical double movement in these constructions. This is a culturalization of politics in the sense that ideas of what good citizenship means very often are represented as both particular and – in a certain sense – universal (Mouritsen, 2006a). They become invested with meaning because they are definitions of the accomplishments of *this* community or nation, and as unchallengeable because, by losing them, we lose the bearings of who and what we are. But they are not just important in a relativist-communitarian sense. Their status is enhanced because they are conceived as *also* universal, i.e. more modern, civilized or liberal.

This movement whereby values and practices are *both* pseudo-anthropological culture and a species of universal high Culture is part and parcel of the civic turn. On the one hand, the values and practices of a group are associated in the blunt categories of public discourse with universally shared values such as democracy, human rights and equality – often in connection with a critique of old-fashioned nationalism (immigrants need do no more than love our 'political' values). On the other hand, these abstract principles are presented as accomplishments of distinct national histories and circumstances. General de Gaulle once stated that 'these values are universal, because they are French' (cited in Holm, 1993), just as liberty in the US is intimately linked to the frontier and flight from European persecution. These narratives are sometimes innocent or benign and may contain kernels of truth, but they often assume exclusive forms. In Denmark, narratives of co-operative, freedom-loving peasants' and workers' movements, even the development of a particular brand of Lutheran 'secularism', imply that democracy, the welfare state and free-spiritedness are only *genuine* here, and that those born and bred in less fortunate places will find it difficult to learn civic practices, particularly if these places are Islamic countries (Mouritsen, 2006a).

The dual pathos invested in ways of life, which are claimed to be both universal and intrinsically ours, involves a paradox, captured with a final meaning of culturalization. Here, what we *do* in fact share, or share in a significant degree, often remains – culture. Culture here signifies habits, cognitive frames and mutual expectations about how to interact, deliberate or solve conflicts, which we hardly speak about, let alone explain to others. Culturalization of politics here is the *lack* of scrutiny of, or debate about, the taken-for-granted nature of political ways of life. Politics here *remains* in a realm of culture, in the anthropological sense of micro-habits and goings on that are often too obvious to be reflected upon, unless we let ourselves be challenged to do so, and which are maintained simply as an unobserved background, as we busily talk of something else – such as 'our common values' and 'our culture'.

This predicament places in perspective a stable of all theory strands discussed above, i.e. the need for self-critical appraisal of a community's own values, identity and practices, most eloquently expressed in Laborde's idea of civic patriotism. Yet, it is probably *not* the case that political culture, unlike wider culture, is 'comparatively easy to elucidate' (Parekh, cited in Laborde, 2002: 611). Indeed, I submit that there is something in the culturalized nature of public (non-)debates that makes this ideal extremely difficult to achieve.

Political theory and realism

These culturalization-of-politics syndromes should not be blamed on political theory. After all, theory should supply normative measures and standards for public life, to be used by politicians and citizens who struggle to improve the latter. Rawls famously warned political theorists not to let their trade become political in the wrong way, i.e. in a way that simply adapted to the imperfectly just circumstances of the day (Rawls, 1985). Yet, we also need theory – including theories of political culture – which can link the claims and ideals of normative theory to accounts of politics and public life, which takes social science knowledge about it seriously. Such theory needs to accommodate at least three kinds of contingency.

First of all, the new focus on how to achieve cohesion and civic competences is already concerned with sociological questions and background ontologies of human motivation. Yet engagement with social science knowledge remains unsystematic, even anecdotal. Moreover, debates on constitutional patriotism and liberal nationalism exhibit a tension, rarely acknowledged, between more sociologically inclined work and traditional moral philosophy, which restricts itself to modelling certain background assumptions, or – as in Rawls' *Political Liberalism* (1993) – to discussing realism and 'stability', in terms of morally reasonable motivations to support a system of justice.

Secondly, conceptual registries of community and pluralism are linked to real-life discourses and contests. Theory is much less autonomous, more reflective of national ideological traditions, including blind-spots and agony points, than authors admit (Triandafyllidou et al., 2006). Should political theory produce more context-*independent* concepts and arguments? This is only a half-solution. The bluntness and institutional dependency of concepts is not merely analytical but also normative. For instance, French, American, British or Danish meanings of secularism are different. They correspond to different political and social forms, traditions of church – state relations and views on education and socialization, each with its advantages and disadvantages. The same can be said of the embeddings of democracy, citizenship, equality and autonomy. Indeed, and further to the first point, theory may reflect diverse *empirical sources* of cohesion, solidarity and trust in different countries – in part to do with different histories of political settlement, or differently established roles and commitments of different groups, civil society and the state. Abstract normative theory cannot always settle which national embedding is intrinsically better, although it certainly should help us criticize some manifestations of them all.

If this leads theorists to cast themselves as interpreters, reconstructing the critical potential of this or that constitutional tradition or public philosophy, they should also, as a third contingency, take seriously the way that public discourse *itself* generates identity and solidarity and more particularly the way that theoretical arguments and principles become inserted into real-life debates. Political theory – or some of it at any rate – needs to be self-reflective and to engage with the murky business of power, rhetoric and strategy, and the constructions of antagonistic *Feinbilds* – constructions which not only emerge with the old-fashioned registers of nationalism but also take on civic guises.

Constituting communities: culture, identity and identification

Some authors would argue that the new call for civics is exaggerated. Powerful states have always found ways to integrate their populations and manage diversity (Eder, this volume), of course. Arguably, the first conditions of minorities' wish to belong are effective policies of social and labour market integration and effective anti-discrimination – and possibly a set of multicultural rights which balance the bias of national public spaces with certain liberal exception rights, protections of minority heritage and symbolic recognitions. That the latter is positively damaging is certainly disputed (Banting and Kymlicka, 2006). Even so, the engagement in political theory with issues of civic education, the reconstruction of political identity, the cultivation of civic virtue and democratic competences are here to stay.

However, if real-life civic languages often freeze into complacent self-description and stereotypes of inherently uncivic values, identities and practices on the part of others, could it be that an idea of political community should be sought neither at a level of observable *cultural traits* nor at a level of *identity*?

As regards the former, if understood as actual political practices and ideals of a group, it is true that modern states require citizens with strong civic *Culture*, as distinct from uncivic passivity and lack of reflection. But there is more than one way to be a good citizen, just as there is more than one conceptualization of the universal values of liberal constitutions. Such conceptualizations continue to divide the proponents of influential, yet competing strands of political theory. In real life, they neither internally unite all groups inside nations nor clearly differentiate among the latter. Languages of *identity* often involve us in strongly politicized representations of particular traditions, character traits and memories, which we ought to share. The conceptual ambiguity of a purely political patriotism, bridging the imaginations and projects of groups with different lineages of community entry, loyalty and desert, as well as what we know of real-world representations of 'our' values, identities and practices as essential, unchanging and sacred, suggests caution for a normative programme. Education in democracy, respect for human rights and tolerance are stable elements of liberal non-neutrality and may need further strengthening in schools. Also, familiarity with ways of social and political interaction and main aspects of political history and discourse is extremely important for newcomers who wish to make their mark as active citizens. However, forcing the specific political ways and identities of a national majority onto minorities in an unreflective and self-congratulatory way is arguably no more feasible or morally defensible than old-fashioned cultural assimilation.

Instead, narratives of belonging, value and good citizenship could perhaps – ideally – become not just fixed entry requirements, but stakes in a debate with many voices. So could the micro-parameters of actually practised political debate, decision-making and being-together of national political cultures. With yet one more conceptual spin on the pregnant signifiers at hand (Mouritsen, 2006b: 5), political languages or traditions are really *un*civic or *un*political when their meanings and references, their key ideals and defining practices, are themselves not contested and disputed, either because they belong to layers of practice which are barely reflected upon, or because they partake in ideological imagery, which is much too heavily identity-invested to be touched. Thus conceptualized, the constitution of a political community is less about sharing a given culture or identity, however thick or thin, and more about maintaining a political space where such cultures and identities are negotiated and contested.

This still leaves us with relatively demanding ideas of citizenship. Citizens of a public realm, short of a substantial identity, must still have *identification* with this realm. Identification denotes not being the same but being together or doing something together – in a civil way. Both aspects – sameness and interaction, maintenance of common culture/ identity and sharing in activities – are ancient republican themes, found from Machiavelli to Rousseau, and brought into normative sociology through Durkheim (Durkheim, 1992; Mouritsen, 2005b). In fact, Durkheim did not think moderns would be integrated by talking about the meaning of political citizenship or even by practising it. It is possible – despite this book, written largely by political theorists, political scientists, and historians of political concepts – that the problem nowadays is the obsession with *political* virtues and practices in advanced welfare states, which really require so much more from us – getting an education, raising children, finding a job and paying taxes. After all, there were always other ways to contribute and share and to imagine such sharing, than those which reflect or take place in the public square.

References

Abizadeh, A. (2002) 'Does Liberal Democracy Presuppose a Cultural Nation? Four Arguments', *American Political Science Review*, 92(3): 495–509.

Anderson, B. (1983) *Imagined Communities. Reflections on the Rise and Spread of Nationalism*. London: Verso.

Arendt, H. (1958) *Origins of Totalitarisnism*, 2nd edition. New York: Meridian Books.

Bader, V. (1999) 'For Love of Country', review essay, *Political Theory*, 27(3): 379–97.

Banting, K. and Kymlicka, W. (eds) (2006) *Multiculturalism and the Welfare State: Recognition and Redistribution in Contemporary Democracies*. Oxford: Oxford University Press.

Barth, F. (1969) *Ethnic Groups and Boundaries. The Social Organisation of Culture Difference*. Prospect Heights: Waveland Press.

Bauböck, R. (1996) 'Cultural Minority Rights for Immigrants', *International Migration Review*, 30(1): 203–50.

Bauböck, R. (2002) 'Farewell to Multiculturalism? Sharing Values and Identities in Societies of Immigration', *Journal of International Migration and Integration*, 3(1): 1–16.

Bauman, G. (1999) *The Multicultural Riddle. Rethinking National, Ethnic and Religious Identities*. New York: Routledge.

Benhabib, S. (2002) *The Claims of Culture: Equality and Diversity in the Global Era*. Princeton, NJ: Princeton University Press.

Buchanan, A. and Moore, M. (eds) (2003) *States, Nations & Borders. The Ethics of Making Boundaries*. Cambridge: Cambridge University Press.

Canovan, M. (2000) 'Patriotism is not Enough', *British Journal of Political Science*, 30(3): 413–32.

Commission for Racial Equality (2007) 'Integration, Multiculturalism and the CRE', http://www.cre.gov.uk/diversity/integration/index.html.

Dagger, R. (1997) *Civic Virtues: Rights, Citizenship, and Republican Liberalism*. Oxford: Oxford University Press.

Danish Ministry of Refugee, Immigration and Integration Affairs (2007) 'Declaration on Integration and Active Citizenship in Danish Society', http://www.nyidanmark.dk/NR/rdonlyres/7A32FAD0-E279-467C-91E3-3074249ED586/0/integrationserklaering_engelsk.pdf.

Eder, K, and Giesen, B. (eds) (2001) *European Citizenship. National Legacies and Postnational Projects*. Oxford: Oxford University Press.

Faist, T. and Triadafilopoulos, T. (2006) 'Beyond Nationhood: Citizenship Politics in Germany since Unification', Occasional Paper 1. Toronto: Munk Centre for International Studies, University of Toronto.

Favell, A. (2001) *Philosophies of Integration*, 2nd edition. London: Palgrave.

Føllesdal, A. (2000) 'The Future Soul of Europe: Nationalism or Just Patriotism? A Critique of David Miller's Defence of Nationality`, *Journal of Peace Research*, 37(4): 503–18.

Goodhart, D. (2004) 'Too Diverse?' *Prospect*, 95: 30–7.

Habermas J. (1990) 'Grenzen des Neohistorismus', in *Die nachholende Revolution*. Frankfurt: Suhrkamp. pp. 149–56.

Habermas, J. (1992) 'Citizenship and National Identity: Some Reflections on the Future of Europe', *Praxis International*, 12(1): 1–19.

Habermas, J. (1994) 'Struggles for Recognition in the Democratic Constitutional State', in A. Gutmann (ed.), *Examining the Politics of Recognition*. Princeton, NJ: Princeton University Press. pp. 107–48.

Hedetoft, U. (1999) 'The Nation-state Meets the World. National Identities in the Context of Transnationality and Cultural Globalisation', *European Journal of Social Theory*, 2(1): 71–94.

Holm, U. (1993) *Det franske Europa*. Aarhus: Aarhus University Press.

Honohan, I. (2002) *Civic Republicanism*. London: Routledge.

Ingram, A. (1996) 'Constitutional Patriotism', *Philosophy and Social Criticism*, 22(6): 1–18.

Joppke, C. (2003) 'The Retreat of Multiculturalism in the Liberal State: Theory and Policy', *The British Journal of Sociology*, 55(2): 237–57.

Koopmans, R. and Statham, P. (2003) 'How National Citizenship Shapes Transnationalism: a Comparative Analysis of Migrant and Minority Claims-making in Germany, Great Britain and the Netherlands', in C. Joppke and E. Morawska (eds.), *Towards Assimilation and Citizenship: Immigrants in Liberal Nation-States*. London: Palgrave Macmillan, pp. 195–238.

Kymlicka, W. (1995) *Multicultural Citizenship*. Oxford: Clarendon.

Laborde, C. (2002) 'From Constitutional to Civic Patriotism', *British Journal of Political Science*, 32(4): 591–612.

Laborde, C. (2006) 'Female Autonomy, Education and the *Hijab*', *Critical Review of International Social and Political Philosophy*, 9(3): 351–77.

Lacroix, J. (2002) 'For a European Constitutional Patriotism', *Political Studies*, 50(5): 944–58.

Levinson, M. (1997) 'Liberalism versus Democracy? Schooling Private Citizens in the Public Sphere', *British Journal of Political Science*, 27(3): 333–60.

Markell, P. (2000) 'Making Affect Safe for Democracy? On Constitutional Patriotism', *Political Theory*, 28(1): 38–63.

Maynor, J. W. (2003) *Republicanism in the Modern World*. Cambridge: Polity Press.

Miller, D. (1995) *On Nationality*. Oxford: Oxford University Press.

Modood, T. (1994) 'Establishment, Multiculturalism and British Citizenship', *Political Quarterly*, 65(1): 53–73.

Modood, T. (2007) *Multiculturalism*. London: Blackwell.

Modood, T. and Kastoryano, R. (2006) 'Secularism and the Accommodation of Muslims in Europe', in T. Modood, A. Triandafyllidou and R. Zapata-Barrero (eds), *Muslims, Multiculturalism and Citizenship: A European Approach*. London: Routledge. pp. 162–78.

Modood, T., Triandafyllidou, A. and Zapata-Barrero, R. (eds) (2006) *Muslims, Multiculturalism and Citizenship: A European Approach*. London: Routledge.

Mouritsen, P. (2005a) 'Four Models of Republican Liberty and Self-government', in I. Honohan and J. Jennings (eds), *Republicanism in Theory and Practice*. Routledge, London. pp. 17–38.

Mouritsen, P. (2005b) 'The Republican Conception of Patriotism', in H. G. Sicakkan and Y. Lithman (eds), *Changing the Basis of Citizenship in the Modern State. Political Theory and the Politics of Diversity*. New York: Edwin Mellen Press, pp. 133–60.

Mouritsen, P. (2006a) 'The Particular Universalism of a Nordic Civic Nation: Common Values, State Religion and Islam in Danish political Culture', in T. Modood, A. Triandafyllidou, and R. Zapata-Barrero (eds), *Muslims, Multiculturalism and Citizenship: A European Approach*. London: Routledge. pp. 70–93.

Mouritsen, P. (2006b) Editorial in special edition on 'Concepts of Politics', *Distinktion, Scandinavian Journal of Social Theory*, 12: 5–10.

Müller, J.-W. (2007) 'Is Europe Converging on Constitutional Patriotism? (And if so, is it be justified?), in *Critical Review of International Social and Political Philosophy*.

Nunez, X.-M. (2001) 'What is Spanish Nationalism Today?' *Ethnic and Racial Studies*, 24(5): 719–52.

Palonen, K. (2006) 'Two Concepts of Politics: Conceptual History and Present Controversies', *Distinktion, Scandinavian Journal of Social Theory*, 12: 11–26.

Parekh, B. (1997) 'A Commitment to Cultural Pluralism', *The Power of Culture*, http://www.powerofculture.nl/uk/archive/commentary/parekh_sum.html.

Patten, A. (1996) 'The Republican Critique of Liberalism', *British Journal of Political Science*, 26(1): 25–44.

Pettit, P. (1997) *Republicanism: A Theory of Freedom and Government*. Oxford: Clarendon.

Phillips, A. (2007) *Multiculturalism without Culture*. Princeton, NJ: Princeton University Press.

Phillips, T. (2006) The Isaiah Berlin Lecture, delivered at Hampstead Synagogue, 11 July 2006, http://www.cre.gov.uk/Default.aspx.LocID-0hgnew0hn.RefLocID-0hg00900c002.Lang-EN.htm

Pocock, J. G. A. (1975) *The Machiavellian Moment: Florentine Political Thought and the Atlantic Republican Tradition*. Princeton, NJ: Princeton University Press.

Putnam, R. (2007) 'E pluribus unum: Diversity and Community in the 21st Century', *Scandinavian Political Studies*, 30(2): 137–74.

Rasmussen, A. F. (2005) The Prime Minister's New Year's Speech, 31 December 2005, http://www.dansketaler.dk/tale.lasso?tale_id=366.

Rawls, J. (1985) 'Justice as Fairness: Political not Metaphysical', *Philosophy & Public Affairs*, 14(3): 223–51.

Rawls, J. (1993) *Political Liberalism*. Oxford: Oxford University Press.

Raz, J. (1994) 'Multiculturalism: A Liberal Perspective', *Dissent*, 41(1): 67–79.

Rosenblum, N. L. (1994) 'Civil Societies: Liberalism and the Moral Uses of Pluralism', *Social Research* 61(3): 539–63.

Rossteutcher, S. (1997) 'Between Normality and Particularity – National Identity in West Germany: An Inquiry into Patterns of Individual Identity Constructions', *Nations and Nationalism*, 3(4): 607–30.

Rothstein, M. (2005) *Social Traps and the Problem of Trust*. Cambridge: Cambridge University Press.

Rusconi, E. G. (1993) *Se cessiamo di essere una nazione*. Bologna: Il Mulino.

Sandel, M. (1996) *Democracy's Discontent. America in Search of a Public Philosophy*. Cambridge, MA: Harvard University Press.

Schiffauer, W. (2006) 'Enemies within the Gates: The Debates about the Citizenship of Muslims in Germany', in T. Modood, A. Triandafyllidou and R. Zapata-Barrero (eds), *Muslims, Multiculturalism and Citizenship: A European Approach*. London: Routledge, pp. 94–116.

Schnapper, D. (2001) *Community of Citizens: On the Modern Idea of Nationality*. New York: Transaction Publishers.

Skinner, Q. (1998) *Liberty before Liberalism*. Cambridge: Cambridge University Press.

Taylor, C. (1989) 'Cross-purposes: The Liberal Communitarian Debate', in N. L. Rosenblum (ed.), *Liberalism and the Moral Life*. Cambridge, MA: Harvard University Press, pp. 159–82.

Triandafyllidou, A., Modood, T. and Kastoryano, R. (2006) 'European Challenges to Multicultural Citizenship: Muslims, Secularism and Beyond', in T. Modood, A. Triandafyllidou and R. Zapata-Barrero (eds), *Muslims, Multiculturalism and Citizenship: A European Approach*. London: Routledge, pp. 1–22.

Turner, B. S. (1990) 'Outline of a Theory of Citizenship', *Sociology*, 24(2): 189–217.

Turner, B. S. (2001) 'The Erosion of Citizenship', *British Journal of Sociology*, 52(2): 189–210.

Viroli, M. (1995) *For Love of Country*. Oxford: Clarendon.

Wodak, R., de Cillia, R., Resigl, M. and Liebhart, K. (1999) *The Discursive Construction of National Identity*. Edinburgh: Edinburgh University Press.

2

Symbolic Power and Cultural Differences: A Power Model of Political Solutions to Cultural Differences

Klaus Eder

Political solutions to cultural differences?

History as a laboratory

History gives us a big laboratory for finding political solutions to cultural differences. In talking about political solutions, we exclude solutions by force, i.e. by military conquest. Political solutions imply more than violence, that those who are subject to a political order accept it more or less as legitimate.

Thinking about the political in these terms we can start to classify political solutions from a comparative macro-sociological perspective. A first type is the political integration of groups through marriage – you integrate the other by marrying him.[1] This creates segmentary social structures that have probably been the dominant mode of politics throughout human history. A second type is the imperial solution: under the emperor people are integrated into a hierarchy, their position depending on power and lineage to the top of the hierarchy (an extreme case is traditional India). This type found an interesting variant in the early modern and modern period when, under the emperor, all people were considered (formally) equal. (An extreme case is the Hapsburg Empire.)

The third type of solution is the fraternal, embodied in the idea of the nation. It is a strange hybrid, characterized equally by violence and freedom, inclusion and exclusion, fraternity and ethnic-cleansing. It is a paradoxical type that has conquered the world. It is ideal since it starts from the premise of free and equal people. But it is violent because it is based on the suppression of cultural differences which forces on people a language and a culture at the expense of their own. It succeeds to different degrees.[2] This paradoxical solution was legitimated by the assertion that all people speaking one language and sharing one culture were equal. These claims, however, were not sufficient to achieve social stability in the political order. A symbolic reference was required beyond the claims of freedom and equality: the people had to be members of a community that ties them together as a *particular* people. This is the solution we as members of a society live with.

My basic claim is this: the problem of making theoretical sense of this solution lies not in its ideal assumptions of free and equal people acting together politically. The problem is to establish what it means to be a *particular people* made up of free and equal human beings. Making sense of the national situation might help make sense of the emerging transnational situation. Then we would have a better idea of the mechanism that produces a particular people among free and equal human beings. We might even be able to weigh up the options for political solutions to cultural differences in a transnational situation.

The theoretical eye

To focus my problem: I am interested in how free and equal people are coordinated as a particular people. Since such people are necessarily culturally different (this I take as a given), the explanatory problem is this: Which particularity is chosen to describe the unity of this people? And how is this particularity accommodated to the universalistic claims of these free and equal people? All this is to reformulate the problem of nation-building on a more abstract level.

I see two types of answer to this question: we can either look at the ideal (or at least appropriate) solution or we can look at real solutions. 'Idealist' are those models that start from the normative premise of a universalistic mode of coordination that then is compared with the real situation. Normativists tell us what we should do regardless of the real situation in which such normative rules should operate (Offe, 1998; Barry, 2001). They express a lot of goodwill, but have nothing to offer to solve real problems. Other normativists (for example, Taylor, 1992; Kymlicka, 1995), introduce social reality to their normative model of cultural diversity. Kymlicka in particular has offered us a series of empirically accommodated normative models of how to live together with cultural differences. He varies the empirical situations from which the constraints on the liberal model he defends result. This latter approach offers an interesting insight into the variability of situations for a normative model, but it lacks an explanation of how particularistic models of coordinating differences emerge in such situations. It lacks a theoretically meaningful idea of the mechanisms of coordinating cultural differences.

'Realist' are those attempts that seek to understand the social mechanisms of coordinating cultural differences. In a realist perspective normative claims are a contextual condition for the processes of coordination which are to be described empirically and explained by identifying the modes of coordination of differences at work in a historically-specific situation.

This is our starting point. I will first present elements of a realist (non-normative) model of coordinating cultural differences and then test the model against the national and post-national situation. It should be noted that I am not speaking of a post-national situation in the sense that the national age is beig replaced by a post-national age. Rather, I take the evolutionary view of emerging structures that are added to existing ones while changing their function. (The function can be uselessness which means the death of a structural configuration; but this depends on contingent factors.) This analysis will offer material in terms of political solutions to the problem of coordinating cultural differences. Finally, I will identify options (6 + 1) regarding political solutions to cultural differences in the transnational context.

A realist model of explaining the coordination of cultural differences: the inevitable scandal of inclusion

Why do we need a realist model? This has to do with basic assumptions about acting together, or 'collective action'. When people act together, they necessarily exclude others. Who acts with whom is based on qualifying criteria of 'membership' in collective action. Not everybody is expected or even wants to participate. Only those with whom there exists a particular obligation are expected to act together. They are members of a group which share a special or 'particular' social relationship.

Another argument which explains the necessity of such particularistic social relationships is Olson's theory of collective action, which states that people do not act together unless they expect to gain something from it (Olson, 1965). To make people act together beyond their individual interests, we need incentives. Olson has proposed providing selective incentives as a mechanism to produce collective action. Others have proposed the mechanism of normative obligation which is based on external force (policing) or internalized obligation. Thus we can conclude that in order to provide collective goods we always have to exclude some from collective action in order to produce strong particularistic bonds among those engaged in group action.

The exclusivity of those included in collective action contains a power dimension. Power is thereby the simple fact of excluding others from being trusted co-actors. Power is also there by the force a group exerts on those cooperating: they have to comply with the group norms that emerge from the very process of inclusion. This mechanism has been described by Russell Harding as explaining the use of power against others in groups which defend a collective good (his example is the conflict between Serbs and Bosnians where such power has run wild) (Harding, 1997). Thus we have to start with the realist assumption that social life is permeated by particularistic bonds which exclude some and which serve as a basis for social power. This is the inevitable scandal of social inclusion: inclusion produces exclusion.

Linking social exclusion with cultural differences complicates the mechanism of social coordination. The easiest and clearest case among equal people is to conflate cultural difference with social exclusivity. This is obviously the solution of the nation-state. However, this is not what empires did – rather, they relied on the obligation resulting from religion in which people could not move out of their social class, which allowed inclusion of cultural differences and set them somewhere in that religion. The unity of differences was constructed through a ruler who claimed sacred legitimacy. This solution is not open to societies founded on equality.[3] When they have to accommodate cultural differences they do so by reference to equality, by locating differences in places of equal rank.

Is there a solution as elegant as the imperial one which could use the hierarchical (i.e. religious) order to include cultural differences while keeping a particularistic bond among diverse peoples?

The modern solution

The nation as a discursive space of free and equal people

The modern – equally elegant – solution is based on a special mode of justification of exclusiveness: the nation as a discursive space of free and equal people. Here you got both: free and equal people *and* boundaries. Thus the question in societies without a religious (hierarchical) order is this: On which grounds can you justify the exclusion of others? And on which grounds are those included selected?

For a group to select members they need to know who 'we' are. All those with whom we cooperate preferably are part of a 'we'. We do something together, whereas 'you' or 'they' do something separately, not with us. Thus a double relationship on the level of personal nouns exists: we versus you or they. But how do we know who 'we' are and who is not? Who knows who the Danish are? How do we know who is Danish? Who knows exactly who is unmistakably Danish?

The point can be made clear by an example. To know who is a Jew you need a widely accepted 'core' group that knows who is a Jew. This group defines whether somebody else fulfils a set of criteria they deem necessary, such as having a Jewish mother, sharing a certain creed and a set of symbols. Jews can also be those whom others consider to be Jews. The others' criteria for defining someone as a Jew do not necessarily coincide with the in-group criteria. Finally, you could consider yourself to be a Jew, but not be recognized by the core group of Jews as actually being a Jew. This process of defining whether or not somebody belongs to a group is what collective identity of a particular group, its particularity, is about.

The definition of who a German is is no less complicated. There are some who know unmistakably who is a German: those whose parents are Germans and who share a particular language. Others recognize Germans according to traits which Germans themselves would not necessarily consider, such as authoritarianism or certain virtues such as punctuality. There are also people who believe themselves to be Germans but are not recognized by the core Germans to be German; examples are those Germans excluded on racist grounds such as German Jews in Nazi Germany. I assume the same holds for knowing who is Danish.

Thus it is not at all clear who constitutes 'we'. They are selected according to certain criteria. Therefore we first have to clarify selection mechanisms. I will distinguish two mechanisms: one based on universalistic grounds and the other based on particularistic grounds. From this will follow a central distinction between a general 'we' of free and equal humans and a particular 'we' of humans with a special relationship to each other.

Selecting members of a group on universalistic grounds

Selecting members of a group on universalistic grounds is based on the free and fair agreement among actors to cooperate. In principle, everybody can enter such a contract. Nobody is excluded in principle. This is a universalistic 'we', which in principle includes everybody. Ideally, this group is identical to humankind.[4] Its ultimate ground is the modern idea that everybody is equally capable of sharing with everybody else the logical space of meaning and understanding.[5] This is the universal 'we' of humanity, an idea embraced by cosmopolitans and today by some positive thinkers on globalization and human rights theorists.

This universal 'we' is not practical since there is no political solution to the coordination of everybody in the world. It lacks a 'them'. But there is one concept for this universalistic kind of selective membership on universalistic grounds: citizenship. Not all human beings have citizenship.

Citizens share membership in a group linked to obligations resulting from a mutual contract. Membership in a group is a decision among contracting partners to accept reciprocal rules that are compatible with the rules governing a political community. This is what citizenship means: a negotiated membership in a community based on the principle of fairness.

Citizenship is a form of membership based on universalistic principles: fair and equal consideration of the interests of all entering a contract to act together. This has become the symbolic referent of modern revolutions, and has been radicalized into the idea of brothers (*Genossen*) who share a particular and universalistic obligation to each other and the whole. It is certainly the primary candidate to consider when looking at political solutions to coordinate different peoples to make them one.

This universalistic conception of citizenship has certain implications: it has to be open to everybody; nobody should be excluded by rules of membership that make it impossible to become a citizen. The only overriding rule that excludes membership is when somebody does not adhere to the rules of fair and equal social relationships. Such behaviour we normally regard as criminal or pathological. This is the reason why those in jail temporarily lose some of their citizenship rights. This makes criminalizing the other a useful mechanism for denying citizenship to foreigners.[6]

This universalistic conception of selective membership in a group (such as a nation) comes close to a republican notion of citizenship which derives its selectivity from a special obligation to a *res publica* defined in legal terms, i.e. as contractual arrangements among free and equal people.

Selecting members of a group on particularistic grounds

There is, however, a limiting condition to this universalistic account. Members of a group not only share an existing group's rules of fair treatment, they also enter the group's past. This provides a more restrictive criterion of membership. Those acting together should be able to do so while recognizing the past of the groups to which those acting together belong. This makes it difficult for a range of people to join a group. The acceptance of the rules of justice and fairness in dealing with each other is not sufficient to qualify for membership. What people share is a particular experience that they do not share with others. What we 'particularly' share with others is a past experience of acting together, which shapes the terms of trust and distrust among those sharing this experience.

Adding the criterion of a shared past, we rely on experiences we do not share with others. Thus there is a 'we' which is based on bonds beyond contractual relationships. It might even be that this relationship cannot be understood fully by others who do not share this experience of a past. We can tell each other about a past, but this does not mean that the others have the same feelings of obligations that I share with a particular group, but not with humankind.

Thus the basic argument for a particularity of a group is its *collective memory*. A collective memory is by definition 'particular' since it includes only those who are participants in a life-world. Observers cannot join. Such collective memory is inevitable. Which collective memory counts varies. It can be the collective memory of a family, a class, a nation, a civilization – in any case such boundaries between members of a group sharing a collective memory constitute necessarily particularistic groups (Halbwachs, 1992).[7]

Based on the distinction between membership in a group based on universalistic grounds and membership in a group based on particularistic grounds we come close to the central dilemma of societies based on the principle of equality: finding a political solution to membership in a group made up of equals which is compatible with both universalistic and particularistic grounds for selective membership.

This problem requires a mechanism beyond discourse: nobody will ever agree to be excluded even if we find good grounds for it. Thus we will necessarily end up in *dissensus* about who should be our fellow and who should not. Since a society cannot include everybody on universalistic grounds, it has to make a choice. It has to exert power in order to provide a stable solution to excluding some and including others given the basic consensus that all people are equal. This is the core question that comes up finally in a realist explanation of political solutions to cultural differences in societies made up of equals.

Symbolic power – the power of legitimate selection

How are people included in a social space where unequal ranks exist but equal chances are assumed? The realist sociology of equality says that the inclusion of people is based on a mechanism of naming those who are 'we'. Society uses its symbolic power to select people for inclusion in the social space.[8] A 'we' is the result of social struggles over naming. Symbolic struggles (Eder, 2002) are the key to explaining the emergence of a 'we' in societies based on the principle of equality.

Thus we have to expect in nationally defined societies an evolutionary increase in symbolic struggles. The more these societies are forced to communicate what they consider to be similar or different, the more we will have an increase in struggles over definitions and over names. In democratic societies in which permanent communication is the *raison d'être*, the opportunities for using symbolic power will increase. This includes symbolic violence, which has never been as fierce as in societies based on equality.[9]

In the transnational situation the evolutionary speed of communication increases and with it the importance of symbolic power. The 'ethnicization' of political action is a manifestation of its symbolic turn: Ethnicization is naming, which is communicated to state differences in public. Politics is an act of naming which says who belongs to the 'we' and who does not. It differentiates between friends and foes. Since we are not sure who is our friend and foe, permanent work on constructing such differences is necessary. The dissolution of the uniqueness of a national identity in the transnational space provokes further communication. It produces more symbolic power and increases the risk of symbolic violence.

To clarify this mechanism of symbolic power I will discuss first the national solution of institutionalizing particularistic grounds of membership in addition to the universalistic grounds of membership in a society of equals. This will be done using a realist model of explaining the naming of those who are considered to be part of a 'we'.

The national solution to cultural differences

The standard account of the selectivity of the modern nation-state

How has the nation-state resolved the problem of getting the universalistic and the particularistic aspect of membership in a group together? The standard account is the narrative of the nation as a group of equals proud of itself. This pride can be based on a revolution (how terrible it might have been) or on literary culture (the poets and thinkers of a linguistically defined group) or victories or defeats from which the nation emerges like a phoenix from the ashes (Giesen, 1998).

The nation as a promise of equality and the obligation to die for this promise are two sides of the same coin. They combine the universalistic and the particularistic aspect: the nation is a community made up of contracts and a community to die for (i.e. to kill those excluded from this community). Sharing a formal-legal institutional framework, the modern democratic state, provides the universalistic selectivity. The nation provides the unquestioned background of commonness among these equals.

There is a reflexive version of this narrative. Instead of being proud of one's cultural past, a group of equals could be proud of its achievement to have become a group of equals. This is the 'patriotic' version of being part of a political community – the citizen as a patriot who is proud of his/her constitutional history. This is again an argument linking a past to being a group of equals.

Both versions, the classical 'national' and the reflexive 'patriotic', tell us about the criteria used to exclude and include. But it does not tell us how such criteria could be applied to limit the space of communication among free and equal people. My proposal is to turn to a realist version by explaining how the state succeeded in limiting a space of communication to those sharing a cultural idiom.

A realist account of the selectivity of the modern nation-state

The realist version asks how the nation-state arrived at the cultural homogeneity of the nation. This is the question of the mechanisms that 'really' have coordinated cultural differences. Two mechanisms created the unity of the nation-state: popular appeals to equality and symbolic power. The democratic sense, how well justified it is on the normative level, works as a mechanism in terms of raising and meeting popular demands that may have hitherto been neglected. The making of the nation has been a violent process of imposing a linguistic idiom through educational institutions and of legitimating this imposed culture by producing events that allowed for positive identification, i.e. victories over those excluded. This mechanism of symbolic power worked well in a situation where communication started to increase exponentially. Karl W. Deutsch has explained nation-building as being produced by intensified communicative links among people. I would like to extend this argument by proposing that the use of symbolism is contingent upon such dense communication.

What these groups consider as their past are invented narratives or reorganized older narratives recounting a triumphant past.[10] In these stories a community of equals is created by imposing through public discourse a shared history. This guaranteed the exclusivity of the group. The particularistic nature of a social group was mediated with the universalistic claims of being a group of equals through the social mechanism of symbolic power by imposing through education and cultural policing a unity in the midst of cultural difference. The history of nation-building has often been a history of symbolic violence even to those included politically, yet who were culturally different. In this way Bretons were made French, Bavarians or Prussians made German, Friesians made either German or Danish, etc.[11]

The realist model therefore argues that political solutions to cultural difference are contingent on the availability of social mechanisms for creating a unitary culture in the midst of differences. The national situation provided such mechanisms: schools imposed by the state, military conscription, mobilization of the population in associations which told people what they had in common and provided rituals in which this collective memory was enacted 'day by day'.[12]

This is the national version of collective identities. Its characteristic has been to generate a unity where none existed before – this is even the revolutionary aspect of this invention of a cultural unity which can vary from a strong to a soft ethnic idiom (French or German versus American or Canadian).[13] Combined with the idea of equals it became an evolutionary success story.

The costs of this solution have been increased violence among different groups of equal people. People, no longer kings, were fighting each other. Again, the realist model appears: physical violence among people led to the finalization of borders – even with latecomers such as the Balkan and Central African countries since the 1990s.[14] As a result we now live in a world of politically organized nations, i.e. nation-states.

The national solution to cultural differences turns out to have been costly, yet effective. Placing the nation above cultural differences, the universalistic inclusion of citizens and the particularistic exclusion of non-fellows aspect were realized via the institutionalization of symbolic power in the form of the nation-state.

The transnational solution to cultural differences

The standard account of Europe as a transnational space of citizens

Can this institutional success story be reproduced in the emerging transnational situation? I will use the case of European integration to discuss the issue of political solutions to the problem of cultural differences beyond the nation-state.

In its standard version the debate on what constitutes the (emerging) unity of Europe is found in the debate on European citizenship. The argument is that citizenship emerges as a strong *idée directrice* in the development of a European society. This European development proceeds along the path taken by the nation-state. The nation-state model was conceived as a political centre controlling and regulating a society of *national citizens*. The national solution was based finally on identifying the nation with the state.

Europe certainly owes a lot to its nation-building past. The *idée directrice* of a European citizenship cannot be imagined without the tradition of democratic nation-building in Europe. Yet the closure of Europe cannot follow the national pattern since it has to reckon with the diversity of the nations in one political community. This gave rise to a variant of the citizenship debate which started with citizenship before the nation-state.

The variant is that European citizenship is traced back to the model of non-nationally defined communities, to the self-organization of citizens, which historians have observed in city-states, in empires, in enlightened absolutism and finally in the early nation-state. This European community of citizens continues – by replacement – the idea of a Holy Empire of souls that shaped Europe in its beginning. It also replaces the idea of a universal community of reasonable and discursive individuals invented as a model of the cultural unity of Europe. In Europe's institutional design the idea of civic participation takes the vanguard which previously had been salvation and education. The mytho-moteurs of religious transcendence and of inner-worldly transcendence by enlightenment and scientific progress are substituted by the mytho-moteur of collective self-creation through participation in public activities.

The mytho-moteur of citizenship transcends the limits of the myth of the nation and decouples the practice of citizenship from being the member of a national community defined by birth or territoriality. It mobilizes the myth of an association of free and equal beings living together harmoniously, i.e. the myth of a community of citizens brought into existence through the practice of citizens, the myth of a European Community and ever closer Union.

Such a myth continues a specific European tradition of framing a social order. The Church provided the frame of a community of souls striving for heaven; whoever failed to be saved was condemned to hell. Science and education provided the frame of a society in the pursuit of becoming perfectly rational and reasonable; whoever failed to join progress and rationality was bound to relapse into barbarism. Citizenship provides the frame of a self-creation of a community of citizens. Those who take part in this process will be included. The discourse on citizenship has become the transnational master-narrative of democratic self-organization in Europe.

These are powerful representations of a transnational space beyond the nation based on strong narratives of people living together as free citizens. Europe as an enlarged city-state – this seems to be the model of thinking a society of equals beyond the nation.[15]

This model of a unity of diversity is an idealist one, based not on explanatory accounts, but on *declarative* accounts: it declares how Europe could (and some would even go further and say should) be conceived as a unity. However, it does not tell us how Europe might get to this point. The question again arises: Which available mechanisms might produce a European society able to include some and exclude others while representing itself as a unity made of equal people?

A power-based account of Europe as a transnational space of cultural differences

The transnational situation, like the national situation, is characterized by cultural differences. It is even confronted with more cultural differences. This has to do with three phenomena.

The first is the simple fact of migration which has added cultural differences that did not previously exist in Europe. This is obvious. Secondly, transnationalization has led to a reaffirmation of particularistic identities, especially of what is called 'ethnic' identities. Europe is a case of the return of ethnic claims. This has to do with the stress European integration has put on national sentiments, and it has to do with the intensification of legal and illegal migration to Europe which increases the potential for claiming cultural differences. Thirdly, the nation itself has become a case of cultural differences within an emerging transnational community; national sentiments have become normal cultural differences. We might even consider national sentiments a variant of ethnic sentiments after having lost their primacy which was tied to the exclusivity of the nation-state.

The third phenomenon is particularly interesting, since it reduces the nation to a normal cultural difference, taking away its capacity of universalistic inclusion *and* particularistic exclusion. Thus the symbolic power that the nation-state had concentrated dissipates; what is left is the nation with a weakened state, left to play with its particularism in a transnational space which regulates the processes of inclusion and exclusion. Nations become collective actors like other 'ethnic' actors, still imbued with more power than other 'ethnic' collective actors defending a cultural particularity, but deprived of the ultimate legitimacy of representing in its particularity the universality of a modern political community.

The increase in differences in a transnational space such as the European Union is linked to a redefinition of clear identifiers of who is a European. Who belongs to these Europeans and who does not can no longer be decided according to criteria such as language or culture. Belonging becomes contingent on being a member of a member state. The other, the non-European, turns into a category of a member of a non-member state (in Italian they have a word for it: *extra-communitari*, in English: non-EU nationals).

We could call this transformation of cultural differences in the transnational space a process of *collective individualization*. This paradoxical term indicates that collectivities are disembedded from their traditional bonds. There are no longer traditional collectivities – they turn into individualized collectivities in search of their collective identity. They are turned into collectivities without tradition. What is left is a collective memory of this tradition.

The process of collective individualization turns out to be ambivalent. It fosters the construction of differences through which collectivities find out about their diverse 'we'. These individualized 'we' distinguish among themselves by difference construction, by producing often very fine, sometimes brute distinctions. This ranges from multicultural tolerance to competition and conflict which includes even the increasing probability of violence. In such situations the opportunities for 'ethnic' collective action increase exponentially.

Confronted with this effect political solutions to cultural differences encounter increasing restraints: symbolic power must be extended to the extent that opportunities for ethnic collective action increase. The transnational inclusion of a diversity of such ethnic 'we' (such as their inclusion into the European Communities, above all the European Union) produces a situation in which the coordination of a multiplicity of mobilized 'we' requires even more symbolic power than in the national situation. This is the realist conclusion: the more we enter the transnational space of individualized 'we', the more the mechanism of symbolic power will structure the process of the coordination of cultural differences.

This proposition is compatible with the theory that modern societies are societies that reproduce themselves through communication. Already the nation as the solution is contingent on communication as Karl W. Deutsch argued half a century ago. The transnational situation is even more contingent on communication. It is confronted continually with the communication of difference. Coordinating differences requires counter-communication, which necessarily implies symbolic power.

We have to expect that symbolic power comes from both sides. Those on top will try to communicate their policies more efficiently and engage in political campaigning. Those at the bottom will mobilize their voices by staging differences. Symbolic power and symbolic counter-power interact, producing spirals of communicating differences and thus increasing opportunities for symbolic power.

Symbolic power then reproduces real differences. First it does so by inclusion which is necessarily accompanied by exclusion. It produces legitimate exclusion from membership. In addition, it works within the space of the included by reproducing real differences through the unequal distribution of 'symbolic capital'. Those internally excluded are excluded by their lack of symbolic capital, which defines the 'value' of what those included possess as their real capital. Social classes within the space of those included differ not only in legal terms such as ownership of the means of production, but also in symbolic terms such as ownership of a symbolically highly valued 'habitus'. The most dramatic internal exclusion would be to construct a difference between those who share a common past and those who do not.[16]

Thus we have to expect an increase in symbolic struggles the more the transnational situation is extending its hold on defining the outer border of a space of included members and on reproducing cultural differences within the emerging transnational space.

Solutions: six + 1

Six political solutions to cultural differences in the transnational situation

The options available in this transnational situation of increasing symbolic struggles vary from legitimate symbolic power to symbolic violence. To capture this variation I will distinguish six options of political solutions to cultural differences in the transnational situation:

Option 1: The first option is to apply at the transnational level the national model which is the strategy of assimilating cultural differences through educational measures, the other into the orthodox dominant culture; this option requires the capacity of traditional symbolic power, i.e. the exclusive right of the state to control education. All included have to adhere to a cultural formula (*Leitidee*) which is similar to what universalistic religions or the nation have required from their members. Since transnational institutions will probably lack such capacity, this solution would require that we have to turn those making their ethnic claims of difference into Germans or French or Danes. However, this collides with the fact that transnational political institutions have already started to make national membership a particularistic aspect of being a member of the European Union. Nationality is nothing more than an entrance ticket that loses its validity after entry. This option would probably imply stopping the process of transnationalization.

Option 2: The second option is the strategy of imposing an orthodox idea of unity beyond the differences. This is the strategy of fundamentalist groups based on universalistic religious doctrines (mainly the Abrahamic religions). The Christian world and the Islamic world provide cultural models beyond the nation-state. Orthodoxy pushes symbolic power towards symbolic violence without which such unity cannot be had. It is a real option that can even go hand in hand with transnationalization insofar as it faces a much better opportunity structure than the national solution, i.e. option 1.

Option 3: The third option is a heterodox solution: the creation of a civil society for cultural differences. In this civil society cultural differences can be enacted, confronted, debated and mediated. Institutions act as watchdogs for this civil society (not the other way around) – they are detached from this dynamic of civil society. This option separates the cultural animal from the political animal in human beings: political solutions are left to institutions that provide deliberative spaces for heterodox movements in search of their particular identities. This option seems to be the actual strategy of the Commission, which provides fora for cultural groups to express themselves in their diversity. This is the institutionalization of heterodoxy.

Option 4: The fourth option is the mobilization of human rights discourses; this strategy, mainly followed by liberals/socialists, creates the abstract community of people having human rights; the political solution is to offer transnational courts of appeal if these rights are violated. Here cultural differences are co-ordinated by law. Judiciary institutions can mobilize much symbolic power and step in when nation-states no longer are capable of doing so. However, this requires the real universalistic creed that judiciary institutions will be fair and neutral. This form of transnational legal institutions beyond national legal institutions is an option that can start from a favourable opportunity structure in the transnational situation. This option might open an evolutionary path towards the model of a global political society proposed by global civil society theorists (Kaldor et al., 2003) and world society theorists (Meyer et al., 1997).

Option 5: The fifth option is the generalization of the rationalist code, to overcome cultural differences by mobilizing common economic interests, which excludes the other by separating spheres of interests that are in the interest of some 'we'. This is the old European Economic Community, incapable of coordinating cultural conflicts; however, the strength of neutralizing cultural differences through economic gains would provide a solution to cultural differences at least for those better off in the transnational situation.

Option 6: The sixth option is military power, which separates the world into military blocs within which a cultural unity is constructed by defining the other as the foe. Taking into account so-called 'new wars' (asymmetric conflicts between territorial military powers and deterritorialized terrorism) this option gains in importance. Inclusion and exclusion are regulated by military means, between and within competing cultures (the 'new civil wars', such as in Iraq after the second Gulf War). Such military conflicts are contingent on the success of symbolic definitions of the good and the bad. In this sense military power and symbolic power enter into a new kind of relationship, less substituting than supporting each other.

All these options have costs. A realist account shows to what extent they rest on the use of symbolic power, which in turn needs strong institutions to make their use feasible. Strong institutions capable of exerting symbolic power are at least (too) costly solutions. More probably, they might be incapable of producing the necessary symbolic power to coordinate cultural differences. This brings me to a seventh option.

A seventh option for a political solution to cultural differences

To develop the seventh option we have to abandon the theoretical assumption of a hierarchy of belongings on top of which we add a transnational unity of differences. This theoretical model of layers where the unity is on top still informs most of the debate on how to coordinate cultural differences. On top of the national community we then readily imagine theoretically a new and higher layer of identification.

This theoretical model is poorly placed. Therefore I propose – on the basis of a realist account of the making of particularistic groups – to think of particularity in the transnational situation in terms of cross-cutting identifications which vary in an issue-specific, ethnic-specific, nation-specific and – still – class-specific way. In the transnational situation there is no longer a people on top of class (sic), nation or ethnicity; there are rather a series of people (*demoi*) who identify at times with class, with nation or with ethnicity. The idea of a hierarchy of identifications is to be replaced by the idea of a network of cross-cutting identifications. These many *demoi* are held together by the reliability of an institutional framework they have accepted by voluntary agreement and which guarantees everybody the maximum fairness in real life.

Historically, we have some experiments in that direction. The Union of the American States, the 'first new nation', followed the path of an overarching identity on national and ethnic differences (euphemized in the metaphor of the melting pot). This Union represents the case of a second-layer community integrating diverse nations into one. Canada did not succeed and therefore represents a case that offers elements of a model beyond the national integration/assimilation model. Europe might go beyond the Canadian case, representing the case of a 'first non-nation of equal nations and ethnicities'. We could theoretically imagine Europe as a network of peoples based on a political bond beyond the national boundaries while recognizing the national bonds of these peoples. Unlike the United States, Europe has a long tradition of such tension-prone social structures: a society constructed with reference to a transcendental universal order.

However, this only tells the story of creating multinational societies based on a political bond that these peoples accept as their preferred form of creating a collective good. This is the 'republican' solution: the acceptance of formal rules that provide equal chances in collectively shared policy areas. This solution is deficient in one respect: it does not tell how cultural differences can be handled politically. There is no republican solution to the problem of cultural differences. In this solution symbolic power differences remain, even being circumscribed and civilized by the idea of a republican polity. In such republics the issue of cultural differences is only pushed to the backstage of the political theatre. And there is always the risk that it will return to the front stage, producing dynamics that are often hard to control (as regional protest or minority protest shows).

To solve this issue a different type of social bond is required. Since exclusive national bonds are excluded by definition and political bonds are insufficient, a different foundation of a bond binding culturally different peoples together has to be imagined theoretically. The proposal is to look at social bonds resulting from a shared story, the story built on a common history in a given territorial space. Thus the national peoples united in an encompassing unity (the reference case here is Canada) share a story that dates back to some beginning of their being part of a community (in Canada the colonization of no-man's land). This story provides a possible yet precarious bond. It works as long as the national peoples tolerate their respective memories.[17] Thus the bond is sharing a collective memory with other people with whom we are ready to share a republic.

The New Europe offers a similar option. Here the history of nation-building after the devastating Thirty Years' War and the Treaty of Westphalia provides a memory that binds nations to each other in terms of a shared history. This is at least the basis on which the founding fathers of the European integration process grounded their project: a Europe with nations that cooperate in peace. It turned out to be a strong bond for launching the project.

A peaceful Europe has been considered to be a basis for a republican solution to the peoples of Europe living together. This becomes manifest in the very conception of a European citizenship. The idea is based on the modern myth (or belief into the idea) of free and equal citizens participating in public affairs. To be a citizen in Europe derives from being member of a nation-state, thus becoming a European citizen by birth or descent. This idea is shared by the peoples in Europe; it resonates with past experiences of struggling against authoritarian domination in Europe.

Yet it seems that this double bond, the political bond based on the idea of living together in peace, is not sufficient to keep the process of European integration going. Peace is a necessary, but insufficient condition for grounding a republican political order in Europe, uniting nations and ethnicities in Europe. Therefore the question of a collective European identity is still open. Finding political solutions to cultural differences is ultimately a question of finding a shared cultural basis for living together in a republican world.

What these peoples could share within that space is a particular memory: the experience of a past of acting together beyond force, a feeling of sharing a history of struggle against domination. In this space they can even remake the national histories that had such devastating effects upon each other in the course of the modernization of Europe. A collective identity is created by sharing a space where national memories are combined in a collective myth of the victory of the people against rulers (kings).

Yet this bond carries with it an ambivalence which constrains its bonding capacity. This is the experience of the bitter histories that these people share and that are hard to share among them. The histories are built into traumatic memories which divide these peoples. This is the cultural ambivalence the New Europe is facing.

The model of cross-cutting political projects that exempt the cultural project of sharing a common history has another drawback. It is feasible only to the extent that there is a shared memory of the history of nation-states in Europe (or Canada). This shared history certainly does not include the immigrants/migrants. Thus this type of commemorating a common history is unfeasible as soon as social groups are to be included with whom the national 'we's' do not remember a shared and territory-bound history. This is the issue that comes up with the presence of 'non-national' peoples who are renamed as ethnic groups in a nation (even when they migrate from full-blown nation-states such as Turkey to Europe).

As soon as the republican solution with its internal problem of sharing a traumatic past is confronted with migrants/immigrants, this solution becomes even more problematic. With immigrant groups, renamed ethnic groups (ethnicities), the implicit assumption of sharing a common (hi)story no longer works. A shared memory of what these groups have in common has to be constructed from scratch. What the common history might be is again a question of symbolic power. The solution to this problem will say something about the degree to which symbolic power becomes power that can be distributed equally among the contenders.

So far, a European collective identity that supports a transnational space of equal and free citizens is struggling with a collective identity defined as the sum of its diverse national parts. The European flag with the stars conveys the idea that the sum is more than the parts and manifests Europe's collective identity. To overcome the limits of shared histories as shared national histories, the history of immigrant groups has to be included into a shared collective memory of Europe.

The cultural bond that is viable in such a situation is still hard to imagine. One possibility is to remember another traumatic European experience: its colonization of the world. This history creates a common history between Europeans and Africans, Asians and the peoples of the Middle East.[18] Reconstructing such a common history has merely begun, yet it provides the medium through which symbolic power tamed by republican procedures might act as a mechanism of coordinating cultural differences which provides a basis for the republican solution.

Thus the emergent property of the transnational situation in Europe, the network structure linking nations and ethnic groups and classes in diverse policy fields through republican procedures, has to be complemented by constructing a common history beyond the sum of mere national histories.[19] This is a final condition of creating social bonds which make a republican world in which cultural differences coexist feasible.

The European space in which symbolic struggles for recognizing each other's particular histories, the histories of nations as well as the histories of ethnic groups, are exposed to each other is especially suited for this experiment. It is especially suited since it is a space in which membership is the result of a fair procedure of negotiation that offers equally the options of voice, loyalty and/or exit. Each group can decide whether – given such conditions for voluntary membership – it is ready to share with the others its own history. If there is such a social bond, the decision to live with some other people together in a political community is no longer merely rational, but a reasoned decision, based on one's own identity (Sen, 1998).

This mode coordinating different past histories of national and ethnic peoples would in fact supersede the national solution and its derivatives, the six options mentioned above. Of course it will be exposed to the competition with the other options in the course of history – the outcome is open.

Conclusion

Symbolic power is the key to understanding the process of social bonding. To be able to act collectively and to produce collective goods, not only political bonds but also cultural bonds are needed. This gives to symbolic struggles a central role in creating the social bond. In symbolic struggles the definition is at stake of what a particular 'we' is ready to share as its past with the other's past. Such symbolic struggles easily lead to the disruption of social bonds – they are a highly sensitive medium of collective action. The presence of ethnic and nationalist conflict and their enduring existence is enough proof.

On the other hand, such symbolic struggles have a built-in self-binding mechanism. To the extent that histories of domination immediately enter the memory of the people, a symbolic counter-power emerges which is the recognition of a past in which some were perpetrators and other victims. Based on the memory of past real struggles symbolic power can be turned into symbolic counter-power, thus offering an alternative to violent conflict between social groups and collective identities: i.e. enlarging the capacity of groups to communicate and recognize the traumatic common history that their different pasts have produced. Working through a common past turns this past into a shared past – and on such strong foundations the vicissitudes of a republican solution, which arguably is the best normative solution we know of, can be lived.

Notes

1. A case close to the European tradition: the Romans did this with the Sabines by stealing their women and marrying them.
2. The French have been used as a model for this kind of forceful fraternization in the course of the making of the French nation, but this holds for most cases. See below.
3. The best, yet controversial explication of this difference is provided by Louis Dumont (1977; 1980). The crucial case for hierarchy is the Indian caste system.

4. I leave aside the question to what extent animals or plants can be made part of such agreements (through proxies who give them a voice).

5. This is sometimes denied by those defending the idea of cultural incommensurability. However, the self-defeating logic of this argument (how to argue for incommensurability when it is clear that the other will not understand?) is a deadly strike against it.

6. Such criminalization permeates empirically modern societies: analyses of media discourses on foreigners show that the criminalizing naming of foreigners has entered the discourse to such an extent that even 'liberal' media do not escape it.

7. This poses a problem, e.g. for those who want to become members of German society: do they take on the collective memory of the group or are they in a sense exempted from the past? The fact that there is no research on this question has to do with the problem that the integration of foreigners has only been discussed under the universalistic premise of citizenship.

8. Foucault's discourse theory is based on the idea of institutional orders which use their symbolic order for social control. This theory offers a provocative question: Is symbolic power a functional equivalent to physical power? Does the mobilization of symbolic power offer the possibility to avoid the recourse to physical power when power turns into physical terror?

9. This may sound paradoxical. However, equality-based societies no longer offer a natural place for the others. Therefore, killing the others might be a rational choice in such situations.

10. Where this triumphant past did not exist the narrative went to a glorious past further back in history (e.g. the past of the Serbian nation) or projected a failed past into the future as a project to realize. In this case the defeat in the past is the starting point of a triumphant future.

11. A famous book on the creation of cultural unity out of cultural differences is Eugen Weber (1976), who describes how rural peasants were transformed into Frenchmen, including the violence that was necessary to do so.

12. This is the realist version of Renan's formula of the nation as 'un plébiscite de tous les jours' (Renan, 1992).

13. This is a contested issue. The established distinction is between the ethnic German version and the republican French version. This seems to me to be a misplaced difference since it underrates the central difference of long versus short historical memories which are used to define the particularity of a people.

14. These latecomers again produced a lot of violence which turned symbolic violence into physical violence. In this way the civilizing effect of nation-building was interrupted and led to ethnic cleansing.

15. I have to admit that I too contributed to that idealist narrative without realizing the distance necessary to provide an explanation of its making (see Eder and Giesen, 2001).

16. This can be constructed in different ways. For example, Turks in Germany have to pass exams to prove that they not only 'know' the German language, but that they have what is considered knowledge of 'good German'. Such exams can easily be failed.

17. Canada provides a particularly interesting example of the importance of memory as a conflictual yet shared history: the phrase 'je me souviens' appears

on the licence plates of cars in Quebecois Canada, the less powerful national group within the Canadian nation.
18. Interestingly enough, Turkey's relation to Europe is outside such a common colonial past. Another past relates the European bond in a highly problematic way: the issue of Armenia and shared commemoration of victims and perpetrators. In this perspective, Turkey is closer to the national commemoration issue than to the immigrant-related issue of sharing a past.
19. For a discussion of these points, see the contributions to Eder and Spohn (2005).

References

Barry, B. (2001) *Culture and Equality. An Egalitarian Critique of Multiculturalism.* Cambridge, MA: Harvard University Press.

Dumont, L. (1977) *Homo Aequalis, I. Genèse et épanouissement de l'idéologie économique.* Paris: Gallimard.

——— (1980) *Homo Hierarchicus. The Caste System and its Implications*, revised edition. Chicago: University of Chicago Press.

Eder, K. (2002). 'Zur Logik sozialer Kämpfe'. *Mitteilungen des Instituts für Sozialforschung*, 13, 51–68.

——— and Giesen, B. (eds) (2001) *European Citizenship. National Legacies and Postnational Projects.* Oxford: Oxford University Press.

——— and Spohn, W. (eds) (2005) *Collective Memory and European Identity. The Effects of Integration and Enlargement.* Aldershot: Ashgate.

Giesen, B. (1998) *The Intellectuals and the Nation. Collective Identity in German Axial Age.* Cambridge: Cambridge University Press.

Halbwachs, M. (1992) *On Collective Memory.* Chicago, IL: University of Chicago Press.

Harding, R. (1997) *One for All. The Logic of Group Conflict.* Princeton, NJ: Princeton University Press.

Kaldor, M., Anheier, H. and Glasius, M. (2003) 'Global Civil Society in an Era of Regressive Globalization', in *Global Civil Society Yearbook 2003.* Oxford: Oxford University Press, pp. 3–33.

Kymlicka, W. (1995) *Multicultural Citizenship. A Liberal Theory of Minority Rights.* New York: Oxford University Press.

Meyer, J. W., Boli, J., Thomas, G. M. and Ramirez, F. O. (1997) 'World Society and the Nation-State'. *American Journal of Sociology*, 103: 144–81.

Offe, C. (1998) ' "Homogeneity" and Constitutional Democracy: Coping with Identity Conflicts through Group Rights'. *Journal of Political Philosophy*, 6: 131–41.

Olson, M. (1965) *The Logic of Collective Action.* Cambridge, MA: Harvard University Press.

Renan, E. (1992) *Qu'est-ce-qu'une nation?* Paris: Presses Pocket.

Sen, A. K. (1998) *Reason before Identity.* Oxford: Oxford University Press.

Taylor, C. (1992) *Multiculturalism and the 'Politics of Recognition'.* With commentary by A. Gutman (ed.), S. C. Rockefeller, M. Walzer and S. Wolf Princeton, NJ: Princeton University Press.

Weber, E. (1976) *Peasants into Frenchmen. The Modernization of Rural France 1870–1914.* Stanford, CA: Stanford University Press.

3
Making Citizens: On the Genealogy of Citizenship Ceremonies

Tine Damsholt

How are loyal citizens made? Politicians have been asking this question since the emergence of statehood, and it appears that citizenship ceremonies are a solution that many older nation-states are resorting to when facing the multicultural challenge at the beginning of the twenty-first century. Countries such as Australia and Canada continue to practise older traditions, whereas other countries have newly invented traditions celebrating naturalization and citizenship. In the following, Britain, Sweden and Denmark serve as examples of the latter.

The ceremonies in these five countries follow two different agendas. In Australia, Canada and Britain, the core element of the citizenship ceremony is the oath of allegiance, framed by an official welcoming speech, presentation of certificates of citizenship, the singing of the national anthem and concluding with light refreshments. These ceremonies follow a national matrix, though they are conducted locally with some variations. In Denmark and Sweden, there is to date no national legislation concerning the form, much less whether there should be ceremonies at all,[1] but several local authorities have taken the initiative to hold celebrations for new citizens in their municipalities.

The Nordic ceremonies do not include swearing-in or other communal core elements, but are fairly informal public celebrations that vary greatly, though they often include an official welcoming speech, flags, music, refreshments and the national anthem. Nevertheless, multiculturalism informs all rituals in both the Nordic and Commonwealth countries: food and beverage are adjusted to a heterogeneous audience, and it is possible to choose alternative versions of the pledge according to religious convictions. We will return to these dimensions and particularities of the ceremonies later.

The reasons for creating ceremonies are similar: becoming a citizen is valuable and therefore something to celebrate. The ceremonies 'have an important symbolic role because they formally welcome new citizens from many cultures into the Australian family', as expressed on the Australian government's homepage. In the Commonwealth countries, the ceremonies are a formal part of the naturalization process. You become a citizen on the day you attend the ceremony and make the pledge. The ceremony thereby replaces an official letter, which was earlier the only notice of newly gained citizenship, whereas the ceremonies in the Nordic countries are voluntary supplements to the letter.

The point of departure for the newly created British ceremony was a White Paper, *Secure Borders, Safe Havens: Integration with Diversity in Modern Britain* (Home Office, 2002), which made clear the importance of the new citizens gaining a 'fuller appreciation of the civic and political dimensions of British citizenship and, in particular, to understand the rights and responsibilities that come with the acquisition of British citizenship'. Ideally, British citizens should 'positively embrace the diversity of background, cultures and faiths that living in modern Britain involves, and that new citizens should be encouraged to play an active role in society and feel a sense of belonging to a wider community' (*Citizenship Ceremonies. Consultation Document*: 6). Much greater emphasis was to be placed on the 'value and significance of becoming a British citizen' by celebrating the granting of citizenship. Furthermore, the ceremonies normally should be conducted in groups to 'reinforce the community nature of citizenship'.

Thus far, no national legislation has been enacted in Sweden and Denmark concerning such ceremonies and, when conducted, they are voluntary. Here, the welcoming and celebration of new citizens and cultural diversity seem to be the core of the initiatives by creating an 'extra festival'.[2] Further, the ceremonious and festive components are emphasized by holding the ceremonies on so-called national days.[3] The idea is to make new citizens feel welcome, but also to mark the occasion with something special to make it more memorable, thereby making the rights and obligations of citizenship felt more deeply.

In Australia, citizens by birth or by choice have, since 1999, been given the opportunity to renew and affirm their commitment to their country by taking part in an affirmation ceremony. These affirmations are extremely popular and are often held as part of citizenship ceremonies, by organizations and schools, or on days of significance to Australian citizenship, such as Australia Day or Australian Citizenship Day (16 January and 17 September).

The idea of the importance of making the occasion memorable inscribes citizenship ceremonies into the 'experience economy', since 'the engagement of customers in a memorable way' is the exact definition of an experience following Pine and Gilmore's concept (1999: 4). However, experiences seem not to be the goal but only the means for something deeper. One general purpose of these new rituals of citizenship is to create a sense of belonging, to produce citizens with a special kind of subjectivity. But how is this civic self established? What can guarantee that individuals as citizens will actually experience the sense of belonging that is considered necessary to feel an obligation towards the state, the nation or the fatherland? Which kind of causal ideas are the invented traditions based on?

This chapter investigates these questions primarily from a cultural history perspective. Following Foucault's genealogical approach (Foucault, 1971), the focus is on extraction (*Herkunft*) rather than origin (*Ursprung*), and this history of the 'kinship' of cultural phenomena is heterogeneous, dissolving the idea of a single truth or essence (Dreyfus and Rabinow, 1983: 107–15). Therefore, several genealogies are possible in the case of citizenship ceremonies, but the analysis is conducted along two lines of kinship: similarities with political rituals in the era of the French Revolution; the cult of federation in France and the local interpretations of this political culture in other countries in the same period, e.g. the multi-ethnic Danish–Norwegian state. This new political culture was permeated with religious forms in structure and iconography. Thus, the second line of investigation concerns communal ritual and religious structures in the ceremonies.

Political culture of the French Revolution

Though citizenship ceremonies have an ancient origin in the classical republics of Greece and Rome, this genealogical analysis focuses on their reinterpretation on the European political stage in the late eighteenth century, since a number of historians have described the French Revolution as a laboratory, highlighting a series of changes in political culture (e.g. Hunt, 1984; Outram, 1989; Schama, 1989; Landes, 1998). It led to the implementation of the political theory of the contract which is still the core of most prevailing political philosophies, which regards the people as the true sovereign body. Only power exercised in agreement with the will of the people is legitimate.

Jean-Jacques Rousseau, in his *Du Contrat Social* (1762), defines *la volonté générale* as something different from and more than the sum of individual wills (*la volonté des tous*). The general will is determined by the interest of the general good. In this sense, the people came into existence in their aspiration for the general good, with the individual subordinating his/her own interests out of concern for the collective. The citizen's ethical imperative consists of loyalty by putting aside his/her own interests in favour of the general will and for the sake of the general good. This ideal subjectivity was called love of the fatherland, i.e. the political community above cultural differences. According to this logic, the subjectivity of the individual as a *citizen* became essential for political Utopia.

The French Revolution thus engendered a new political culture that tried to legitimize a new form of state, through both rhetoric and visual symbolism (Hunt, 1984) and through physical expressions of the utopian civic subjectivity. In this production of political forms, symbols and practices, the individual bodies in the new, sensitive public space played a decisive role. Part of the bourgeois revolution was that 'the gaze of society', which previously had been directed at the person and body of the king, focused instead on the interiors of the citizens (Outram, 1989: 42, 80), but also that this virtuous interior had to be staged in the public space as a form of theatre.

As the historian Joan Landes suggests, the paradox of popular representation must be taken into consideration 'when the sovereign is faceless and in the majority, when the ability to speak on behalf of the people or to represent it is always in danger and subject to objection. For the same reasons, the democratic body politic requires a stage and must be constantly performed' (Landes, 1999: 163).

With the end of absolutism in France or, as in the Danish-Norwegian state, with a new interpretation of absolutism,[4] the public space became the stage upon which the utopian subjectivity of the citizens and the people was to be embodied. The celebration and staging of princely power in the public space was already an integral part of absolutism. The French Revolution, however, created a new cultural phenomenon in the form of didactic state festivals, which instead staged abstract values such as reason, equality among citizens and the shared duty to the fatherland. One such new ritual was the *Fête de la Fédération* in 1790, which inspired local political performances in several European countries (e.g. England; see Colley, 1992). For the festival, the Champ de Mars was transformed into a huge amphitheatre with an 'altar to the fatherland' at the centre. Thousands of national guards swore their loyalty to the constitution at this altar, with its inscription proclaiming that all mortals were equal and that virtue, not birth, made the difference. A new revolutionary religion was created, 'a cult of federation', which was more or less in opposition to the Catholic Church, but simultaneously borrowed from its iconography (Schama, 1989: 414, 502, 768). Emotional outbursts played a major role in these rituals; all the events ended in collective 'patriotic tears and embraces' (Vincent-Buffault, 1986).

One prerequisite for understanding this change in the political culture was the eighteenth-century European culture of emotion, which focused on feelings as the seat of a person's proper moral responsibility for society. The historian Simon Schama shows how a 'cult of sensibility' combined with a fascination with classical citizen republics was an integral part of the cultural construction of the citizens of France in the late eighteenth century. The same was true in many other parts of Europe, where the educated class of nobles, citizens and intellectuals cultivated the same ideas. Unlike the rococo court's concentration on external formalities (manners and style), the focus was now on the interior (virtue and morality). Powerful feelings and the possession of *un cœur sensible* were seen as preconditions for morality (Schama, 1989: 149).

One important element of this interest in the self was the aesthetic theory of the *sublime*, of soul-shaking experiences as a central field in self-knowledge. It is in encounters with unfathomably large phenomena of the senses and nature that the sublime arises. A transcendent meeting with 'terrible beauty' means that the individual has to relate to new sides of his/her character and hence get to know him/herself. The focus on emotions was also based on philosophical discussions suggesting that sensory experiences constitute the self, and therefore were accompanied by the associated scientific investigations of the nervous system as the seat of sensibility (Barker-Benfield, 1992). The objectification of feelings in science and art, the detailed description and textualization of how emotions are felt and expressed, may be regarded as discursive practices and a condition for the ability of individuals to recognize such emotions in themselves (Abu-Lughod and Lutz, 1990), thereby resulting in a process of subjectification.

Subjectivity

I have emphasized some cultural preconditions for the emergence of a specific form of subjectivity. One of the main theorists examining the relation between culture and subjectivity is Foucault, who describes his objective as a 'history of the different modes by which, in our culture, human beings are made subject' (1983: 203).[5] His analyses of discourse and discipline (e.g., Foucault, 1969/1972, 1975/1979) are thus about how specific types of subjectivity are formed. However, these analyses are somewhat narrow, as Foucault puts the greatest emphasis on subjection and domestication, whereas an actual analysis of the formation of subjectivity as self-awareness is insufficient. Analysing subjectification concerns the constitution of free subjects with a consciousness, not mechanically obedient slaves. More productive is Foucault's later work on what he calls

> technologies of the self, which permit individuals to effect by their own means or with the help of others a certain number of operations on their own bodies and souls, thoughts, conduct, and way of being, so as to transform themselves in order to attain a certain state of happiness, purity, wisdom, perfection, or immortality. (Foucault, 1988: 18)

Foucault's point here is that it is precisely via individuals' work with themselves and via their 'freedom' and self-ethics that subjectification takes place. The subjectification process simultaneously constructs and recognizes the subject's self-determination. One characteristic of modern society is that the relation between citizens' freedom and subjection is problematic, and solutions are sought in both political philosophy and practice. In his later courses of lectures, Foucault defines and explores what he calls 'governmental rationality', or using his own neologism, governmentality (Gordon, 1991: 1). Governmentality is the encounter between technologies for the domination of others and those of the self (Foucault, 1988: 18). In this chapter, we are interested in the relationship between an emerging European governmentality based on the government of the self (Rose, 1999) and the development of new forms of technologies of the self that support this new way of governing. The government of oneself (the subjectivity, morality or, in the terminology of the period, love of the fatherland) was the key problem for this form of government, which was different from earlier forms based on physical coercion. The governmentality of the emerging nation-states presupposed moral imperatives, such as an inward urge or emotion, to be heartfelt. Thus the cult of citizenship, of civic morality and patriotic emotions, can be interpreted as part of the gradual development of a modern Western form of governmentality.

The political discourse was based on 'the fiction of a neutral but embodied (because natural) subject, an individual capable of subjecting passion and interest to the rule of reason' (Landes, 1998: 132). This civic subjectivity was an ideal, but the subjectivity of the actual population deserved great attention, according to the patriotic logic of the period. The actual population had to be improved. What is interesting here is that it was an *emotion* like love of the fatherland that became a central virtue in the complex of political ideas. The cult of sensibility naturalized feelings as the entity ensuring the ideal responsibility and subjectivity of the population, and established a specific causal connection between emotional movement and the creation of the patriotic or civic self.

Technologies of the civic self

This relationship between emotion and virtue informed the citizen rituals in the political culture of revolutionary France. The repetition of the same activities and the use of the same symbols, such as liberty trees and female representations of the republic, were important elements in the construction of a sense of community (Hunt, 1984). The speeches and choreography of tactile experiences and physical presence formed rituals in which the nation was symbolically created. This didactic of citizenship is in keeping with the logic developed by Jean-Jacques Rousseau in his *Du Contrat Social* (1762), in which he argues that because political and social unity in society are necessary, they must be supported by what he calls a civil religion. A civil religion works by making the fatherland the object of the citizens' veneration and by teaching them to serve the state. It thereby secures the feeling of unity and the morality of the single citizen. Traditional religion might work in this way, but it also implies dangers or defects, since, for example, Christianity detaches the citizens' hearts from all earthly things. And as Rousseau states: 'I know of nothing more contrary to the social spirit' (1997: 147). Furthermore, Christianity preaches nothing but servitude and dependence, which are extremely favourable for tyranny. However, since it certainly matters to the state that each citizen has a religion that makes him/her love his/her duties, it is up to the sovereign to fix the articles of such a purely civil profession of faith. The dogmas of this religion are only of concern to the state insofar as they 'bear on morality and on the duties which everyone is bound to fulfil toward others' (1997: 150). The articles of civil faith should be formulated as 'sentiments of sociability, without which it is impossible to be either a good citizen or a loyal subject'. 'Beyond this everyone may hold whatever opinion he pleases', Rousseau argues, confirming the eighteenth-century idea of religion as a private matter. Religion constituted an inner, non-political zone in opposition to a secular, political space; both culturally-specific constructions (McCutcheon, 2003).

The ideas of faith, emotion and morality tied together and as the agents that would secure a heartfelt inward urge or subjectivity also call for new technologies of the utopian civic self. Rousseau develops the didactic reflections further in his exemplary *Considerations sur le gouvernement de Pologne et sur sa réformation projecté* (1772). Here he reflects on the necessity of inscribing the constitution in the hearts of the citizens, which in his philosophy is one of the central locations in the interior, moral topography of the self:

> There will never be a good and solid constitution unless the law reigns over the hearts of the citizens; as long as the power of legislation is insufficient to accomplish this, laws will always be evaded. But how can hearts be reached? That is a question to which our law-reformers, who never look beyond coercion and punishment, pay hardly any attention; and it is a question to the solving of which material rewards would perhaps be equally ineffective. . . . How then is it possible to move the hearts of men, and to make them love the fatherland and its laws? Dare I say it? Through children's games; through institutions which seem idle and frivolous to superficial men, but which form cherished habits and invincible attachments. (Rousseau, 1772/1991: 165)

With reference to leaders in antiquity, he thereby argues for the benefit of public ceremonies as a perfect institution for engendering love for the fatherland in the hearts of citizens: national religious ceremonies, games, exercises and spectacles that 'touched their hearts, inflamed them with a lively spirit of emulation, and attached them strongly to that fatherland with which they were meant to be incessantly preoccupied' (Rousseau, 1772/1991: 166). This, Rousseau emphasizes, is 'the art of ennobling souls' (p. 170). In keeping with Foucault's characterization of the emerging governmentality, Rousseau finds education and setting a good example more successful than prohibition. Education can give souls a 'national formation' and make them 'patriotic by inclination, by passion, by necessity'. Civic subjectivity must become an inward urge rather than an outer claim. And festivals and rituals are perceived as technologies by which the civic self is transformed and generated.

Rousseau's ideas and the political culture of the French Revolution echoed all over Europe and also in the multinational conglomerate of the Danish-Norwegian state. Professor Laurits Engelstoft lived in Paris for several years during the Revolution, and the didactics of citizenship he developed after his return to Denmark are more or less a 'Rousseau light' or Rousseau's theory of civic education interpreted within absolutism. Ceremonies as the means for forming the desired subjectivity are exemplarily expressed in *On the Influence that Education, Especially Public, Can Have for Instilling Patriotism: An Essay in State Pedagogy* (1802). Here, the author operates with classical didactics of citizenship: tuition in history, narratives about exemplary conduct and physical training.

In keeping with Rousseau, Engelstoft suggests 'promoting patriotism via sensuous means'. He emphasizes the necessity of influencing the heart, which he claims can be done through the senses. Ceremonies and national festivals have to be created so that one can stage 'instants' that 'shake a young person' so they will not be forgotten. He therefore proposes the institutionalization of a youth festival that could fill the heart with the noblest sentiment; for this it had to have 'a stamp of importance' and 'a solemn pledge must be made and certain symbolic actions performed, intended to move and elevate the heart' (Engelstoft, 1802: 57).

Tacitus' account of the Germanic tribes, Roman antiquity and the rituals and *inscription civique* of the French Revolution formed the basis for Engelstoft's description of a 'festival of the Fatherland': the (male) youths who complete an education in their obligations as citizens should form a solemn procession that proceeds to a temple dedicated to the fatherland. A kind of throne should be created for the spokesman of the state, who is responsible for communicating the fatherland's expectations to its sons about being industrious, virtuous and willing to defend it. In the centre, an altar dedicated to the fatherland is to be set beneath the national flag, decorated with emblems of civic virtues. Here, the Statute Book should be waiting for the pledge to be taken by each of the young men. After the ceremony, a 'humble more than costly meal' is to be arranged.

We recognize here core elements in the French didactic festivals and Rousseau's didactics. With their soul-shaking properties, the solemn ceremonies can be understood not just as staging patriotic utopia, but also as a technique for subjectification via the creation of the emotions meant to generate the matching civic subjectivity.

A religious matrix

The prevailing religious features of Engelstoft's citizenship ceremonies – a performance at a *temple* with an *altar* and the ritual named a civic *confirmation* – are hardly a coincidence. Besides the clearly classic model for Rousseau's didactics, the Christian Church no doubt played an important role in his ideas concerning civil religion, just as the political culture of the French Revolution drew strongly on the established iconography of the existing church.

Recently, Anthony D. Smith argued that sacred belief remains central to national identity, even in the increasingly secular, globalized modern world. In *Chosen Peoples* (2003), Smith is in search of the deep Judeo-Christian roots of the many manifestations of national identity: the national myth of origin, the sacred homeland, the golden age, the commemoration of the glorious dead. Similarly, the French Revolution marked the transition from representations of charismatic individuals to mass celebration and commemoration. David's painting, *Marat assassiné* (1793), depicting a Christ-like wounded position, and the *Pantheon*, as a mausoleum not just for famous French men, but also as a temple in which citizens can reflect upon the virtues and greatness of France itself, became, among other central elements in the new idea of the nation, sacred communion. In Germany, the early national festivals were modelled on the Lutheran services, as acts of worship, at once Christian and national (Smith, 2003: 218–40). In the case of Rousseau and his heirs throughout Europe, it seems that a religious matrix prevails in a broader sense than merely in politics of nationalism, i.e. in weaving the fabric of Western political culture emerging in the era of the French Revolution.

The strong emphasis on emotional devotion in the cult of people and citizens can also be interpreted along a religious axis as a legacy of the inwardness and fervour of Pietism. Moreover, this is in keeping with Rousseau's ideas about the self-worship of the people. The pivotal point in both Pietism and the political rituals seems to be the issue of self-improvement. Foucault also points to early Christianity as one of the sources of the gradual development of technologies of the self, in a genealogical perspective (1988).

Foucault describes the evolution of the hermeneutics of the self primarily in two different contexts: the care of the self, self-interpretation and self-exercise in Greco-Roman philosophy and self-examination, self-confession and verbalization in early Christian monastic principles. These different technologies among others gradually constitute the idea of an inner, true core entity: the self. Foucault's primary object is the technologies of self-confession later to be reinserted in the field of psychoanalysis, since he conducts this genealogy in relation to his history of sexuality. However, by exploring this issue, he fails to see the field of technologies of the self developed in later versions of Christianity, and he thereby misses Pietism and its fellow versions as obvious cases for a genealogy of technologies of self-improvement.

Several scholars propose Pietism as a central phenomenon for understanding enlightenment and the rise of a public sphere (e.g., Fulbrook, 1983; Gawthorp, 1993; van Horn Melton, 2001; Bredsdorff 2003; Horstbøll, 2003). Pietism can be understood as part of a wider crisis in confidence in the late seventeenth century. The Pietists and their spiritual father P. J. Spener called it a 'reformation in the reformation' or an 'inner reformation'. Moral and religious reform demand genuine repentance and conversion, not through mere outward consent to doctrinal principles, but only through an inwardly cultivated faith. True Christians carry out their obligations voluntarily and with conviction. One of the key Pietist terms *Innerlichkeit* stresses this inwardness, which is accompanied by a determined social activism. The Pietists' spontaneous, conversational, religious meetings – the conventicles – had strong egalitarian implications, emphasizing feeling and emotion over intellect, with participants from both sexes and all social groups. They can be seen as forerunners to the coffeehouses and political meetings of the late eighteenth century and the rise of the public sphere (van Horn Melton, 2001: 314), though this alternative genealogy will not be pursued here. Instead, I would like to suggest that Pietism (and the similar reform movements within Protestantism and Catholicism) is a central field in the development of new technologies of self-improvement within theology and education. In Pietist theology, conversion is portrayed as a gradual process, with a refined description of its distinct stages. Pietism also established educational institutions and practices for the improvement of the individual and the population as a whole, in their educational complex from compulsory schooling to university. Self-discipline, a sense of obligation and industriousness were the core values in these education programmes, and the students were provided with tools for their own improvement.

Thus, Pietism was optimistic about creating disciplined, Christian citizens through instruction and reading, especially with new versions of the catechism. As for enlightenment, one of the key concepts of Pietism is light. Besides the dimension conditioned by reason, light has another inconceivable, emotional dimension, which is the prerequisite for the rebirth of the individual (Horstbøll, 2003: 89). The primal object of Pietist enlightenment was the reformation of the heart, establishing a reborn, sin-conscious and self-correcting person. And to prepare, examine and celebrate this desired inner reformation, several Lutheran countries reintroduced the ecclesiastical confirmation of youth.[6] As noted above, the heart also holds a central place in Rousseau's idea of an interior and moral topography. The similarities between key Pietist concepts and rituals and Rousseau's ideas, mentioned earlier, are therefore striking, as are the structural similarities between Pietism, enlightenment and the new political ideals. In Pietism, one catches a glimpse of the eighteenth century's new, self-assured, social individual. The individual possessed with a moral sentiment (Horstbøll, 2003: 93). Pietism implied confidence in individuals' options to improve themselves. Thus, the individualization and the technologies of the self generated within Pietism can be seen as one of the conditions for the development of the new political culture and didactics of citizenship in the era of the French Revolution and for a new governmentality, the government of the self, based on the citizens' individual, heartfelt, inward urges to do right.

Didactics of citizenship in a new millennium

British citizenship ceremonies can serve as an illustration of a modern ritualization of citizenship. They were introduced in 2003 and the first took place in London 2004. The process of naturalization, of which they are a formal and final part, has already been made more demanding: starting in November 2005, one needs to demonstrate knowledge of life in the new country as a condition for being granted citizenship. The British ceremony begins after the registration and examination of the invited participants. After this ritual of identification, they receive their pledge cards with the words of the oath or affirmation and the pledge that they have to say during the ceremony. The ceremony opens with a short welcome speech, at which time an official 'formally welcomes those who wish to join us into full membership of the British family and into Citizenship of the United Kingdom'.[7] The metaphor of the multicultural nation as a family can be retrieved from a number of the websites concerning naturalization and citizenship in Western countries.[8] The welcome is followed by the core elements: the oath or affirmation of allegiance and the pledge. The wording of the oath runs: 'I [name] swear by Almighty God that on becoming a British citizen, I will be faithful and bear true allegiance to Her Majesty Queen Elizabeth the Second, her Heirs and Successors, according to law.'

If the affirmation is chosen, the words 'swear by Almighty God' are replaced with 'solemnly and sincerely affirm'. After the oath or affirmation of allegiance, the new citizens take the citizenship pledge: 'I will give my loyalty to the United Kingdom and respect its rights and freedoms. I will uphold its democratic values. I will observe its laws faithfully and fulfil my duties and obligations as a British citizen'.

Then the new citizens receive their citizenship certificates and information packs. Later, the audience, made up of friends and family members of the new citizens, is encouraged to rise and give a 'warm round of applause for our new citizens', and is kindly asked to remain standing for the playing of the national anthem.[9] After the ceremony, a reception with light refreshments is recommended, which emphasizes the commonalities of the structures of the new ceremonies and the rituals of the revolutionary era, as illustrated by Engelstoft's description.

The features of the British ceremony are very similar to the Australian and Canadian ceremonies; in the latter, the wording of the oaths is almost identical. In the Australian version, 'From this day forward, (under God), I pledge my loyalty to Australia and its people, whose democratic beliefs I share, whose rights and liberties I respect, and whose laws I will uphold and obey',[10] the monarch is replaced with 'the people', i.e., the subject and sovereign of the democracy. Nevertheless, according to the official guidelines, a portrait of the queen is requested; therefore, the monarch is not absent. Neither is God, though the possibility of making the oath or pledge in a form with or without the reference to God is a common feature of the British Commonwealth ceremonies. It is striking nevertheless that, in the British and Canadian affirmations, in the alternative instance one may refer to 'solemnly and sincerely' and this seems to be an inner core entity – a true self – that the affirmation is in correspondence with. The idea of the self and the sentiments of the heart as the instance that guarantees the moral virtue of citizens, the sense of belonging and obligation, are completely in keeping with the eighteenth-century ideas described above.

Though it is possible to leave reference to God out of the pledge, God is unavoidable in the national anthem, which is the final element of the ceremonies. In *God Save the Queen* and in *O Canada* (with the line 'God keep our land glorious and free'[11]), although they are not exclusively Christian, but at least monotheistic, a religious framework is invoked.[12] Despite the attempt to establish a political ceremonial setting beyond cultural and religious differences, the Christian legacy of the European monarchies is inevitable. Without doubt, the ceremonies could be interpreted as a form of civil religion as characterized by Robert N. Bellah (1967) and his followers within the sociology of religion (e.g. Pierard and Linder, 1988). Here Rousseau's concept of civil religion is transformed and used to describe phenomena within the framework of secular, republican states with religious pluralism. In the new form civil religion emphasizes how political features often are informed with a religious authority with references to transcendent elements in spite of their explicit secularism. The analyses of civil religion, as a need every state has, nevertheless tend to retain a functionalistic interpretation of ceremonies, taking for granted how they work and reducing the complex relationships and interfaces between the political and the sacred.

A broader anthropological approach to rituals and sacralization could be fruitful. The ceremonies follow the general form of rites of passage with their separation (tests, applications), stage of transition or liminality (naturalization process, pledge-making) and reincorporation in society with a new status (receiving the citizenship certificate, final reception, sharing a meal).[13] In *Secular Rituals* (1977), Sally F. Moore and Barbara

G. Myerhoff argue that ritual is a way of conveying a message as if it were unquestionable. The unquestionability is a quality of the sacred, but the sacred is a wider category than is the religious. Secular rituals therefore also establish a form of sacredness and are able to present doctrines as unquestionable and dramatize social/moral imperatives, attempting to structure the way people think about social life. The ceremonies of modern life use a variety of symbols, having both religious and non-religious referents. Citizenship ceremonies represent such a complex relationship and combination in establishing the sacred zone of statehood, patriotic sentiments, citizenship rights and obligations, and their unquestionability.

Thus, the various documents on how to arrange a ceremony strongly emphasize securing and maintaining dignity and the bipartisan significance and atmosphere. This requirement also means that a suitable room is necessary for the occasion, and the flag, the Commonwealth Coat of Arms and a portrait of the Queen are to be displayed during the ceremony to establish an official quality. The Prince of Wales, who participated in the first British ceremony, said he hoped it 'added something to the significance'. 'Being British is something of a blessing', he said, thereby implicitly referring to a secular form of sacredness – and the ceremony was meant to 'reinforce your belief . . . that you belong here and are very welcome'. One of the new citizens, a 32-year-old Indian-born male, confirmed this meaning of the celebration by saying: 'The ceremony idea is an excellent one. It puts extra emphasis on becoming a citizen and makes it feel more important.'[14]

The idea of the ceremonies and the interpretations of the participants thereby follow the causal connections between ritual, being moved and self-improvement established in eighteenth-century political and religious discourse. The pivotal point is that ritualization should create key events, thereby making the sense of belonging, rights and obligations inwardly felt, a matter of individual emotion, of self. Ritualization thus is a matter of emotionalization. The official symbols, the national anthem, the elevated, dignified atmosphere that is created can be interpreted as a way of establishing a secular sacredness meant to secure a sublime, soul-shaking and unique experience, which is believed to be a prerequisite for the improvement of the self and thereby the subjectivity of the people. However, in the eighteenth century, the issue of a utopian subjectivity was a challenge concerning the whole population (though adult males were mainly the focus). In the twenty-first century this seems to be limited to an issue for immigrants (of both sexes) in the Scandinavian countries, whereas in Australia the challenge also is a question of strengthening the consciousness of being a citizen among citizens by birth – a question of improving their citizen subjectivity by their taking part in affirmation ceremonies.

The multicultural challenge

In all the analysed countries, citizenship ceremonies are primarily invented to celebrate immigrants, or their children, becoming citizens.[15] This multicultural group, however, challenges the political culture of the Western countries, which are pervaded with Christian forms and symbols. The informational material describing the arrangement of ceremonies gives a list of 'do's and don'ts'. One of the fixed 'don'ts' is the inclusion of alcoholic beverages in the refreshments. In the Australian Ceremonies Code, one is also instructed to take into account any special dietary or religious requirements that people from different cultural backgrounds may have concerning food. Another 'don't' is using the event for political or other reasons: the recommendation is for speakers to avoid issues that might be contentious from a political, racial or sectarian perspective. The aim is to create a 'welcoming atmosphere', to form an including ritual and to use constitutional core elements to create a sacred zone above ethnic, cultural and religious differences. The idea is to create a sense of belonging and communality by avoiding specific cultural or religious embedding (which, as argued above, is difficult) or by strongly demonstrating an openness and willingness to respect cultural diversity.

As mentioned, metaphors of family and kinship are often used, just as the websites are full of pictures of happy people of all colours and ethnicities, sometimes even holding hands standing in a circle. Though the official website includes a video recording of a simulated British ceremony using volunteer staff, the multicultural ideal is displayed: the group of new citizens consists of several people of colour and disabled individuals. In the Australian ceremonies, candidates who wish to make the pledge on a holy book may bring one of their own choosing, just as it is possible to recite a translation of the pledge in one's native language if one does not speak English. Cultural diversity and multiculturalism seem to be core values in the Australian case.

Compared to these examples of explicit multicultural politics,[16] the Scandinavian examples seem to be more problematic in spite of their informality. In Denmark and Sweden, to date, there is no national legislation concerning the ceremonies,[17] and since they are not a formal part of the naturalization process, they are voluntary and diverse. Since 2003, local authorities in Copenhagen have arranged a 'festival of integration' at the town hall, to which they invite all the new citizens of the municipality.

The core of the celebration is an official speech welcoming the new citizens, which often thematizes democracy and the awarding of the newly instituted 'Integration Prize'. The national anthem is sung, and after this light refreshments are served in the form of the symbolic 'town hall pancakes', which on this occasion are prepared without alcohol.

The first year included entertainment by a popular pop singer, who sang Danish national songs. However, this was not successful; a majority of the invitees left the ceremony, to the disappointment of the organizers. In following years, music 'of their own', i.e., so-called ethnic music, has been chosen, since 'it appears to be what they want'.[18] Thus, in spite of the multicultural discourse and the wish to create a welcoming atmosphere, the rhetoric of 'othering', of us and them, prevails.

In Sweden, there are great variations in the way local authorities choose to welcome their new fellow citizens.[19] As in Copenhagen, the day of choice is the National Day (already laden with meaning). The idea of materializing the welcoming is also a core element here, as is the emphasis on 'diversity and civic pride', as the publication from *Integrationsverket* states. This publication displays the same explicit multiculturalism as the Australian Code, but the means for creating rituals of inclusion are different. Commemorative certificates are often awarded, but cultural elements such as national costumes, Swedish (folk) music, together with gifts like pins and flags, are also integrated in several of the rituals. Religious dietary restrictions are taken into consideration, as in the other countries, but the refreshments seem to be more regional and culturally specific: coffee and cake,[20] open sandwiches and regional dishes. This may be a way of materializing the new community and the new citizens, following the popular health slogan 'You are what you eat'. In the Scandinavian countries, eating (national dishes) can be interpreted as one of the important technologies of the national self.

For the organizers in several of the Swedish localities and in Copenhagen, the goal is to create both a ceremonious atmosphere – a festival – and at the same time to have a 'social hour', an informal celebration with elements that are often included in private family parties (flags, songs, cakes etc.). The Danish concept of *hyggeligt* (homely, cosy) permeates the Danish organizers' aspirations. But it takes cultural competence to embody the Danish or Swedish sense of informality and homeliness. Thus, the informality of the Scandinavian ceremonies can potentially undermine the intended inclusiveness of the celebrations. The celebration of multicultural diversity with 'every culture performing and contributing with music and dance' (Integrationsverket, 2002: 6) may simultaneously cement the idea of difference and 'the other'. It may transform the willingness to include into processes of 'othering' and 'exotizing'. As Gerd Baumann argues in *The Multicultural Riddle*, on the aesthetic cultivation of cultural difference: the multi-ethnic parade as a kind of stage show rhetorically celebrates diversity,

> yet they represent not so much a pluralist multiculturalism as a difference 'multi'-culturalism that parades the distinctiveness of each so-called cultural group and remains in thrall to each reified understanding of culture. Instead of breaking down cultural barriers, which is its chief claim, it has to reinscribe these cultural borders and fix them as if they were given by nature. (1999: 122)

Instead of politicizing citizenship on a level above cultural differences, the ceremonies are made into a matter of enculturation.

As noted above, the Commonwealth ceremonies are neither entirely political nor above cultural differences. All are permeated with religious and sacred forms, and even our very idea of the secular public sphere is culturally specific. The modern citizenship ceremonies draw on a heterogeneous genealogical tree including the political culture and cult of sensibility of the revolutionary era in Europe. As argued, a specific causal relationship was established connecting ritual, being moved emotionally and self-improvement. Through the rituals' soul-shaking experiences, a utopian civic self is both to be performed and generated. This connection draws on Christian and especially Pietist technologies of the self and ideas of the heart and an interior core self to be the topography of conviction and moral sentiments, and hence the object of improvement.

At the citizenship ceremonies, religious technologies and iconography also inform the attempts to establish secular sacredness in order to improve their significance, and to make their moral imperatives concerning civic obligations and sense of belonging unquestionable and fervent. The citizenship ceremonies analysed here thereby are embedded in a specific culture with eighteenth-century European and Christian roots. Within secularism not only a culturally specific notion of the public sphere as independent of religion was constructed, but also national and culturally specific versions of secularism gradually developed. In a comparative point of view citizenship ceremonies can be interpreted as practices in which specific articulations of secularism are embedded, performed and reformulated.

Thus, the idea of making new citizens and including them with rituals, from a genealogical perspective raises questions. Religious forms and technologies operated as a kind of matrix for Western political cultures in one of their formative periods. Thereby our very idea of a universal secularized public space as a space beyond religion and culture can be problematized, just as simplistic expectations for political solutions to cultural differences can be.

Notes

1. The Danish parliament invited all new citizens to a ceremony on 26 March 2006 after this chapter was completed. Currently, a comparative ethnographic analysis of this and other citizenship ceremonies in Western countries is being conducted by the author.
2. Swedish: *ekstra högtidsstund*.
3. 6 June has been the Swedish National Day since 1983 and a national holiday since 2005. Since 1916, it has also been the festival for the Swedish flag. 5 June, *Grundlovsdag*, is the day the Danes celebrate their constitution. It is a half-day holiday and is considered the closest thing to a national day.
4. For an elaborated analysis, see Damsholt (2000).
5. Though it may be argued to be a case of post-rationalization.
6. In Denmark-Norway, the decree commenced the Jubilee year of the Protestant reformation in 1736 (Horstbøll, 2003: 85).
7. This and the following quotations are from the homepage of the British Home Office.
8. As Benedict Anderson (1983) has argued, the family metaphor is prevalent in national discourses.
9. This description and the quotations follow the website of the British Home Office: 'What Happens at a Citizenship Ceremony'.
10. Quoted from Appendix 3, p. 56, *Australian Citizenship Ceremonies Code*.
11. Quoted from *How to Host a Citizenship Ceremony*, from the Canadian Home Office website: *Citizenship and Immigration Canada*, p. 8.
12. The Australian national anthem *Advance Australia Fair* does not include any reference to God, but if the Queen or any member of the Royal Family is present, *God Save the Queen* should be played at the beginning of the ceremony, *Australian Citizenship Ceremonies Code*, p. 33.
13. Following the stages as described first by van Gennep (1909/1977).
14. Both quoted in BBC News, 26 February 2004.
15. Though it is possible to renew the affirmation in Canada and Australia, and in the latter case, these affirmation ceremonies are extremely popular according to the homepage.
16. The Australian ceremonies are managed by the Department of Immigration and Multicultural and Indigenous Affairs, a name that says a lot.
17. In Denmark, new citizens were invited to visit the Danish parliament for the first time in March 2006. It has been debated whether oath-making is a good idea and whether a test of knowledge about Denmark is to be a condition of citizenship. The latter was introduced in 2007.
18. Interview with the organizer, 6 July 2005.
19. However, the different experiences in various municipalities in Sweden are gathered in a publication from the integration office in one of the larger towns, Norrköping.

20. The way this is eaten and its symbolic meaning in the Scandinavian countries make it culturally specific.

References

Abu-Lughod, L. and Lutz, C. A. (eds) (1990) *Language and the Politics of Emotion.* Cambridge: Cambridge University Press.

Anderson, B. (1983) *Imagined Communities. Reflections on the Origin and Spread of Nationalism.* London: Verso.

Australian Citizenship Ceremonies Code (2003) Department of Immigration and Multicultural and Indigenous Affairs.

Barker-Benfield, G. J. (1992) *The Culture of Sensibility. Sex and Society in Eighteenth-century Britain.* Chicago: Chicago University Press.

Baumann, G. (1999) *The Multicultural Riddle: Rethinking National, Ethnic and Religious Identities.* London: Routledge.

BBC News (2004) 'First Citizenship Ceremony for UK', 26 February.

Bellah, R. (1967) 'Civil Religion in America', *Daedalus*, 96: 1–21.

Bredsdorff, T. (2003) *Den brogede oplysning.* Copenhagen: Gyldendal.

Colley, L. (1992) *Britons. Forging the Nation 1707–1837.* New Haven, CT and London: Yale University Press.

Damsholt, T. (2000) 'Being Moved', *Ethnologia Scandinavica, A Journal for Nordic Ethnology*, 29: 24–48.

Dreyfus, H. L. and Rabinow, P. (1983) *Michel Foucault. Beyond Structuralism and Hermeneutics.* 2nd edition. Chicago: Chicago University Press.

Engelstoft, L. (1802) *Om den Indflydelse Opdragelsen, især den offentlige, kan have paa at indplante Kiærlighed til Fædrelandet. Et Statspædagogisk Forsøg.* Copenhagen.

Foucault, M. (1969/1972) *The Archaeology of Knowledge.* Paris and London: Routledge.

——— (1971) 'Nietzsche, Genealogy, History', in D. F. Bouchard (ed.), *Michel Foucault: Language, Counter-Memory, Practice: Selected Essays and Interviews.* New York: Cornell University Press.

——— (1975/1979) *Discipline and Punish. The Birth of the Prison.* Harmondsworth: Penguin Books.

——— (1983) 'The Subject and Power', in H. L. Dreyfus and P. Rabinow (eds), *Michel Foucault. Beyond Structuralism and Hermeneutics*, 2nd edition. Chicago: Chicago University Press.

——— (1988) 'Technologies of the Self', in L. H. Martin, H. Gutman and P. H. Hutton (eds), *Technologies of the Self. A Seminar with Michel Foucault.* Amherst, MA: University of Massachusetts Press.

Fulbrook, M. (1983) *Piety and Politics. Religion and the Rise of Absolutism in England, Württemberg and Prussia.* Cambridge: Cambridge University Press.

Gawthorp, R. (1993) *Pietism and the Making of Eighteenth-Century Prussia.* Cambridge: Cambridge University Press.

Gordon, C. (1991) 'Governmental Rationality: An Introduction', in G. Burchell, C. Gordon and P. Miller (eds), *The Foucault Effect. Studies in Governmentality.* Chicago: Chicago University Press.

Home Office (2002) *Secure Borders, Safe Havens: Integration with Diversity in Modern Britain.* London: The Stationery Office.

——— (2003) *Citizenship Ceremonies.* Consultation Document. London: The Stationery Office.

Horstbøll, H. (2003) 'Læsning til salighed, oplysning og velfærd. Om Pontoppidan, pietisme og lærebøger i Danmark og Norge i 17- og 1800-tallet', *Fortid og Nutid. Tidsskrift for kulturhistorie og lokalhistorie*, 2: 83–104.

How to Host a Citizenship Ceremony. Canadian Home Office website: Citizenship and Immigration Canada.

Hunt, L. (1984) *Politics, Culture, and Class in the French Revolution*. Berkeley, CA: University of California Press.

Integrationsverket (2002) *Du gamla du nya. Sveriges kommuner välkomnar nya medborgare*. Norrköping.

Landes, J. B. (1998) 'Bodies in Democratic Public Space. An Eighteenth-century Perspective', in S. Hardy Aiken et al. (eds), *Making Worlds. Gender, Metaphor, Materiality*. Tucson: University of Arizona Press.

——— (1999) 'Køn og forskel i forskningen om den franske revolution', *Den jyske Historiker*, 85.

McCutcheon, R. (2003) *The Discipline of Religion. Structure, Meaning, Rhetoric*. London: Taylor and Francis.

Moore, S. F. and Myerhoff, B. G. (eds) (1977) *Secular Rituals*. Amsterdam: Van Gorcum.

Outram, D. (1989) *The Body and the French Revolution. Sex, Class and Political Culture*. New Haven, CT: Yale University Press.

Pierard, R. and Linder, R. (1988) *Civil Religion and the Presidency*. Grand Rapids, MI: Academie Books.

Pine, B. J. and Gilmore, J. H. (1999) *The Experience Economy*. Boston, MA: Harvard Business School Press.

Rose, N. (1999) *Governing the Soul: The Shaping of the Private Self*. 2nd edition. London: Routledge.

Rousseau, J. J. (1762/1997) *The Social Contract and Other Later Political Writings*, ed. V. Gourevitch. Cambridge: Cambridge University Press.

——— (1772/1991) 'Considerations on the Government of Poland', in S. Hoffmann and D. P. Fidler, *Rousseau on International Relations*. Oxford: Clarendon Press.

Schama, S. (1989) *Citizens: A Chronicle of the French Revolution*. London: Vintage.

Smith, A. D. (2003) *Chosen Peoples. Sacred Sources of National Identity*. Oxford: Oxford University Press.

Van Gennep, A. (1909/1977) *The Rites of Passage*. London: Routledge.

van Horn Melton, J. (2001) 'Pietism, Politics and the Public Sphere in Germany', in J. E. Bradley and D. K. Van Kley (eds), *Religion and Politics in Enlightenment Europe*. Notre Dame, IN: University of Notre Dame Press.

Vincent-Buffault, A. (1991) *The History of Tears. Sensibility and Sentimentality in France*. London: Macmillan.

4
The Politics of Discourse towards Islam and Muslim Communities in Europe[1]

Ricard Zapata-Barrero and Islam Qasem

> 'Houston, we have a problem.'
> (Commander James Lowell on board Apollo XIII, Monday, 13 April 1970, about 2100 h)

Introduction: the discourse of politics and the politics of discourse towards Muslims

In Europe conflicts related to Muslim communities are not a matter of fact, but a matter of interpretation. And when interpretations govern human behaviour and political decisions we enter the realm of hermeneutics where discourse is better understood as a framework that articulates a set of interpretations that are politically significant (Zapata-Barrero, 2005a). Events related to Muslim communities generate much rhetoric. The political discourse has an almost magical component, shaping ordinary citizens' perceptions of and reactions to cultural pluralism. Rhetoric by political representatives with respect to Muslims, whether it is true or false, is ultimately politically motivated.

It becomes clear that the discourse on Muslims is a political gambit, since political statements by European governments serve a clear purpose: to avoid losing votes to the Far Right parties. This is the primary concern of many governments, the only intentional logic that directs the political body. As such we are not in the realm of the *discourse of politics* but of the *politics of discourse*. Discourse becomes a political option, a common and deliberate practice for most traditional European political parties, especially when they have to communicate their positions on cultural diversity. These *politics of discourse* aim to gain and maintain power by securing the majority of votes through traditional and populist rhetoric.

This discursive strategy is mainly based not only on stereotypes and negative pictures of Muslim people as well as other defence mechanisms of the social structure (Zapata-Barrero, 2004a), but also on a simplistic, reductionist and monolithic interpretation of Muslim communities. Political discourse generates problems instead of solving them, fracturing society in two: pro- and anti-Muslim. In citizens' terms, the difference between Muslim and non-Muslim citizens becomes in itself an explanatory category.

The case of *adhan* (calling Muslims to prayer) is well known, and for many it is an illustration of the process of multiculturalism in Europe. However, there are also cases of confrontations ('conflict zones') that arise as a result of failure to allow religious identities to be manifested in public spaces. Recently, new issues have arisen, such as the establishment of set times in municipal swimming pools for Muslim children (in France). These situations are very different, but all share one feature: 'contact zones' between two religious traditions (the Christian and the Islamic), which tend to turn into 'conflict zones'. The reasons for the change from contact to conflict zones vary across European countries, but they are also very similar in that they have a clear electoral restriction in discourse-building on cultural pluralism. It is true that we cannot say that a conflict arises every time there is contact between an immigrant/citizen of Muslim origin and a non-Muslim, but in general Muslims often have serious problems performing their culture and religion in a public space originally created and occupied by non-Muslim citizens. In short, we are faced with what would qualify as a structural problem of multiculturalism (Parekh, 2000: 196–238).[2] There is a tendency to identify Muslims by what they are (their religious affiliation) rather than by what they do (like any other citizen) (Martín Muñoz, 2003: 38). These negative interpretations are the main variable explaining why contact zones are transformed into conflict zones.

Conflicts related to cultural pluralism are a matter of interpretation. Indeed, one of the channels where this picture is produced and enforced is the media, which convey at least three negative pictures of Muslims that serve to legitimate racist and xenophobic attitudes: Muslims are linked to Osama bin Laden, to criminal activities and to terrorism; Arab people are opposed to democracy because their Islamic practice violates the most elementary human rights; and finally, as a corollary, Islam is identified with barbarism.

In Europe, 'circumstances of multiculturality' are mainly related to religion and the interrelation between Muslim communities and non-Muslim European citizens.[3] This chapter argues that reflections on Muslim communities and political management of cultural pluralism necessitate an analysis of political discourses – a reflection not so much on the *discourse of power*, but on the *power of discourse* is necessary. We present a conceptual framework of why and how interpretations are constructed to manage cultural pluralism in general and regarding the Muslim communities in Europe in particular. Three case studies demonstrate how different political traditions and powers employ discourse and integration models as a barrier for exclusion rather than inclusion of the Muslim communities.

What makes the Muslim community a problem in Europe is the distorted and hostile discourse on Islam that sprung up from historical misrepresentations as well as contemporary misperceptions propagated by the media. Although these images are based on gross generalizations and stereotypes, they have shown durability and continuity over time to the extent that they have dominated the European discourse as facts.

Conceptual framework: the reactive discourse based on the populist rhetoric and the rhetoric of tradition

From a social psychological point of view we know that when there is social fear of an unknown community, citizens tend to search for arguments to explain their feelings. This helps them to rationalize their emotions. The media, tradition and political discourse generate a large part of these interpretations. The argument to be defended is not that Islam is a source of social and political instability, but that it is the citizens' perception of Islam and the interpretation politicians intentionally and tacitly follow that are the main sources of instability. For instance, it is not the presence of a mosque that provokes instability, but the citizens' perception of a mosque that transforms this previous contact zone into a conflict zone.

In most surveys, the media are seen to consolidate the perception that Muslim communities are not only extremely different from us but can also threaten our values and current ways of life. When the media try to correct this tendency, they are inclined to go to the other extreme and build an exotic icon of the Muslim, close to the Rousseauvian universe, as an uncivilized but benign human being, who reminds us of the philosophical discourses after the conquest of America in the sixteenth and seventeenth centuries (Todorov, 1991). In reality, the public's perception of Muslims is based on media discourse rather than direct contact. The *politics of discourse* nourishes these arguments. It builds a reactive and conservative discourse against the cultural and religious demands of pluralism. From the viewpoint of the reactive discourse, cultural pluralism

may transform the various spheres of life. Circumstances of multiculturalism are seen as negative. Two main rhetorics occupy the political space:
the populist rhetoric and the rhetoric of the tradition.

The populist rhetoric uses the argument of democracy in a way that
appeals to and satisfies citizens. But in reality it appeals only to a sector
of society in the name of the whole society. It creates conflicts of interests
between the societal majority (non-Muslim citizens) and the minority
(Muslim immigrants/citizens). This rhetoric is nourished by the 'popular'
referent, linking it with the security and maintenance of the socio-
economic level (Zapata-Barrero, 2004a: 260–2). Populism is, in fact,
'democracy poorly understood'. It supposedly addresses the interest of
the whole society, but in reality it addresses only the interest of a sector
of the society (non-Muslim citizens), but not the Muslim citizens.

Populism is a discourse that dismantles and fractures society. The populist rhetoric has a 'reactive' function as its arguments are built on the
'complaints' of common citizens with the objective of translating them
into social action against other sectors of society, confusing the reality
and the ideal of society. Populism has an 'essentialist' component, since
the interests and needs of the non-Muslim citizens are seen as unchangeable, and as the only criteria to be politically considered in managing
'circumstances of multiculturalism'. It uses the perception of one part of
the citizenry as democratic truth. It also has a dualistic logic given arguments to the extreme that the needs of some (non-Muslims or Muslims)
are seen as incompatible with the needs (social, cultural, economic) of
others.[4]

The rhetoric of the tradition does not have the interest as reference
framework (the interest of the Muslim/non-Muslim citizens), but a set of
beliefs and values homogenizing society. By contrast to the link between
security and maintenance of the socio-economic level, which characterizes
the populist rhetoric, this conservative discourse produces arguments
based on identity. Its basic framework is that tradition, understood as a
set of established values and beliefs that have persisted over several generations and as a process of transmission of customs from generation to
generation (Friedrich, 1972: 18), breaks with cultural pluralism. Tradition
is a defence to maintain the sacred chain of the self and his/her history.
It has, then, a vital function in the political body – the sacred purpose to
maintain social cohesion. This new rhetoric is opposed to the process of
change in which we are, since cultural pluralism affects the values of the
most essential tradition: values tied to identity and community. Before
the process of structural change provoked by the politics of cultural pluralism, this rhetoric seeks, in the words of Hirschman (who analyses the

rhetoric of reaction in the nineteenth and twentieth centuries provoked in the process of acquisition of rights), to 'turn the clock back' (Hirschman, 1991: 9).

But this is not an historical exception. In all processes of structural change, beginning with the French Revolution, a conservative reactive line of thought is generated. Indeed, the conservative tradition began to produce its arguments inspired by the context of the French structural revolutionary change. For example, Edmund Burke's framework of reference was to defend respect for the tradition of the English Revolution set against the French one, which literally broke the chain of historical transmission (Burke, 1987). This rhetoric of the new conservatism takes tradition as the main source of arguments. It argues for the Apostolic, Roman Catholic and Christian tradition as a source of identity, against other religious sources of identity. Tradition is our cultural *alter ego*. It nourishes politics against the demands of cultural pluralism. Tradition is the last source of recognition and plays an almost sacred role, since from some initial rational arguments we can penetrate easily to strong emotions directly related to our identity.

In sum, populism and tradition govern the *politics of discourse* towards Muslim communities and are at the forefront of the management of cultural pluralism. In turn, *politics of discourse* upholds a cultural rather than a religious view of culture, as we shall see in the case studies of Spain, Great Britain and France. But first a brief background of the European discourse on Islam and Muslims.

Re-imagining European discourse towards Muslims today: from the past to the present process of pluralizing the view of Islam

The presence of Islam in the European discourse is not new; it dates back to the Middle Ages. What is new, however, is that Muslims in Europe are now part of this discourse. Today, it is estimated that more than 15 million Muslims live in Europe, making Islam Europe's second largest religion. Their increasing presence, coupled with their demands for cultural and religious recognition, however, have given rise to the so-called 'Muslim problem'. Islam is portrayed as an absolute antithesis to European culture. Thus, Islamic practices and symbols, such as mosques and headscarves, are turning into 'conflict zones', causing social alienation and political discrimination.

While secular Europe is still haunted by its own religious past (too complex to be discussed here), it is sufficient to say that after painful and bloody experiences, a sort of accommodation in the public space has been made for Christianity and Judaism. Thus far no comparable place has been made for Islam. By and large the Islamic presence in terms of mosques, schools and dress code has been fiercely objected to and viewed with fear, contempt or both. A shallow analysis reveals that these attitudes are largely based on simplistic interpretations, ignorance and gross generalizations, which begs the question: how have such perceptions come to dominate the European discourse? Attempting to present a comprehensive explanation of the origin, evolution and circumstances surrounding and promoting today's image of Islam is beyond the scope of this chapter. Moreover, the numerous factors across time and space render such a task ever incomplete. Two factors, however, are quite evident and significant in shaping the political discourse on Islam: past Muslim – Christian relationships and present geopolitical conflicts.

European discourse still sees Islam from an historical perspective, as images rooted in historical Christian–Muslim rivalries and violent confrontations. These images have had an enduring impact beyond time and space, as John Esposito observes: '[p]ast images of the Christian West turning back the threat of Muslim armies seeking to overrun the West are conjured up and linked to demographic and political realities' (Esposito, 1999: 233). The growing presence of Muslims, therefore, is seen as part of an historical continuum, attempting to conquer or Islamize Europe from within. Such fear of Islam is aroused at the sight of a mosque, a Muslim school, a veiled woman or any other Islamic expression. Today European Muslims are tolerated only if they are invisible, when no cultural or religious claims are made.

Ever since Islam erupted out of Arabia, '[t]he Islamic empire and the flourishing of Islamic civilization posed a direct danger to Christendom's place in the world both theologically and politically' (Esposito, 1999: 35). In response, Christian kings waged six Crusades and a mounting anti-Islam literature emerged and dominated European thought. Islam was portrayed as a 'demonic religion of apostasy, blasphemy, and obscurity' (Said, 1981: 5), preached by 'a false prophet, an impostor, and a hypocrite' (Hichem, 1985: 13). Christian Europe was not worried about the religious aspect of Islam alone, but the Muslim world as a whole and its political ideology and different civilization (Rodinson, 1987: 64). The vilification of Islam resumed during colonialism 'with arguments dating back to the Middle Ages, but with modern embellishments' (Rodinson, 1987: 66).

Ultimately, what emerged from colonialism and settled in European consciousness was the perception of two separate cultures – a superior

European culture and an inferior and backward Islamic culture. Samuel Huntington's thesis of the clash of civilizations is one example that illustrates how Islam as a civilization and religion to the present day is regarded as being at odds with the European civilization and Christianity. The perception of Islam as an intruder religion from the East and Muslim immigrants as not 'really' European (even those born in Europe) is prevalent in Europe. Muslims are by virtue of their religion considered part of a different culture, an extension of the Muslim world. Therefore, they are associated with all kinds of events unfolding in far-off lands from what they have come to call home. Moreover, this culture is considered monolithic and extremist. Domestic and international political conflicts, especially those connected with fundamentalist and militant activities, are all taken out of geopolitical context and reassembled to reflect a global and fundamentalist Islamic culture of which European Muslims are seen as an integral part.

Without a doubt, all media have played an important part in this regard, homogenizing Islam as a fundamentalist religion and culture.[5] In the evening TV news or the morning newspaper, Islam is the focus of attention when it comes to reporting on anything pertaining to the Muslim world, from the wars in Iraq and Afghanistan and terrorism to female circumcision in Africa, economic stagnation and human rights violations. In short, Islam as a religion and culture is politicized and portrayed as violent. 'The Iranian revolution, the Rushdie affair, the surge of Islamist-inspired antioccupation and antiregime militancy', among other events, as Sami Zemni notes, '[a]ll have been held up as examples of a fundamentally different culture dynamic and trajectory' (Zemni and Parker, 2002: 233). No matter how disparate and separate in ideology, reason and space, these events are perceived by European discourses as unquestioned testimony to a global fundamentalist 'Islamic' culture. Unless they do change their religion, European Muslims are by default part of this culture. Consequently, their political allegiance is in doubt, their religious practices are suspected, their cultural and religious claims are controversial – their whole presence in Europe is a problem.

To sum up, the European discourse has for centuries misrepresented Islam as 'anti-Christian', 'anti-democracy', 'oppressive', 'uncivilized', and so on. The underlying theme, however, is that Islam is monolithic and violent. This double image is not accidental, but intentional. Islam is purposely defined as a monolithic bloc to facilitate the generalization of fundamentalism from the few to the many. Despite coming from many diverse ethnic, linguistic and cultural backgrounds, European Muslims are imagined as a cultural minority called Islam, and not simply a religious minority. It is true that for the vast majority of Muslims, Islam is an all-embracing way of life, with fixed spiritual principles, moral and legal codes, and an economic doctrine. Yet, there is a good argument to be made against the monolithic claim when we consider Islam as a religion and as a civilization.

As a religion, Islam is divided into different groups – Sunnis, Shi'ites, Isma'ilis and Zaydis to name just a few. These groups can be found all over the world, and follow different theological and legal interpretations of Islam. Moreover, there are different levels of personal religiosity within Islam in general – moderates, extremists and fundamentalists – and they too have different, and sometimes conflicting, interpretations of Islam. Seyyed Hossein Naser observes that as a civilization, '[t]here is nothing more erroneous than thinking that Islam is a monolithic reality and that Islamic civilization did not allow the creation or subsistence of diversity' (Nasr, 2003: xxii). Islam, indeed, wherever it spread, underwent a process of contextualization whereby a synthesis of Islam and the domestic culture emerged. Thus, there is the Islam of Saudi Arabia, of Turkey, of Africa, of Persia, of China and more recently of America and Western Europe. And while these different groups do belong to the same faith in the same way say a Lutheran German and a Catholic Lebanese belong to Christianity, they do not belong to the same ethnic, cultural or linguistic group.

Second, this monolithic Islam is depicted as a violent and fundamentalist religion. The European discourse casts the fundamentalist net so wide that hardly any Muslim who is not fully secular escapes. It hardly distinguishes between the majority, who practise a peaceful interpretation of Islam, and the minority who practise militancy against Muslims and non-Muslims alike. A 2004 Pew's survey shows such perceptions.[6] Among the three Abrahamic religions (Islam, Judaism and Christianity) the large majority of Europeans considers Islam the most violent religion and express concerns about Islamic extremism in their countries. Such fears are partly a by-product of the recent acts of terrorism in Europe, such as the Madrid bombing committed by a band of extremists following an aberrant interpretation of Islam. What is noteworthy and relevant is that the overwhelming majority of Muslims in Europe did not have a hand in these crimes, nor do they subscribe to a violent interpretation of Islam. And while the tragedy was strongly denounced by the vast majority of Muslims in Europe and elsewhere in the Muslim world, the European discourse is reluctant to view the new citizens beyond the shadow of terrorism and disloyalty. Too often violence and terrorism are equated with Islam itself and generalized from the few to the many. And yet, the clash is not between militant Islam and Europe. The best proof of this is the wave of terrorism that has swept through many Islamic countries – Jordan, Egypt, Saudi Arabia, and others – with Muslims as its victims.

In short, historical tendencies that conceive Islam as a bellicose enemy of the Christian West persist in contemporary European discourse. These historical tendencies, however, now face a new reality in Europe: a multicultural, multiethnic, multi-religious society. Islam is no longer confined to the East; it is now part of Europe's religious landscape, and Muslims are now European citizens by birth or naturalization, and are demanding cultural and religious recognition like any other citizen.

So, how is Europe dealing with this new reality? And how are European politicians responding to Muslims' demands? We shall answer both questions in three national contexts: Spain, Great Britain and France. These countries are selected primarily due to the large number of Muslims living there and the different models of accommodation. As we shall see, however, they share a common discourse on Islam and Muslims.

Muslim communities and conflicts in Spain, Great Britain and France

The Spanish Maurophobia tradition

Since the tragedy of El Ejido in February 2000,[7] but undoubtedly also as a consequence of the attacks on 11 September 2001 in New York and Washington and 11 March 2004 in Madrid, there has been an explicit policy favouring Central and Eastern European and South American immigrants over Moroccans. Moroccans were until recently the most numerous foreign nationality in Spain (about 21.8 per cent of the foreign population), followed by Ecuadorians, who accounted for 7.6 per cent. The latest statistics (2004) show that Ecuadorians have overtaken Moroccans.[8] Moreover, the first bilateral agreements for admitting immigrant workers were signed with Ecuador and Poland. The only feasible explanation for this policy is based on race and the Christian identity, for example, protection of the Spanish identity against those viewed as potential 'cultural invaders', or even as a new Arab invasion (de Lucas, 2002), or the re-Islamization of Spain (Martín Muñoz, 1996: 9–16).

An historical Spanish tradition of Maurophobia is found in social and political discourses, and is used to legitimate citizens' attitudes to Muslim immigration to Spain (Zapata-Barrero, 2005b). This Spanish identity-building is also fostered by the media, which constantly remind us that the most negative news is related to Muslims' presence and practices. Islam has historically been excluded from the formation of the Judeo-Christian

Spanish identity in which the formation of a Christian 'us' has been opposed to an Islamic 'other' (Zapata-Barrero, 2005b: 14). The process of Islamization of Spain through the presence of Muslim immigrants is also driven by the Spanish authorities, who draw on these historical stereotypes to restrict the public space available to the Muslim community, forcing its members to close in on themselves and search for their own identity, since the identity of Spanish citizenship is not open to them. In this situation, the construction of Muslim facilities acquires vital importance and so, too, the Muslim presence in schools and the redesigning of cemeteries to allow for Muslim funeral rites.

This evidence forms the premises for an analysis linking the Muslim community and Spanish tradition. The analysis is approached from two perspectives. One argues that Islam is part of the Spanish cultural tradition and identity; the other that Islam is alien to the Spanish cultural tradition and identity, which is based on the Greco-Roman and Judeo-Christian heritage. Consequently, each perspective employs a different political discourse.

The first approach defends the idea that there is one tradition rather than two. It demonstrates that Spain is the only Western European context in which the Islamic tradition developed a cultural society and a political system that lasted centuries. Spain is the only country in Western Europe to have been Islamized (we acknowledge that the Balkans and Sicily were also Islamized). Thus this perspective gives rise to a political discourse emphasizing what is common.

The second perspective portrays two separate traditions that have been historically at odds. It follows a political discourse that stresses what is different between the Muslim and Spanish traditions, what separates them. It has also constructed a hostile tradition by drawing a negative picture of the Moroccan, synthesized in 'the Moor' (*el moro*). The main line of this argument is that Spanish tradition is the result of the Christian victory over Islam. Muslim people are by nature incapable of being integrated into a society and a public sphere that is replete with Catholic customs. The Spanish public sphere is structurally Catholic.

Instead of having a socializing and pedagogic effect, this political discourse generates divergence and instability in society. Politicians not only avoid talking about immigration, but when they do talk about it, their discursive behaviour is alarmist and even contains populist components linking the Muslim community to insecurity and social instability. The reality is that there is an absence of integrationist politics in Spain, a lack of political will to include Muslims in the public sphere. In an integrationist framework that favours the sentiment of social belonging, Islam could develop in Spain, and in Europe, without conflict. Instead, it tends to turn into a closed and hostile space where Muslims search for their identity and their community (Martín Muñoz, 1994: 24).

It is important to stress that immigration has been incorporated into the political discourse at the expense of one specific ethnic group: Moroccans. The case of El Ejido has been symbolically constructed as the extreme case of the danger of multiculturalism and lack of socialization. It is multiculturalism seen in its most essentialist form (Modood, 2000). Two years later the situation has hardly changed, but with an important difference: the majority of workers are no longer Moroccan, but come from Central and Eastern Europe. If it was just a legal problem (the majority of workers were undocumented), why replace the Moroccans with another ethnic group? The government's reading of events is straightforward: religion and culture matter. It is supposed, notwithstanding the Arab legacy in the Spanish identity and disregarding eight centuries of coexistence, that Morocco's culture is more remote than that of Central and Eastern Europe. These cultural and religious criteria are not new, and have already been used for the formal selection of immigrants. It is even said that it is not immigrant selection that is being applied in Spain, but really an 'ethnic filter' and even some 'Darwinist politics of immigration' (López García, 2003). These criteria are present not only in the Aliens Law but also in the Spanish citizenship acquisition code, which lists seven nationality preferences: South Americans, Portuguese, Filipinos, Andorrans, Equatorial Guineans, Gibraltarians and Sephardic Jews.

Language and religion are the only criteria to explain this shift in immigration management. In general terms, we can say that in Spain the labour market attracts immigrants, but politics selects them, using colonial and national identity criteria. In the management of its new multicultural society, Spain is currently at the beginning of a *Hispanidad* revival.

Hispanidad is a political term coined precisely to comprise the whole Spanish area of influence, designating a linguistic (Spanish) and religious (Catholic) community and creating a sense of belonging, to the exclusion of non-Spanish speakers, atheists, Masons, Jews and Muslims. The Franco regime (1940–75) reconstructed it as a symbol of homogeneity and unity, as a cohesive society, with the slogan *Una, Grande y Libre* (One, Great and Free) (González Antón, 1997: 613). *Hispanidad* was a political construction separating people in a Manichaean fashion (Vila Selma, 1996: 551). Those following the regime were good citizens, those having some doubts about it (i.e. republicans) were bad citizens. The political construction of *Hispanidad* aimed at creating the notion of the Hispanic race in order to foster a sentiment of loyalty and patriotism. Patriotism, race and religion were an explosive mixture that dominated the conservative political discourse (and academic arena) for the first half of the twentieth century (García Morente, 1938) and legitimized the Francoist regime (Carbayo Abengózar, 1998).

This binary logic still exists, though now with a different dimension. Bad citizens are those who do not speak Spanish and hold beliefs other than Catholic: Moroccans are the first candidates and are constantly used in a political discourse that reminds us of this imagery of *Hispanidad*. Society's perception of immigration is usually that of Muslims as a religious minority. At the same time, there are conservative discourses on European identity and civilization that advocate Christian tradition and politically construct Islam as anti-European and Christian.

Multiculturalism and the Muslim Community in Great Britain

The integration of Muslim communities into British society suffers from a lack of political will and a pervasive negative view of Islam. Since the 1960s, and because of the large numbers of South Asian and Afro-Caribbean immigrants who refused to assimilate, multiculturalism was born by the advent of certain policies. Today, multiculturalism is recognized as the primary integration policy of immigrants and their offspring in Great Britain. In a multiculturalist model, 'immigrants and their succeeding generations are not expected to shed their cultures of origin' (Michalak and Saeed, 2002: 155). Thus, in theory, there is a place in the public space for cultural diversity backed by political discourse and the protection of law. In practice, however, British multiculturalism has not fared well in integrating the various ethnic Muslim groups into society. The problem is primarily due to politicians' failure to accept that Britain is not only a multicultural but also a multi-religious society.

Immigration has drastically changed the religious landscape of Great Britain. Muslims, Hindus, Sikhs and others brought with them not only their different cultures, races and colours but also their religions. Anticipating problems of discrimination, the government enacted the Race Relations Act 1965, which was amended in 1976. The 1976 Act prohibits discrimination on 'the following grounds: race, colour, nationality, citizenship, and ethnic or national origin, *but not religion*'.[9] By excluding religion, the state fails to take measures to prevent discrimination of some minorities on religious grounds. While certain religious minorities, such as Jews and Sikhs, are given protection under the law as ethnic groups, Muslims are not. Muslims receive some indirect protection as members of ethnic groups (i.e. as Pakistanis, Indians, and so on), but they are not protected from religious discrimination and offensive speech.

For the most part, the political response has been dismissal of Muslim grievances and claims, with no serious intention of giving Muslims the same status that has been accorded to other religious minorities. Not until December 2003 did a law take effect making discrimination in employment on religious grounds unlawful. However, the new Religion or Belief Regulations do not apply to housing, education in its entirety, criminal justice or the supply of goods or services.[10]

The lack of political will is apparent in the state's procrastination in taking anti-Muslim discrimination seriously, despite findings in many studies. For instance, the Derby Project, commissioned by the Home Office to examine discrimination against Muslims and other religions, states that even when religious discrimination is identified, courts are unlikely 'to proscribe legal protection if it is seen to inconvenience the majority' (Vertovec, 2002: 28).

Similar findings were described by the Runnymede Commission in a report published in 1997 entitled 'Islamophobia: A Challenge for Us All'. The report describes many instances of anti-Muslim discrimination in various aspects of life and particularly emphasizes 'a dramatic aspect of social exclusion, the vulnerability of Muslims to physical violence and harassment'.[11] Moreover, the lack of adequate anti-Muslim discrimination measures is not the only area where the absence of political will is evident.

A second problem is the inequality between Islam and other religions as demonstrated by the following two examples: state funding of schools and the blasphemy law. Muslims' request for state funding of Muslim schools rests on the fact that such financial support already exists for '30 Jewish schools, 28 Methodist schools, and 2160 Roman Catholic schools' (Vertovec, 2002: 31). After repeated requests and a long political battle, the Labour government approved funding for two Muslim schools in 1997. A second example is the blasphemy law, which is best illustrated in the Rushdie affair. The book burning and the riots that took place in Bradford on 14 January 1989 were not only expressions of discontent with the novel, but also with the application and scope of the blasphemy law, not freedom of expression. Steven Vertovec observes that British Muslims 'were concerned with the kinds of offences that were included under the British law of blasphemy and, most important, which religions it covered' (Vertovec, 2002: 25). The law to this day applies only to Christianity. British Muslims who do not have the protection from blasphemy enjoyed by Christians found the law discriminatory and unjust.

Another cause hindering integration of Muslim immigrants is the image of Islam. Oddly enough, Islam enjoys minimum protection under the current laws of multiculturalism, while many Britons view Islam and Muslims adversely. According to the Pew's survey, 63 per cent of the British perceive Islam as the most violent religion in comparison with Judaism (4 per cent) and Christianity (8 per cent); 70 per cent express concern about Islamic extremism in Great Britain.[12] With so much fear of and anxiety, the daunting challenge of integrating the growing Muslim population becomes apparent. In 2001 it was estimated that 1.6 million Muslims were living in Great Britain, comprising 3 per cent of the total population. Equating Islam itself with violence implies that the Muslim community at large is a potential source of violence and extremism. The consequences of such perceptions can hardly be ignored. This negative image of Islam is bound to turn into discrimination, provoking resentment and sometimes violence on the part of the Muslim community. In effect the multiculturalism logic is undermined. There is no recognition of the 'other' culture as espoused by the multiculturalism model; instead there is a multicultural society without 'ism' and two competing and conflicting identities, Islamic and British. According to the majority of Britons (63 per cent) in Pew's survey, the Islamic identity is rising. Ironically, the public identifies the Muslim population by its faith, yet the law deals with it as an ethnic group.

Two issues follow. The Islamic identity is not only widely seen as a source of extremism and violence, but also obscures the diversity of the Muslim population. A 2001 survey by the Home Office shows diversity along the lines of ethnicity, culture, language and place of birth. For instance, 39 per cent of British Muslim immigrants are from Asia (Pakistan, Bangladesh and India), 9 per cent from African, 3 per cent from Turkey and 1 per cent from former Yugoslavian countries. But the largest Muslim group (46 per cent) were born in Great Britain.[13] While these different groups are Muslim by faith and entitled to religious claims like Jews and Christians, they have different Islamic views and practices. In other words, there is no overarching Islamic identity broad and common enough to account for the diversity within the Muslim population. The term 'Islamic identity' itself is highly contested. It is true that Islam plays an important role in the various life spheres of many Muslims, but when it comes to the question of identity many Muslims see themselves as British nationals. Almost two-thirds of Muslims (65 per cent) aged 16 and over described their national identity as British, English, Scottish or Welsh. And the overwhelming majority of Muslims (93 per cent) who were born in Great Britain described themselves as British nationals.[14] In other words, British Muslims make the distinction between national identity and faith.

In sum, while the multicultural model is a promising solution for cultural diversity, discrimination and prejudice are inherent in the British political discourse against Islam and Muslims. Claims made on behalf of Islam have fallen off the edge of British multiculturalism. The absence of anti-religious discrimination laws in general and the dismissal of anti-Muslim discrimination in particular frustrate many British Muslims. The failure of British multiculturalism to integrate different ethnic Muslim groups is a product of the hostile perceptions of Islam and Muslims. The perception of Islam as a violent religion and Muslims as fundamentalists complicates and hinders integration. As Steven Vertovec notes, political demands made by British Muslim communities are often seen against the backdrop of Islamic fundamentalist threats (Vertovec, 2002: 23–4).

Secularism and the Muslim community in France

Nowhere has the question of Muslim integration been more controversial and painful than in France. The November 2005 riots smashed the republican rhetoric of liberty, equality and fraternity. Simmering social, political and economic exclusion over many decades came to the boil on a scale not seen since the student riots of May 1968. The riots broke out after two youths of Maghreb origin were electrocuted when they hid in a power station to avoid a police check. For more than three weeks, in many cities and towns, angry young people armed with with rocks and Molotov cocktails clashed with riot police armed with tear gas and rubber bullets. Thousands of cars were torched and thousands of arrests were made. A devastating but unequivocal wakeup call was sent to French politicians: the current integration (or lack of) policies are not working. As stated in simple terms by an 18-year-old French of Algerian descent: '[French leaders] know the conclusion to draw. We are sick of being discriminated against. That is all.'[15] The message is simple but cut to the heart of the republic, to the founding ideals of liberty, equality and fraternity enshrined in the French Revolution.

Historically, these ideals were put forth to establish a society where citizens are free from oppression, enjoy equal political and economic opportunities, and share a common sense of brotherhood. In reality they seem to have been overlooked with respect to a significant portion of the population: Muslim immigrants. The growth of the Muslim community and demand for religious rights gave rise to a traditional and populist rhetoric. It is often argued that 'Islam challenges France's long national history of relations between religion and the state' (Kastoryano, 2005: 63). In other words, Islam challenges the public neutrality established by the 1905 law, which called for the separation of church and state. Islam, however, is not the only visible religion in France. To this day, Catholics, Protestants and Jews continue to own places of worship, religious schools and chapels in the army (Caldwell, 2000: 30–1). For example, there are 40,000 cathedrals, churches and chapels for the Catholic population of 45 million; 957 houses of worship for a Protestant population of 900,000; 82 synagogues for a Jewish population of 500,000; and only eight officially recognized mosques for a population of four million Muslims (although there are many small informal praying rooms) (Caldwell, 2000: 31).

Therefore, to deny Islam accommodation already enjoyed by other faiths is clearly not a matter of division between public and private. The problem seems to lie in the rhetoric in which Islam is depicted as incompatible with French culture, and as a backward, monolithic and extreme culture. Oppression of women and extremism are the typical images of Islam transmitted to the French by the media and political elites.

Both stereotypes are seen in the case of the *foulard* and the *faubourgs*. The *foulard* was politicized in 1989 when a headmaster in Creil, Ernet Chenière, expelled three female students of Moroccan origin for not removing the *foulard* in a public school 'on the grounds that it would contravene the Republican principle of secularism' (Jane, 2004: 11). The affair polarized society and triggered various lines of provocative and exaggerated rhetoric, linking the *foulard* to the 'Islamization of France', 'the destruction of the Republic', 'a challenge to secularism' or 'Islamic fundamentalism'. The tension culminated in September 2004 with a law banning the *foulard* and other 'obvious' religious symbols in state schools.

While various justifications were offered, fear of Islamic fundamentalism was the decisive factor. For many the *foulard* is not simply what it is, an act of religious devotion, but as Remy Leveau and Shireen Hunter note, 'a symbol of *jihad* (holy war)' (2002: 22). In Pew's survey, the majority of the French (78 per cent) favour the ban, and 81 per cent of those who approved it are concerned about Islamic extremism. Yet, the relationship between the *foulard* and extremism is forged with no clear explanation of why, except that it is the case.

Such a popular and exaggerated view of Islam has had disastrous consequences in the French suburbs where mostly Muslim immigrants are housed. David Ignatius observes that, '[France] was so worried about Muslim extremists that it ignored the more immediate problem of the soulless and sullen suburbs' (Ignatius, 2005). They are grouped together in deteriorating housing projects, 'which no longer appears to be the result of individual choice but rather of the failure of the project of immigration' (Kastoroyan, 2005: 66). As a result, two unequal societies are living side by side, a reality which diametrically contradicts the ideals of the republic.

In response to the riots, political rhetoric failed to recognize and acknowledge the true cause, namely the social and economic discrimination of immigrants and their offspring. On the contrary, the riots generated racist and insensitive rhetoric that is hardly appropriate in tone and content to the problems facing French society. Both the head of the centre-right party and the employment minister partly blamed polygamy. The employment minister Gerard Larcher suggested that polygamous families breed 'anti-social' behaviour among young people, making them unemployable. The inflammatory remarks of the former interior minister (now president), Nicolas Sarkozy, to flush out the scum from the suburbs with a water hose, exacerbated rather than calmed the tension. Moreover, his remarks depicted the riots as simply a criminal act, without acknowledging the underpinning claims and grievances driving many of these angry young people to riot.

Government statistics estimate that the unemployment rate among French-born children of immigrants is more than double the national average (Moore, 2005). According to some estimates, the unemployment rate is nearly 40 per cent among second- and third-generation immigrants. For many French Muslims, a non-French sounding name like Mohammad is enough to lose a job offer. The French sociologist Jean-François Amadieu has shown that applicants with 'French' names obtain five times more job offers than applicants with Arab-sounding names (Geary and Graff, 2005). In addition to discrimination in the job market, many of these young people live in poverty and experience social exclusion and police harassment.

These social and economic ills have largely contributed to the failure of the integration process. Clearly, xenophobia and discrimination are incompatible with liberty, equality and fraternity. To make matters worse, a long political tradition has steadfastly considered cultural differences a threat to the cohesiveness of French society and the nation. So the assimilation model in France expects immigrants 'to completely give up their cultures of origin and adopt the culture of the country to which they have come' (Michalak and Saeed, 2002: 155). Its implication that culture is something that can easily be changed, especially religion, is increasingly recognized not only as unrealistic but also as a source of tension.

Considering that faith is deeply embedded in the hearts and minds of people, it is hardly likely to vanish on crossing the border. To reject legitimate religious claims, such as building mosques and wearing the *foulard* in school, is a denial of basic human rights much the same as the right to freedom of speech and assembly.

The riots forced France to re-evaluate the problems of immigrants. The important question now is how French politicians and society at large will deal with unemployment and discrimination in particular, and the question of Islam in general. Irresponsible comments by politicians criminalizing the protesters or blaming polygamy for unemployment exemplify the rhetoric that has partly caused the problem. It will take a new kind of political rhetoric, more responsible and sensitive to the cultural and religious diversity of French society, and a major transformation of the legal structure to effectively remedy the current ills and prevent future riots.

Conclusion

The presence of Muslims and their demands for recognition have sparked an extensive political rhetoric. Despite the various political and cultural circumstances across Europe, European political rhetoric has two common features: it is largely based on interpretation and gross generalizations, and it is calculated to win the majority of voters by deploying traditional and populist rhetoric. Such rhetoric has had an enormous effect on Muslims' integration, by drawing on past Muslim–Christian relationships and present global political conflicts and wars to construct an image of Islam as a violent and oppressive religion. Images of the violence on the West Bank, in Iraq and Afghanistan and the bombings in Madrid and London, among many more, are juxtaposed without objective and accurate explanations. Consequently, Islam is widely perceived as a monolithic and violent culture and European Muslims are naturally perceived as part of this culture. Thus, Muslims continue to face major obstacles when integrating into European societies.

European politicians and a societal majority have fiercely objected to a place for Islam in the public space, as shown in the case studies discussed in this chapter. The Spanish case shows how Islam has been excluded from the Spanish Judeo-Christian tradition, despite the fact that an important and rich Islamic tradition lasted in Spain for 800 years. Today Muslims in Spain are seen primarily through the hostile prism of the Moors. Meanwhile, politicians in Great Britain for the most part avoid confronting anti-Muslim discrimination. Unlike Jews and Sikhs, Muslims are not directly protected by law. The riots in France bear witness to the social and economic discrimination of mostly Muslim Arabs and Africans immigrants. What is more, republican rhetoric is often deployed to counter demands for mosques, state-funded Muslims schools, wearing the head-scarves, and so on.

To sum up, European politicians have yet to accept and publicly recognize the cultural and religious diversity of their societies. The Muslim problem facing Europe today echoes the words of Commander James Lowell on board Apollo XIII: 'Houston, we have a problem!' The only way to solve it is for politicians to treat Muslim citizens with the same respect shown to any other European citizen, regardless of religion, place of origin or colour. However, this first and foremost requires a responsible rhetoric, free of stereotype and distortion of Islam and Muslims as seen in the discourses of populism and tradition. The 'alliance of civilizations' promoted by the Spanish President José Luis Rodriguez Zapatero is a promising start.

Notes

1. This chapter is part of a research project financed by the Spanish Ministry of Education and Science (Ministerio de Educación y Ciencia) entitled *The politicization of immigration: the relationship between the political and the social discourse in Spain and the EU immigration politics* (*La politización de la inmigración: relación entre el discurso político y social en España y políticas de la UE entorno a la inmnigración*) (SEJ2004-04775/CPOL, 2004–2007).
2. For information on the process of multiculturalism in Spain, see Zapata-Barrero (2004b).
3. Kelly defines 'circumstances of multiculturality' as a 'Context within which the problems raised by group differences arise and in which the issues addressed by multicultural theorists can be located' (Kelly, 2002: 1–17).
4. For additional information on populist rhetoric, see among the most recent works: Taggard (2000); Perrinau (2001); Meny and Surel (2000); Ihl et al. (2003); Taguieff (2004); Laclau (2005).
5. For a good demonstration of how the media covers Islam, see Said (1981).
6. Pew Global Attitudes Project. http://pewglobal.org/
7. El Ejido is a market-garden town in the province of Almeria (Andalusia) in south-eastern Spain where violent riots against Moroccan workers took place (Zapata-Barrero, 2003: 523–39).
8. *Anuario de Extranjería 2004*, Ministerio de Trabajo y Asuntos Sociales, Secretaria de Estado de inmnigración y emigración (December 2005). http://extranjeros.mtas.es/es/general/DatosEstadisticos_index.html.
9. http://www.cre.gov.uk/legal/rights_religion.html.
10. http://www.cre.gov.uk/legal/rights_religion.html.
11. http://www.runnymedetrust.org/publications/pdfs/islamophobia.pdf.
12. Pew Global Attitudes Project. http://pewglobal.org.
13. Office for National Statistics. http://www.statistics.gov.uk.
14. Office for National Statistics. http://www.statistics.gov.uk.
15. As quoted in *The Washington Post* (9 November 2005) p. A22.

References

Anuario de Extranjería 2004, Ministerio de Trabajo y Asuntos Sociales, Secretaria de Estado de inmnigración y emigración (December 2005). http://extranjeros. mtas.es/es/general/DatosEstadisticos_index.html.

Burke, E. (1987) *Reflections on the Revolution in France*. London: Collier Macmillan.

Caldwell, C. (2000) 'The Crescent and the Tricolor', *Atlantic Monthly*, 286(5): 30–1.

Carbayo Abengózar, M. (1998) 'La Hispanidad: un acercamiento deconstructivo', *Revista de estudios literarios*, 10.

de Lucas, J. (2002) 'Algunas propuestas para comenzar a hablar en serio de política de inmigración', in J. de Lucas and F. Torres (eds), *Inmigrantes: ¿cómo los tenemos?* Madrid: Talasa Ediciones. pp. 23–48.

Esposito, J. L. (1999) *The Islamic Threat: Myth or Reality*. New York: Oxford University Press.

Friedrich, K. (1972) *Tradition and Authority*. London: Macmillan.

García Morente, M. (1938) *Idea de Hispanidad*. Buenos Aires: Espasa Calpe.

Geary, J. and Graff, J. (2005) 'Restless Youth', *Time*, 21 November. http://www.time.com/time/europe/magazine/printout/0,13155,901051121-1129484,00.html.

González Antón, L. (1997) *España y las Españas*. Madrid: Alianza.

Hichem, D. (1985) *Europe and Islam*. Berkeley, CA: University California Press (Translated by Peter Heinegg).

Hirschman, A. O. (1991) *The Rhetoric of Persuasion*. Cambridge, MA: The Belknap Press of Harvard University Press.

Ihl, O., Chêne, J., Vial, E. and Waterlot, G. (2003) *Le populisme au coeur de l'Europe*. Paris: La Découverte.

Ignatius, D. (2005) *The Washington Post*, 9 November.

Jane, F. (2004) 'Secularism as a Barrier to Integration? the French Dilemma', *International Migration*, 42(3): 11.

Kastoryano, R. (2005) 'French Secularism and Islam: France's Headscarf Affair', in T. Modood, A. Triandafyllidou and R. Zapata-Barrero (eds), *Multiculturalism, Muslims and Citizenship: a European Approach*. London: Routledge.

Kelly, P. (2002) 'Introduction: between Culture and Equality', in R. Kelly (ed.), *Multiculturalism reconsidered*. Cambridge: Polity Press. pp. 1–17.

Laclau, E. (2005) *La razón populista*. México: Fondo de Cultura Económica.

Leveau, R. and Hunter, S. T. (2002) 'Islam in France', in S. T. Hunter (ed.), *Islam, Europe's Second Religion*. Westport, CT: Praeger.

López García, B. (2003) 'El islam y la integración de la inmigración en España', *Webislam*, 212 (May). http://www.webislam.com.

Martín Muñoz, G. (1994) 'El islam en España hoy', in L. Martín Rojo, C. Gómez Esteban, F. Arranz and A. Gabilondo (eds), *Hablar y dejar hablar (sobre racismo y xenophobia*. Madrid: Universidad Autónoma de Madrid.

——— (1996) 'Prólogo', in P. Balta (ed.), *El islam* (Spanish edition). Madrid: Salvat-Le Monde. pp. 9–16.

——— (2003) *Marroquíes en España. Estudio sobre su integración*. Madrid: Fundación Repsol YPF.

Meny, Y. and Surel, Y. (2000) *Par le peuple, pour le peuple. Le populisme et les démocraties*. Paris: Fayard.

Michalak, L. and Saeed, A. (2002) 'The Continental Divide: Islam and Muslim Identities in France', in N. Al Sayyad and M. Castells (eds), *Muslim Europe or Euro-Islam: Politics, Culture, and Citizenship in the Age of Globalization*. Lanham, MA: Lexington Books.

Modood, T. (2000) 'Anti-essentialism, Multiculturalism, and the "Recognition" of Religious Groups', in W. Kymlicka and W. Norman (eds), *Citizenship in Diverse Societies*. New York: Oxford University Press. pp. 175–95.

Moore, M. (2005) *The Washington Post*, 15 November.

Nasr, S. H. (2003) *Islam: Religion, History, and Civilization*. New York: Harper.

Parekh, B. (2000) 'The Political Structure of Multicultural Society', in *Rethinking Multiculturalism*. London: Macmillan. pp. 196–238.

Perrinau, P. (2001) *Les croisés de la société fermée*. Paris: Editons l'Aube.

Rodinson, M. (1987) *Europe and the Mystique of Islam*. Seattle: University of Washington Press (translated by Roger Veinus).

Said, E. (1981) *Covering Islam: How the Media and the Experts Determine How We See the Rest of the World*. London: Routledge & Kegan Paul.

Taggard, P. (2000) *Populism*. Buckingham: Open University Press.

Taguieff, P. A. (2004) *Le retour du populisme*. Paris: Universalis.

Todorov, T. (1991) *Les morales de l'histoire*. Paris: Grasset, le Collège de Philosophie.

Vertovec, S. (2002) 'Islamophobia and Muslim Recognition in Britain', in Y. Yazbeck Haddad (ed.), *Muslims in the West: From Sojourners to Citizens*. New York: Oxford University Press.

Vila Selma, J. (1996) 'Hispanidad', *Enciclopedia de la Cultura Española*. Madrid: Editora Nacional, 3: 551.

Zapata-Barrero, R. (2003) 'The "Discovery" of Immigration in Spain: The Politicization of Immigration in the Case of El Ejido', *Journal of International Migration and Integration*, 4: 523–39.

——— (2004a) *Multiculturalidad e inmigración*. Madrid: Editorial Síntesis. pp. 168–73.

——— (2004b) *Inmigración, innovación política y cultura de acomodación en España*. Barcelona: Cidob/Bellaterra.

——— (2005a) 'Hermenéutica de la inmigración', *Revista Claves de la razón práctica*, 158: 29–37.

——— (2005b) 'The Muslim Community and Spanish Tradition: Maurophobia as a Fact, and Impartiality as a Desideratum', in T. Modood, A. Triandafyllidou and R. Zapata-Barrero (eds), *Multiculturalism, Muslims and Citizenship: A European Approach*. London: Routledge, pp. 143–61.

Zemni, S. and Parker, C. (2002) 'Islam, the European Union, and the Challenge of Multiculturalism', in S. T. Hunter (ed.), *Islam, Europe's Second Religion: The New Social, Cultural, and Political Landscape*. Westport, CT: Praeger.

5

Constitutional or Agonistic Patriotism? The Dilemmas of Liberal Nation-States

Ephraim Nimni

> Always, however, the intellectual is beset and remorselessly challenged by the problem of loyalty. All of us without exception belong to some sort of national, religious or ethnic community: no one, no matter the volume of protestations, is above the organic ties that bind the individual to family, community, and of course nationality.
>
> (Edward Said, *The Independent*, 1 July 1993, p. 14)

During the last two decades of the twentieth century, with or without irony, a phantom haunted Eastern Europe, the phantom of liberal democracy. The collapse of communism and the end of Marxism as a serious political and ideological contender propelled the supporters of liberal democracy in countries where it had enjoyed a central position for hundreds of years into a triumphal and congratulatory mood. From Francis Fukuyama at the shallow end of the debate, to more nuanced exponents of liberal democratic political philosophy, such as John Rawls and Jürgen Habermas, liberalism triumphantly paraded its values and ideas, as the collapse of communism and the dissolution of most politically organized forms of Marxism relieved liberals of important political and intellectual opponents. However, and in spite of this considerable success, the result in Eastern Europe's former communist states was not always the emerging of liberal political regimes. The causes of this paradox are many, but perhaps one important ingredient can be found in a recurrent problem that haunted liberals for decades, if not centuries. This problem can be summarized as follows. Historically, the (civic) nation-state was the vessel through which liberalism exercised its political philosophy.[1] However, the institutionalization of individual rights, the most potent and persuasive device in the liberal inventory, cannot easily accommodate political demands for collective or group rights for national and ethnic minorities in civic nation-states.

Constitutional patriotism (Verfassungspatriotismus) as a theory distinct from both liberal nationalism and republican patriotism was elaborated in post-war West Germany. Following the traumatic German experience, it was designed to overcome the early ethnic bias of nation-states by producing a model of governance that can win the loyalty of all citizens to established constitutional civic values without resorting to *Völkish* forms of nationalism and social cohesion. The term was coined by Dolf Sternberger, a distinguished political scientist, in the Frankfurter Allgemeine Zeitung (23 May 1979) and Jürgen Habermas further developed it in the mid-1980s (Müller, 2005: 4). In tandem with deliberative democracy, the model promises to provide an ethnically neutral civic space. However, *contra* Sternberger and Habermas, this chapter argues that in the context of the prevailing organizational forms of the nation-state, the alleged neutrality of the civic constitutional space is little more than a chimera, and that in the organizational forms of liberal democratic nation-states, a neutral, procedural form of constitutional patriotism is not possible. The overwhelming majority of civic nation-states are *de facto* multination-states that endorse, implicitly or explicitly, legal and political-cultural mores of dominant nations. Ethnic/national minorities who feel justifiably or unjustifiably alienated by what they claim to be the imposition of the values of dominant nations dressed up in universal liberal values have little redress. The problem is particularly challenging for minorities precisely because the values of the dominant *ethnie* are presented in the guise of neutral procedural principles and of individual universal rights divorced from sectoral affiliation. To compound the problem, when minorities make demands for the protection of a minority culture, these minorities are often accused, in the name of civilization and progress, of holding on to traditional or regressive principles (see e.g. Moller Okin, 1999).

The question of political recognition is of great importance for the evaluation of the demands of ethnic and national minorities. This perhaps points to the liberal democratic dilemma, which is clearly expressed by Amy Guttmann: 'Can citizens with diverse identities be represented as equals if public institutions do not recognise their identities?' (in Taylor, 1992: 3–4). As Guttmann argues, this challenge is 'endemic' to liberal democracies because they are committed in principle to the notion of equal representation. It is in this principled and uncompromising demand for individual equality (unfortunately understood as sameness) that, paradoxically, the equally important need for the recognition of diversity is lost. In the nineteenth century, John Stuart Mill set the tone when he asserted that: 'Free institutions are next to impossible in a country made up of different nationalities. . . . Among people without fellow-feeling, especially if they speak different languages, the united public opinion, necessary to the working of representative government cannot exist' (Mill, 1862/1976: 361). It is indeed remarkable that one of the founding fathers of the philosophical creed most committed to pluralism could *not* reconcile himself to culturally plural forms of governance.

Following Mill's influential assertion and considering its impact on mainstream liberal thinking, it might be more prudent to reformulate Guttmann's question so that it can address the liberal Gordian knot: Can citizens with diverse ethnic and national identities be represented as equals by nation-states that adopt *one* official state culture?

Almost half a century ago, Elie Kedourie provided a categorical answer to this question:

> The national state claims to treat all citizens as equal members of the nation, this fair sounding principle only serves to disguise the tyranny of one group over another. The nation must be, all its citizens must be, animated with the same spirit. Differences are divisive and therefore treasonable. (1960: 127)

The criticism is not new, as this problem has been present since the emergence of the nation-state in seventeenth-century Europe. In post-revolutionary France, the Jacobin deputies Barére and Grégoire presented a report to the constitutional assembly of 1794 under the suggestive title: *On the need and means to destroy dialects* [patois] *and universalize the use of the French language.*[2] A year later the assembly approved the revolutionary slogan: 'In the one and undivided Republic, the one and undivided use of the language of Freedom'[3] (Nimni, 1994: 18–20). Let us not forget that more than half the population of France during this period was unable to speak 'French' (the language of the court of Versailles) fluently. The Revolution's goal was to destroy the ancien régime and its corporate network of sovereign sectional interests. Communities (ethnic, national or otherwise) had no legitimate entitlement to representation or right to mediate between citizens. This vertical dimension of the French polity prevented representation of religious groups and national and ethnic communities, and gave rise to the exclusionary characteristics of the republican concept of citizenship (Lefebvre, 2003: 17).

This shows us that from its revolutionary origins, republicanism was incapable of integrating its ethnic and national minorities into a nation-state without insisting on uncompromising demands for assimilation. All citizens are equals, but that equality requires citizens to embrace the dominant political culture. What is remarkable is that for centuries these impediments were hidden from view, disguised by the seductive rhetoric of the discourse of modernization. To be sure, the rival Marxist tradition did no better: it is sufficient to recall Engels' dubious term 'Non-historic Peoples', and the cry for the assimilation of the so-called South Slavs to German culture (Rosdolsky, 1986; for a more detailed discussion see Nimni, 1995).

However, in the last three decades, mainly through the weakening of the nation-state through globalization (Held, 1995: 278–80), the hidden inequality of minorities has been exposed for everyone to see, driven by the strength of the politics of difference (Taylor, 1994).

There is a long and protracted debate about the meaning of the term 'nation' and the possibility of a nation to be either 'ethnic' or 'civic' (Kohn, 1944; Greenfeld, 1992; Smith, 1998). There is also a more recent argument showing the futility of such a distinction (Kuzio, 2001, 2002). This debate cannot be entered here. For the purposes of our argument, an ideal nation-state is the usually unobtainable symbiosis of a territorial and administrative unit and a complete ethno-cultural community engulfing the totality of its citizens. Except for the principalities of San Marino, Liechtenstein and Andorra and an exceptionally small numbers of larger states (such as Poland and Korea), there is an insurmountable gap between the homogenizing normative prescription of the nation-state and the empirical ethnic diversity of its citizens. In a few cases the nation-state is being slowly replaced by what many call a 'multicultural state' or a 'multination-state' (Norman, 2001: 96–7). This is a state that recognizes the national plurality of its citizens and in a few and extraordinary situations, the collective rights of some minority national communities.[4]

Notwithstanding the recent fiasco on the European Constitution in the birthplace of the nation-state – Western Europe – the original powers of this institution have been considerably diminished. With the European Union, its non-national citizenship and subsidiarity principles, what remains of the nation-state is now is a significantly weakened version of its former self and here EU supporters and opponents agree.

However, these recent momentous changes in the practical standing of the nation-state, in part the result of globalization and in Europe the incremental changes brought about by the EU, have not led to significant conceptual changes in political theory. We continue to use the terms 'nation' and 'state' (or indeed nation-state) as if nothing had happened and we thus remain confused and perplexed by these changes. While we can agree with Halliday (1994: 82) that the image of the nation-state as ethnically homogeneous and politically sovereign is empirically wrong in the contemporary world, no alternative redefinition, let alone conceptualization, of the state has emerged. It is necessary to re-evaluate the terms ethnicity, nation and nation-state, as a first step towards a long overdue conceptual change in these key ideas in political theory. Here, the idea of a 'multi-scale democracy' (*démocratie multiscalaire*), a set of institutional frameworks that prescribe democratic practices at a variety of space scales not necessarily subordinated to the normative political order of nation-state, and that moves away from territorial conceptions of sovereignty, offers a promising beginning (Nootens, 2004: 157–8). This discussion cannot be entertained here.

Minorities and collective rights

A sharp divide between collective and individual rights is sometimes difficult to sustain. Most democratic rights are not restricted to one individual but can only be enjoyed collectively by a plurality of individuals. Van Aaken defines rights as 'legally recognised interests which are to be found in a continuum from individual to collective interests' (Van Aaken, 2005: 9). For the purposes of this discussion, ethnic groups are interactive communities, usually self-defined, bound by ties arising out of shared customs, sometimes a shared language and sometimes a shared mythology. While in some cases there are external markers in the form of a common language, and in a small minority of cases phenotypical characteristics, the sense of belonging is inherently subjective and sometimes held by members against reasoned and/or eclectic arguments to the contrary.

Whatever definition is adopted, nations and ethnic groups are always segmental and open to differing interpretations. Within nation-states, competing definitions of 'the national interest' and which of them prevails is the result of a tussle between contending national ideologies. Much in the same way, what political meaning is ascribed to ethnic and national identities is the preliminary outcome of internal hegemonic tussles. While the plurality of definitions of 'the national interest' is self-evident and accepted, minority nationalisms or minority religious political ideologies are much less commonly understood as temporary outcomes of internal ideological struggles, and this tends to stereotype and obfuscate the character of these communities. Pre-modern religious practices of minorities are often wrongly seen as constitutive of these communities, which are then counterposed to the modernity of the beliefs of the dominant group. This conveniently forgets that dominant groups also have a history or a reality of pre-modern religious practices and that these are subjected to vibrant debates that can take place only because the dominant community does not need to close ranks to protect itself from assimilatory pressures. Consequently, the recognition of group rights in the public domain is not only a critical normative need, but will encourage internal minority debate and more robust group integration into the larger polity. However, liberals are deeply suspicious of collective rights because they violate the individualistic character of the liberal tradition.

There are two main problems in aiming towards recognition of collective rights of ethnic communities. First, because of their interactive attribute – both internal and external – ethnic communities are in continuous flux. As they are not embedded in institutions, there are few if any external referents to determine membership of the group. Yet core members stick proudly to their communities, and a deep sense of loss, alienation and grievance arises when their cultural identity is misrecognized, and they are often prepared to struggle, sometimes violently, to gain political recognition. This subjective feeling is often constitutive of the individual's identity and needs to find an expression in the broader polity if the aim is to encourage an all-embracing, transcultural citizenship. Second, the vital interactivity with other communities sometimes creates 'ethnic hybrids' – individuals or groups linked to more than one community – and 'ethnic stereotypes' – individuals or groups associated with an ethnic community against their will. Individual rights are thus crucial to protect the differentiation of 'ethnic hybrids' from pressures from minority communities and 'ethnic stereotypes' from the prejudices of dominant majorities.

A word of caution is necessary here to avoid misunderstandings about dichotomy between ethnic majorities and minorities. First, it is not possible to distinguish clearly between ethnic and national communities. While national communities are often (but not always) dominant within a (nation-) state, both types of communities include segmental characteristics sustained by a differentiating cultural substratum. It therefore seems more productive to see them as poles of a continuum with fuzzy demarcations, rather than as two unambiguously different phenomena. Second, and as Parekh (1991: 185) argues, ethnic communities are not ethnic because they are minorities. The term 'minorities' has a numerical referent that may confuse the issue. What distinguishes members of one community from another is their real or imagined common bonds and interactivity, and not their numerical qualities. An ethnic/national group will not lose its characteristics by becoming a minority and vice versa. However, numerical qualities are important in one respect. They often determine differential access to common goods and resources in the wider society.

As mentioned, it is misleading to think of ethnic groups and nations as homogeneous communities. More often than not, the identity and prescriptive characteristics of the group is the outcome of internal power struggles in their interaction with the 'outside' world. While the raw material through which the collective identity is constructed is often related to real or imagined historical experiences, contemporary characteristics are invariably the result of internal hegemonic battles that result in one particular (or a combination of) interpretations gaining recognition to the detriment of others. Identity definitions are nearly always the outcome of internal debates that could be protracted and acrimonious. Eriksen (1993: 92–3) observes that nationhood (or ethnic identity) involves shared memories, but also a great deal of 'shared forgetting'. The victorious hegemonic interpretation triggers selective amnesia of the shared memories it dislikes. Ethnic identities and ethnicity are far from immutable and static ideological constructs, it is necessary to explain their mutation and their relation to dominant forces within the community as well as why ethnic and national groups remain distinctive under different social conditions and how they interact with other identities. Ethnicity and nationalism are kindred concepts, and the bulk of nationalisms are ethnic in character. Even if nationalism is understood as an ethnic ideology that protects or demands a state, the insurmountable problem is that the potential number of nations is much larger than the actual number of nation-states and exceeds the practical possibilities of building new ones, and the number of ethnic groups and potential nations is even larger (Eriksen, 1993: 11–18). The problem becomes particularly acute and vicious when the collective abode of alienated ethnic/national communities overlaps. Minority nationalisms are often caught between the hostility of dominant majorities and sheer practical impossibility of building a separate nation-state. This is one of the most significant triggers of contemporary genocides. There is therefore an urgent and compelling need to find a solution that does not require separate statehood to resolve the burning problem of the self-determination of alienated national minorities.

We shall now examine the political implications of these reflections for liberal democracies.

The impossibility of a nation-state-oriented constitutional patriotism

An influential group of liberal thinkers uncritically accepts the ambiguous contrast between 'civic' and 'ethnic' nation-states and uses this distinction as the point of departure for the development of the concept of constitutional patriotism. Jürgen Habermas is the most prominent and vocal among them. As we shall see, Habermas bases his advocacy for the idea of a culturally 'neutral state' on an unequivocal distinction between civic and ethnic nationalism as derived from the work of Hans Kohn (1944; 1967) and Miroslav Hroch (1985) and expanded by Habermas himself.

Habermas contends that in antiquity the term *natio* clearly denoted an ethnic dimension as it was related to the idea of origin and birth. In the Roman Empire the term was used to distinguish between 'barbarian nations' and 'the civilized world' (*civitas*). The former was an ethnic conglomerate of what Habermas calls 'pre-political populations', while the latter was integrated through a political process (Habermas, 1992: 3).

Habermas's defence of constitutional patriotism is presented with passion in his critique of Taylor's politics of recognition. For Habermas, modern constitutions are derived from a conception found in what he calls 'modern natural law'. Citizens come together voluntarily to form 'a legal community of free and equal consociates or to put it clearly rights . . . protect the integrity of legal subjects who are in every case individuals' (Habermas, 1994: 107). In contrast to this, Habermas argues that 'communitarians' like Taylor and Waltzer dispute the ethical neutrality of the law and thus can expect the constitutional state, if need be, actively to advance specific conceptions of the good life (Habermas, 1994: 111).

Habermas further contends that coexistence for different ethnic groups and their cultural forms of life does not need to be safeguarded through collective rights that would overtax a theory of rights tailored to individual persons. For Habermas, the constitutional state is capable of making 'the reproduction of lifeworlds' possible, but it cannot promise this. 'For to guarantee survival will necessarily rob the members of the very freedom to say yes or no if they are to appropriate and preserve their cultural heritage' (Habermas, 1994: 130). The state must remain 'neutral' with respect to differences among cultural communities. The nation is then clearly a 'civic' nation, and it is imperative to separate the political community (or polity) from that of an ethnic or cultural community. With the emergence of the nation-state in Europe, nationhood was both a community of culture and a community of citizens, but in the contemporary world, Habermas argues, there is an increasing tendency for both ideas to clash. Three momentous events highlight this situation: 1) German unification and its implications for republican notions of universality; 2) the ethno-national conflicts in Central and Eastern Europe; and 3) the formidable influx of migrants from poor regions to the more developed regions of the world. For Habermas (1992: 1), these three processes exacerbate the conflict between what he calls 'the universalistic principles of constitutional democracies and the particularistic claim of communities to preserve their integrity and habitual ways of life'.

In discussing the origins of the territorial nation-state Habermas agues that:

> the nation-state laid the foundations for cultural and ethnic homogeneity, on the basis of which it then proved possible to push ahead with the democratisation of government since the late eighteen century, *although this was achieved at the cost of excluding ethnic minorities.* (Habermas, 1992: 2; emphasis added)

From this argument, one is left wondering under what criterion Habermas considers that it is possible to initiate a process of democratization from a discriminatory basis, and how he can justify the exclusion of ethnic and national minorities to achieve greater homogeneity under *any* democratic criteria. Habermas's liberalism is prepared to contemplate the exclusion of ethnic and national minority cultures to achieve that cultural and ethnic homogeneity that is necessary for the smooth operation of the nation-state.

But if the nation-state was initially based on a common ethnic/national identity, then the differences of meaning between nation (as an ethnic community) and 'politically organized people' have gradually been disappearing since the nineteenth century (Habermas, 1992: 3). With the French Revolution the nation becomes the basis for state sovereignty. This finally leads to Habermas's central argument:

> The nation of citizens does not derive its identity from some common ethnic and cultural properties, but rather from the praxis of citizens who actively exercise their civil rights. At this juncture, the republican strand of citizenship completely parts company with the idea of belonging to a pre-political community integrated on the basis of descent, a shared tradition and a common language. (Habermas, 1992: 3)

Habermas argues that 'Only briefly did the democratic nation-state forge a close link between "ethnos" and "demos" '. Citizenship was never conceptually tied to national identity. Habermas further argues that, in the identity of the nation-state, one must carefully separate the ethnic component which has become 'obsolete'. Instead one must build a new sense of national (state) identity in which citizenship is not based on allegiance to an indivisible community, but on a contractual arrangement in which the citizen agrees to respect and tolerate others without requesting a commitment to one cultural tradition (or ethnicity). Unfortunately, Habermas does not tell us how this contractual agreement can create the conditions for tolerance without requesting a commitment to one cultural tradition. This is important because he admitted earlier that the modern liberal-democratic nation-state laid the foundations for cultural and ethnic homogeneity (see above).

Everyone should be in a position to expect that all will receive equal protection and respect for his/her inviolable integrity as a unique individual. According to Habermas then, the abstract idea of the universalization of democracy and human rights forms the basis from which the sense of national identity and national loyalty is constructed. He further argues that 'Germans' (presumably he means citizens of the Federal Republic of Germany) understand themselves as a nation of *Volksgenossen* (ethnic comrades) (Habermas, 1994: 145) and the French, in contrast, are a nation of citizens. However, if one accepts the argument that the nation-state reproduces ethno-cultural dominant practices, French citizens are as *Volksgenossen* as German citizens are in the Habermasian model. The only difference is that in the latter this is implicit in the constitution and political culture, and in the former it is made explicit by constitutional laws. Not a difference of substance, merely one of form.

However, Habermas contends, the French Revolution introduces a crucial distinction: with Abbé Sieyès the third estate becomes the nation and the source of state sovereignty. At this point the term nation is linked to citizenship and loses its ethnic dimension, reinforcing the distinction between 'civic' and 'ethnic' nation-states. This dichotomy helps Habermas to assert that it is necessary to distinguish conceptually between predominately Western European 'civic' nation-states, and predominately Central and Eastern European 'ethnic' nation-states, and he uses this argument to argue for sweeping reforms in the Federal Republic of Germany.

While there is some limited, technical-legal merit in using the distinction between civic and ethnic nation-states, particularly when comparing constitutional laws, as mentioned before, this difference is merely a matter of degree, not of substance. Democratic nation-states, civic or otherwise, require a relatively culturally homogeneous sovereign body of citizens. If *individual* sovereign citizens have rights and duties, the discharge of these responsibilities requires at least a minimal overarching collective framework of values. This presupposes at least a 'thin' cultural consensus[5] concerning some fundamental values that are legally codified and objectified in the nation-state's political institutions. The problem with these codified values is, however, that as culturally 'thin' their supporters might claim them to be, they enlist all citizens' loyalty, including that of ethnic minorities, in the name of an undivided collective that is the recipient of the sovereign will of individual citizens (the 'civic' nation). This leaves the collective will of minorities unrepresented, for this sovereign principle admits no fragmentation. This is what Otto Bauer (2000: 222), following Karl Renner, calls the atomist-centralist representative principle.

The centralizing principle was initially developed by European absolutism, and the centralization of the state had the effect of reducing society to its smallest parts (in Bauer's words, atoms), for example, to single individuals. This idea was developed further by liberalism, which swept away the last vestiges of ancient autonomous associations. As a result, in liberal democracies there are two recognized politico-juridical entities: the sovereign individual and the sovereign will of the undivided collective (Nimni, 1999; Bauer, 2000). This is what Bauer and Renner call the atomist-centralist structure of modern nation-states. This totalizing tendency fails to acknowledge important and meaningful intermediate locations, like the ones occupied by ethnic and national minorities. The inhabitants of the state are nationally identified with the state through habitation and citizenship, irrespective of ethnic affiliations. States are thus seen as nation-states whether they are ethnically homogeneous or not (Ra'anan, 1991: 20). In the liberal nation-state the cultural practice of the dominant nation (the official ethnicity of the state) is disguised by a procedural practice that claims neutrality but is derived from the cultural experiences of the dominant national community. Furthermore, a liberal view of culture is perspectival and cannot avoid seeing every culture from a liberal angle. This creates distortions that have the effect of limiting multiculturalism in liberal democracies through the hegemony of the ethnic majority making the dominant nation to be in effect *a primus inter pares* (first among equals – an oxymoron). Atomist states, however much consideration they might show for individual democratic rights and however egalitarian their practices, are by definition adverse to recognizing intermediate and constitutionally enshrined entities (Ra'anan, 1991: 25). This issue puts defenders of liberal nationalism in a bind. If liberal nationalists consider that it is desirable for states to be nation-states, then multination-states face two equally unacceptable options: either to split the state along national lines, or to enable the larger national group to assimilate the weaker ones (Kymlicka and Straehle, 1999: 76). Both strategies have been tried with equally catastrophic results (Nimni, 1999: 300).

Consequently, in 'ethnic' nation-states cultural criteria are explicit in the constitutional arrangements, and in 'civic' nation-states they are implicit and subtle in the legal system, the cultural mores supported by the state, and in the definition of rights and duties of citizens. Thus, considering the liberal perspective, the ethnocultural core of the nation-state is 'thin' in the case of the civic state and 'thick' in the case of the ethnic state, a difference of degree and not of substance. Consequently, Habermas and other procedural liberals are wrong if they wish to base their claim for the neutrality of the 'civic' nation-state. Neither form of nation-state is culturally neutral and in both cases the salience of ethnicity is a matter of degree rather than of substance. Ethnic and civic nation-states cannot be unambiguously differentiated as they are poles or simply variants within the same continuum.

In contrast, constitutional patriotism in its different variants and forms accepts the idea that a civic nation-state could be procedurally neutral, but it nevertheless suggests constitutional restrictions to political loyalty and focuses all loyalty on a legally enacted constitution. The constitution provides procedural norms to organize public debate and orients it to justifiable ends (Calhoun, 2002: 149). This argument has been challenged by Veit Bader (1997), who questions whether one can separate liberal principles from cultural contexts in which they gain cultural meaning. The second problem is that the idea of a 'civic' political culture blurs and confuses universalist norms with segmental ethnic cultures (Laborde, 2002: 597).

Because of the privileged position that the anonymous individual citizen (depicted in the image of the dominant majority) occupies in the proceduralist liberalism of constitutional patriots, they are confronted by the old dilemma of the impossibility of securing non-assimilationist minority rights, and the concomitant challenge to universalizing patterns that result from the recent success of politics of difference in the West. Here procedural liberalism reaches its conceptual limits. Within the framework of liberal theory, the recognition of special (and differentiated) rights for ethnic and national minorities often conflicts with procedural liberal notions of individual autonomy and freedom of choice. In Taylor's words:

> The fact is that there are forms of this liberalism of equal rights that in the mind of their own proponents can give only very restrictive acknowledgement of distinct cultural identities. The notion that any of the standard schedules of rights might apply differently in one cultural context than they do in another, that their application, that their application may have to take account of different collective goals, is considered quite unacceptable. (Taylor, 1992: 52)

Taylor argues for a different interpretation of liberalism, one that affords protection and recognition of minorities in the same way as more mainstream forms of liberalism protect individual autonomy and freedom of choice. Taylor contends that procedural liberalism and by extension constitutional patriotism are 'inhospitable' to difference. By this he means that this form of liberalism insists on the uniform application of the rules that define individual rights and is suspicious of collective goals. This form of liberalism cannot accommodate the desire for survival of collectivities that are different, and in Taylor's opinion this form of liberalism is guilty as charged by the supporters of the politics of difference. He further argues for a different type of liberalism, one that is willing to weigh the importance of certain forms of uniform treatment against the importance of catering to minorities' anxiety for cultural survival (Taylor, 1992: 60–1). Chantal Mouffe goes one step further and argues that fixing the content and meaning of liberal democratic institutions into a transcendental universalist logic that is the generalization of a parochial perspective effectively disposes of the possibility of a pluralist accommodation of minorities. This type of liberalism searches for an argument that is beyond argumentation and wishes to fix the meaning of the universal. In doing so it makes the same error that it criticizes in totalitarianism: it rejects democratic indeterminacy and the identification of the universal with a given particular (Mouffe, 1996: 254).

In a thought-provoking revision of the Habermasian model, Cécile Laborde argues that the neutralist version of constitutional patriotism advanced by Habermas is 'self-defeating'. Laborde instead develops a model for civic patriotism that while accepting it has little to say about the difficulties of reconciling civic values with deeply divided multinational societies, nevertheless attempts to reconcile the imperatives of democratic legitimacy and respect for cultural diversity through a republican and social democratic model (Laborde, 2002: 591–2). Laborde is also careful to distinguish between national identity and what she calls 'the collective identity of the polity', and argues that the conflation of the collective identity of the polity with the identity of the historical majority cannot be justified on civic patriotic grounds (Laborde, 2002: 598, 607). The form of civic patriotism she promotes prescribes that civic culture must be reshaped to reflect concerns of minority groups, but advocates in line with the main tenets of constitutional patriotism a strong republican concept of political equality. Civic patriotism thus promotes a common political identity whose contents make it compatible with a variety of practices and beliefs (Laborde, 2002: 611). This model meets important objections raised against the Habermasian model of constitutional patriotism, but to implement its laudable goals successfully, it requires to go one significant step further, namely to break with the historical model of the republican nation-state, accept the fragmentation of sovereignty and embrace the need for collective representation of national and ethnic minorities. In short an agonistic collective identity of the polity that includes forms of individual and collective representation of culturally diverse groups.

Is Agonistic patriotism a substitute?

Audi alteram partem
[Listen to the other side]
(Tully, 2000: 474)

An alternative way of cementing the social solidarity that constitutional patriotism yearns for is to take the opposite route and allow for a legitimate and pluralist representation of different national and ethnic communities within a mutually agreed commonwealth, or community of communities and individuals. For this community of communities to forge the collective identity of the polity it must on the one hand include cross-community negotiated operational principles for a democratic multination-state, and on the other accept within these parameters the autonomy and self-determination of both communities and individuals. To achieve this goal, the philosophical monism that permeates much of contemporary liberal theories must be revisited. Bhikhu Parekh describes monism as 'the view that only one way of life is fully human, true, or the best, and that all others are defective to the extent that they fall short of it' (Parekh, 2000: 16). Monists fail to take account of the role of culture in shaping individuals, and to appreciate the significance of cultural diversity. This criticism of monism is categorically not an advocacy of its inverted mirror image, an enclosed and foundational pluralism that fails to see commonalities between peoples of different cultures. On the contrary, it is precisely through the recognition and institutionalization of cultural diversity in the public domain that it will be possible to foster common political goals and stable institutions across diverse communities. As the position of minority communities is institutionally safe, members of ethnic minorities will feel much freer to interact with others across community boundaries in the pursuit of goals that might be opposed by other members of their own community. This is done in the knowledge that their own community is safe as an accepted member of the multination-state.

Recent discussions on agonist democracy laid the foundation for agonist patriotism in the terms discussed above, namely the combination of democracy with cultural pluralism that protects the institutional manifestation of difference. In most circumstances, the critical engagement will generate political agreements, but in a small number of others differences might be irreconcilable. For this reason, it is essential to establish an inter-community agreement over the parameters of what Laborde calls 'the collective identity of the polity' where such differences will meet one another in an agonist setting, establishing a set of guiding principles on how to agree to disagree as well as setting out the structure for common action on agreed issues (Little, 2002: 378). This facilitates a shift to the 'politics of respect', one of the cardinal aspects of agonist democracy. Here there will be wide agreement on the principles of pluralist democracy that will encourage the shift from antagonism to agonism without resort to the neutrality, rationality and impartiality that characterize political liberalism (Mouffe, 2000b).

The term agonism is derived from the ancient Greek άγώη, meaning originally 'a gathering or assembly' and according to the OED was taken to mean 'the contest for the prize at the games', and by extension, 'any contest or struggle'. Agonism (άγώη ι σ μ α) becomes then a contest, or its prize. It was in its original meaning a contest between adversaries who are not enemies but bound rules of the game by which all contenders abided. The term was revived via Foucault and Nietzsche and it is used to define a group of related contemporary democratic theories: agonistic pluralism (for an overview, see Wenman, 2003a). These theories refer to the work of Connolly (1991), Mouffe (2000b) and Tully (1995). These theorists understand agonism to imply the necessary interdependence of social relations and assume the constitutive nature of conflict in the formation of political identities. Tully in particular shows how the doctrine of popular sovereignty seeks to eliminate cultural diversity and how politics can be envisaged as an intercultural dialogue in which diverse citizens negotiate agreements and their form of association (Tully, 1995: 30; Wenman, 2003a: 176). Mouffe's (2000a) aim through her systematic discussion of Carl Schmitt makes a very important distinction between agonism and antagonism, or how to convert enemies into adversaries through the institutionalization of mutually agreed rules of contestation.

On a more specific dimension agonistic patriotism is understood here to refer to the bonding, solidarity and loyalty of differing ethnic and national communities to a common set of transcultural agreements that constitute and make possible the arena of common politics. It differs from constitutional patriotism in that it does not fix a constitutional arrangement once and for all and make it dependent on a single political culture, but it creates rules of the game that, while ensuring the flexible representation of both communities and individuals, creates an autonomous and secure environment for different groups to protect their specific identities. In the conversion of contending players from enemies to adversaries, it allows for political representation across ethnic divides, and permits the participatory integration of minority communities *qua* communities. Agonistic patriotism can take a number of forms, depending on the wishes, desires and possibilities of participating individuals and communities. It incorporates insights from democratic theory, theories of ethnic conflict resolution and from consociationalism. Because of the flexibility in the inclusion process as well as the empowerment it gives to participating citizens and communities to negotiate the agreement that best suits their circumstances, agonistic patriotism cannot provide a blueprint or a fixed model. It can, however, provide a set of parameters in the terms discussed above through which community agreements can be reached.

One possible way to operationalize agonist patriotism is the national cultural autonomy model (NCA). NCA is rarely mentioned in the West nowadays, mainly because there was no English translations available, something we have recently remedied (Bauer, 2000; Renner, 2005). The model is debated in many post-communist states in a diluted and perhaps distorted form and has been enacted in Russia in the form of the National Cultural Autonomy Law, approved by the Duma in 1996. The model has something to say to many contemporary multinational and multiethnic societies governed in accordance with the principles of the nation-state model, but which show a glaring discrepancy between this model and their multinational and multiethnic composition. The model emerged as the brainchild of two Austrian socialist leaders, Karl Renner the former president of Austria, and Otto Bauer, the historical leader of Austrian Social Democracy in the first part of the twentieth century. I have discussed the origins of this model in detail elsewhere (Bauer, 2000: xv–xlv; Nimni, 1999; 2005: 1–14).

In sharp contrast to most other forms of national autonomy, the national-cultural autonomy model rests on the 'personality principle', the idea that autonomous communities are organized as sovereign collectives whatever their residential location within a multination-state. As in the millet system in the Ottoman Empire, peoples of different ethnic identities can coexist in the same territory without straining the principle of national autonomy. The crucial difference from the Ottoman millet system is, however, that the autonomous communities are organized in accordance with the canons of representative democracy and are based on individual consent to belong and internal democracy. The analogy used by Renner is that of religious communities. Much in the same way that Catholics, Protestants and Jews could coexist in the same city, Renner argued, so members of different national communities could coexist with their own distinct institutions and national organizations, provided they did not claim territorial exclusivity. The NCA model acknowledges that national communities require recognition of their specificity and difference in the public domain, and this is achieved through the existence of legally guaranteed autonomous and sovereign corporations. Unlike more conventional forms of autonomy and self-determination, it rejects the idea of ethnically or nationally exclusive control over territory.

The Renner/Bauer model of national-cultural non-territorial autonomy was called by its authors the 'personality principle' (*das Personalitäten-prinzip*). The term is derived from Friedrich Meinecke (1970), who was influential in shaping Renner's ideas. Meinecke criticizes the idea that the nation-state embodies ethical values. Here Renner cites Meinecke when he argues that 'personality is not only the highest form of autonomy, but it is also the highest level of personal autarky and the harmonic unity of all forces and qualities' (Agnelli, 1969: 97). Drawing on Meinecke, Renner calls the system he envisaged the 'personality principle' because it referred to the widest personal choice of its members to partake in a particular national association. This was contrasted by Renner with the 'territorial principle', which is characteristic of the modern nation-state. Renner (2005: 29) describes the territorial principle in the following way: 'If you live in my territory you are subjected to my domination, my law and my language.' This, according to Renner, suggests domination and not equality of rights. It suggests the dominance of the ethnic majority over the ethnic minority, the dominance of settled populations over immigrants, and the dominance of settlers over indigenous peoples. The model proposed by Renner and Bauer is suited to minorities that demand significant autonomy, but for a variety of reasons cannot have separate states. A prime example of such minorities is indigenous peoples in liberal settler societies. In an argument that closely resembles Bauer and Renner's ideas, James Tully (1995: 197–8) argues that political recognition of diversity is one of the most important ways to ensure constitutional allegiance in culturally diverse states.

The model of national cultural autonomy proposed by Renner at the end of the nineteenth century was a model to transform Habsburg Austria into a democratic multination-state. It proposes that all citizens declare their nationality when they reach voting age. Members of each national community, whatever their territory of residence, would form a single public body or association endowed with legal personality and sovereignty and competent to deal with all national-cultural affairs. For example, these corporations would organize the educational system of their members, the legal system, and all other issues of national character. The idea is to eliminate competition between national communities by ensuring a strict separation of competences. The model is based on the premise that the most controversial issues in the relationship between ethnic and national groups are those concerning language, education and the recognition of cultural rights in the public domain. Here, networks of communication across cultural boundaries are crucial because the model recognizes both communities and individuals as legitimate interlocutors. Change is a constant feature of cultural practices. A continuous dialogue within and between communities and between individuals of different communities is the only way to secure and formalize a negotiated public space across community boundaries (Parekh, 1995: 436).

The NCA model proposes a radical reshaping of the liberal democratic nation-state into a two-tier system of government: national and non-territorial and territorial and non-national. The model addresses a key weakness of other models of territorial autonomy: national territorial boundaries always create minorities and propensities for ethnic discrimination. In a world of migration and differential development, territorial boundaries are porous, and population movements tend to upset neat schemes for fortress states. This situation inevitably results in ethnic and national minorities constituting unwelcome pockets in any autonomous or sovereign territories. The second advantage of the model is that it does away altogether with the idea of national minorities and the need for specific minority protection. The status of national minorities is the by-product of a national state that has a sovereign national majority. In the NCA model, even if the citizen inhabits a territory where the majority belongs to a different national group, citizens of different ethnic groups are not subject to the cultural practices of the majority on questions of national and ethnic interest, but can rely on their own trans-territorial national organization, which has the status of a public corporation with sovereign areas of competence. This is an important advantage of the Bauer/Renner model over contemporary liberal theories, as it obviates the need to pursue complex and invidious discussions on the rights and wrongs of minority communities, and more importantly, it obviates the need for patronizing and controversial special cases (Nimni, 1999).

While it could be credibly argued that this model is suitable for societies that face a deep ethno-national conflict or for the cases of national minorities that have been severely alienated by dominant groups, such as indigenous peoples in liberal-democratic settler societies, it is far from clear if all minorities in Western liberal democracies desire such sweeping powers of autonomy, or if such strong forms of autonomy are warranted in less conflictual situations. In cases where the antagonism between national communities is not acute, or where there is a high incidence of cross-community integration, the model could be scaled down to encompass only a few autonomous dimensions as democratically desired by all participating communities. However, in cases of deep national conflicts, the NCA model could help address intercommunity distrust by providing guarantees in the form of constitutionally enshrined collective rights, and aim for a better integrated multination-state. There are those who argue that the NCA overtaxes citizens with two tiers of government. This might be so, but it is a small price to pay to avoid the bloodshed and ethnic cleansing that accompanies deep-seated ethnic conflicts. If a scaled-down model is proposed for Western liberal democracies, it is also a small price to pay to ensure that patriotism and loyalty to the institutions of a multination-state enjoy cross-community support, and the chances of that are greater than in the model proposed by liberal constitutional patriots.

Conclusion

More than any other liberal writer, Habermas shows the conceptual limits of procedural liberalism in coming to terms with demands for cultural recognition in contemporary liberal-democratic multination-states. To the proliferation of demands for cultural and political recognition, through the model of constitutional patriotism, Habermas simply reiterates more of the same. The liberal-democratic nation-state has, in his view, ample resources to accommodate difference, but this is something that cannot be reconciled with the nation-state demand for loyalty and membership of the cultural and political community of citizens. As Engels (Marx and Engels, 1977: 227) argued in the nineteenth century, the democratic state in the long run requires assimilation to the culture of the majority with democracy as compensation. Curiously, procedural liberals and ortho-dox Marxists agree on this point. The point is amply demonstrated by Habermas. First, in his zeal to remain loyal to the values of procedural liberalism, he produces an analytical model based on a logical contradiction. Habermas supports the original cultural homogenization that became the backbone of the European nation-state on the one hand, and on the other, expresses support for a rigorously culturally neutral national state. It can't be both.

What makes Taylor's liberalism interesting is that it allows for the recognition of special rights for ethnic and national minorities in limited circumstances, and thus introduces an element of contingency to the universally prescriptive and deductive liberal model. While there is no doubt that Taylor rescues important elements of the liberal tradition, there is here an important epistemological break with constitutional patriotism and the procedural liberalism of Habermas.

Agonist patriotism proposes an alternative to the totalizing rigidities of constitutional patriotism by advocating a flexible recognition and self-determination of minorities as autonomous communities in a multi-nation-state, it enhances the possibility of minority loyalty in the security of representation and recognition. The NCA model is just one possible application of agonist patriotism, as it provides a flexible model for minority representation, fully-fledged autonomy in societies cursed by deep ethnic divisions, and a scaled-down and limited version of autonomy for Western liberal multination-states.

Notes

1. Of course, there is a minority of left cosmopolitan liberal thinkers who seriously question the contemporary validity of the nation-state as a relevant political institution. See among others Waldron (1995: 93–119) and Nielsen (2003: 437–63). However, the growing numbers of political regimes that operationalize the normative values of liberalism do so in the context of the institutions of the nation-state.
2. *Sur la nécessité et les moyens d'anéantir les patois et d'universaliser l'usage de la langue française* and on 8 pluviôse year II (27/1/1794) Barére asserted: *Le fédéralisme et la superstition parlent bas-breton; l'émigration et la haine de la République parlent allemand; la contre-révolution parle l'italien, et le fanatisme parle le basque. Brisons ces instruments de dommage et d'erreur* (Federalism and the superstition speak low-Breton; the emigration and the hatred of the Republic speak German; the counter-revolution speaks Italian, and fanaticism speaks Basque. Let us break these instruments of harm and error).
3. *La langue de la liberté dans la République une et indivisible.*
4. Indigenous demands for recognition in settler postcolonial liberal democracies play an important role in this. For a European example, see Semb (2005: 531–49).
5. This cultural consensus is of course perspectival, usually understood as 'thin' by the dominant majority and as 'thick' by minorities.

References

Agnelli, A. (1969) *Questione nazionale e socialismo: contributo allo studio del pensiero di Karl Renner e Otto Bauer*. Bologna: Il Mulino.

Bader, V. (1997) 'The Cultural Conditions of Transnational Citizenship: On the Interpretation of Political and Ethnic Cultures', *Political Theory*, 25: 771–813.

Bauer, O. (2000) *The Question of Nationalities and Social Democracy*, ed. E. Nimni. Minneapolis: University of Minnesota Press. Translated by Joseph O'Donnell.

Calhoun, C. (2002) 'Imagining Solidarity: Cosmopolitanism, Constitutional Patriotism, and the Public Sphere', *Public Culture*, 14(1): 147–71.

Connolly, W. E. (1991) *Identity/Difference: Democratic Negotiations of Political Paradox.* Ithaca, NY and London: Cornell University Press. Reprinted 2002, University of Minnesota Press.

Eriksen, T. H. (1993) *Ethnicity and Nationalism, Anthropological Perspectives.* London: Pluto Press.

Greenfeld, L. (1992) *Nationalism: Five Roads to Modernity.* Cambridge, MA: Harvard University Press.

Habermas, J. (1989) *The Neo-Conservatives.* Cambridge: Cambridge University Press.

—— (1992) 'Citizenship and National Identity: Some Reflections on the Future of Europe', *Praxis International*, 12(1): 1–19.

—— (1994) 'Struggles for Recognition in the Democratic Constitutional State', in C. Taylor and A. Gutmann (eds), *Multiculturalism, Examining the Politics of Recognition.* Princeton, NJ: Princeton University Press, pp. 107–48.

Halliday, F. (1992) 'Bringing the "Economic" Back in: The Case of Nationalism', *Economy and Society*, 21(4): 483–90.

—— (1994) *Rethinking International Relations.* London: Macmillan.

Held, D. (1995) *Democracy and the Global Order: From the Modern State to Cosmopolitan Governance.* Cambridge: Polity Press.

Hroch, M. (1985) *Social Preconditions of National Revival in Europe: A Comparative Analysis of the Social Composition of Patriotic Groups among the Smaller European Nations.* Cambridge: Cambridge University Press.

Kedourie, E. (1960) *Nationalism.* London: Hutchinson.

Kohn, H. (1944) *The Idea of Nationalism: A Study in its Origins and Background.* New York: Macmillan.

—— (1967) *Prelude to Nation-states: The French and German Experience, 1789–1815.* Princeton, NJ: Van Nostrand.

Kuzio, T. (2001) 'Nationalising States or Nation Building: A Review of the Theoretical Literature and Empirical Evidence', *Nations and Nationalism*, 7(2): 135–54.

Kuzio, T. (2002) 'The Myth of the Civic State: a Critical Survey of Hans Kohn's Framework for Understanding Nationalism', *Ethnic and Racial Studies*, 25(1): 20–39.

Kymlicka, W. and Straehle, C. (1999) 'Cosmopolitanism, Nation-States and Minority Nationalism: a Critical Review of Recent Literature', *European Journal of Philosophy*, 7(1): 65–88.

Laborde, C. (2002) 'From Constitutional to Civic Patriotism', *British Journal of Political Science*, 32: 591–612.

Lefebvre, E. L. (2003) 'Republicanism and Universalism: Factors of Inclusion or Exclusion in the French Concept of Citizenship', *Citizenship Studies*, 7(1): 15–36.

Little, A. (2002) 'Community and Radical Democracy', *Journal of Political Ideologies*, 7(3): 369–82.

Marx, K. and Engels, F. (1977) *Marx-Engels Collected Works (MECW). Vol. 8, 1848–1849.* Moscow: Progress Publishers.

Meinecke, F. (1970) *Cosmopolitanism and the National State.* Princeton, NJ: Princeton University Press. Translated by Robert B. Kimber.

Mill, J. S. (1862) 'Considerations of Representative Government', in H. B. Acton (ed.) (1976) *Utilitarism, On Liberty and Considerations on Representative Government.* London: J. M. Dent & Sons.

Moller Okin, S. (1999) *Is Multiculturalism Bad for Women?* ed. J. Cohen, M. Howard and M. C. Nussbaum. Princeton, NJ: Princeton University Press.

Mouffe, C. (1996) 'Democracy, Power and "the Political" ', in S. Benhabib (ed.), *Democracy and Difference: Contesting the Boundaries of the Political.* Princeton, NJ: Princeton University Press. pp. 245–56.

——— (2000a) *The Democratic Paradox.* London: Verso.

——— (2000b) 'Deliberative Democracy or Agonistic Pluralism', *Political Science Series*, 72. Vienna: Institute for Advanced Studies.

Müller, J.-W. (2005) 'A Thick Constitutional Patriotism for the EU? On Morality, Memory and Militancy', paper presented at the Law and Democracy in Europe's Post-National Constellation Conference, European University Institute, Florence, 22–24 September. http://www.iue.it/LAW/ResearchTeaching/Cidel/pdf/Muller.pdf

Nielsen, K. (2003) 'Toward a Liberal Socialist Cosmopolitan Nationalism', *International Journal of Philosophical Studies*, 11(4): 437–63.

Nimni, E. (1991, 1994) *Marxism and Nationalism. The Theoretical Origins of a Political Crisis.* London: Pluto Press.

——— (1995) 'Marx and Engels and the National Question', in W. Kymlicka (ed.), *The Rights of Minority Cultures.* Oxford: Oxford University Press. pp. 57–75.

Nimni, E. (1999) 'Nationalist Multiculturalism in Late Imperial Austria as a Critique of Contemporary Liberalism: The Case of Bauer and Renner', *Journal of Political Ideologies*, 4(3): 289–314.

——— (ed.) (2005) *National Cultural Autonomy and its Contemporary Critics.* London and New York: Routledge Innovations in Political Theory.

Nootens, G. (2004) *Désenclaver la démocratie, des Huguenots a la paix des braves.* Montréal: Québec Amérique.

Norman, W. (2001) 'Justice and Stability in Multination-states', in J. Tully and A. Gagnon (eds), *Struggles for Recognition in Multinational Societies.* Cambridge: Cambridge University Press.

Parekh, B. (1991) 'British Citizenship and Cultural Difference', in G. Andrews (ed.), *Citizenship.* London: Lawrence and Wishart.

——— (1995) 'Cultural Pluralism and the Limits of Diversity', *Alternatives*, 20/43.

——— (2000) *Rethinking Multiculturalism: Cultural Diversity and Political Theory.* London: Macmillan.

Patten, A. (1996) 'The Republican Critique of Liberalism', *British Journal of Political Science*, 26: 25–44.

Ra'anan, U. (1991) 'Nation and State, Order out of Chaos', in U. Ra'anan et al. (eds), *State and Nation in Multiethnic Societies.* Manchester: Manchester University Press.

Renner, K. (2005) 'State and Nation', in E. Nimni (ed.), *National-Cultural Autonomy and its Contemporary Critics.* London: Routledge.

Rosdolsky, R. (1986) *Engels and the 'Non-Historic Peoples': The National Question in the Revolution of 1848.* Glasgow: Critique Books.

Semb, A. J. (2005) 'Sami Self-Determination in the Making?', *Nations and Nationalism*, 11(4): 531–49.

Smith, A. D. (1998) *Nationalism and Modernism.* London: Routledge.

Taylor, C. (1992) *Multiculturalism. Examining the Politics of Recognition.* Princeton, NJ: Princeton University Press.

Tully, J. (1995) *Strange Multiplicity, Constitutionalism in an Age of Diversity.* Cambridge: Cambridge University Press.

———— (2000) 'Struggles over Recognition and Distribution', *Constellations*, 7(4): 469–82.

Van Aaken, A. (2005) *Making International Human Rights Protection More Effective: A Rational-Choice Approach to the Effectiveness of* Ius Standi *Provisions*. Preprints of the Max Planck Institute for Research on Collective Goods, Bonn /16.

Waldron, J. (1995) 'Minority Cultures and the Cosmopolitan Alternative', in W. Kymlicka, (ed.), *The Rights of Minority Cultures*. Oxford: Oxford University Press, pp. 93–119.

Wenman, M. (2003a) 'Agonistic Pluralism and Three Archetypal Forms of Politics', *Contemporary Political Theory*, 2: 165–86.

———— (2003b) 'What is Politics? The Approach of Radical Pluralism', *Politics*, 23(1): 57–65.

6
Transnational Europe

Jan Ifversen

Academics, journalists and trendsetters often search for new concepts to denote ongoing transformations. In the 1980s many people were busy conceptualizing a transgression of modernity. Heated intellectual debates on postmodernism and postmodernity took place throughout the Western world. Today, one of the core institutions of the modern era, the nation-state, is under fire. We are witnessing great semantic turbulence around the concept of the nation. Claims about the erosion of the nation-state abound. Often such claims are related to the effects of *globalization*, which has become a key term in the current conceptualizations of transformation. *Globalization* has become what Reinhard Koselleck calls *a basic concept* because it 'combine[s] manifold experiences and expectations in such a way that [it] become[s] indispensable to any formulation of the most urgent issues of a given time' (Koselleck, 1996: 64). Globalization is followed by a host of other terms that indicate change and transgression. Prefixes like *post-* and *trans-* are frequently found. This is certainly the case when the fate of the nation is being discussed. Terms like *transnational –* and to a lesser degree *postnational –* have forcefully entered public and academic debates. The former belongs to a spatial configuration; the latter outlines a temporal movement. In this chapter, I intend to examine the effects of such semantic reorientation on some of our basic concepts for understanding political community. I am particularly interested in how the concept of the *transnational* affects basic points of orientations in our vocabulary related to political communities. Community concepts like identity, culture and citizenship have a long history in common with the concept of the nation. Their liaison with the *transnational* indicates a rupture of that history.

Academics are heavily involved in conceptual reorientation. They discuss and produce forecasts about major changes in the world. Many political analysts are concerned with the fate of the nation-state. I intend to look into the conceptual laboratory emerging from academic debates on current challenges to the nation-state. The debates evolving around the nature and development of the European Union are a case in point in terms of studying how basic community concepts react to the challenge of the transnational. The EU has become a testing ground for a new political vocabulary which takes action with the transnational. I want to highlight some of the conceptual choices in the debate and discuss the epistemological and normative consequences involved.

Transnational – some preliminary remarks concerning the word

Transnational is one of several derivatives of the adjective *national* with different etymologies, e.g. inter-national, multi-national, supra-national and post-national. *International* appeared as early as 1789 – in a famous text by Jeremy Bentham[1] – to designate the legal relations between states. In English, *supranational* can be traced back to the late nineteenth century when it was used to emphasize a legal space above the nation-state (Smith, 1895; Snow, 1912). In German Nietzsche introduced the word *übernational* to describe the European as a new, nomadic type of man.[2] After World War II the term came to denote the new form of cooperation related to the institutionalization of European integration (Schumacher, 1971: 51). According to the OED, *multinational* first appeared in English in 1918. Until the 1950s the word was mostly used to designate nationally composite states or empires. From the 1950s onwards the term shifted to the economic field where it was used to describe new forms of economic transactions. *Transnational* seems to have appeared for the first time in English in 1916, in the form of the noun *transnationality*. The American journalist and writer Randolph Bourne (1886–1918) is credited with it. In an article titled *Transnational America* he talked about America 'not as a nationality, but a transnationality, a weaving back and forth, with the other lands, of many threads of all sizes and colours' (Bourne, 1916). Bourne was using the term to express the mixing and hybridity that followed from the United States being an immigrant society. He viewed the mixing as the result of nationalities coming together. *Transnational* (and its various derivatives) was rarely used until the final decades of the twentieth century when the term became very widespread, at least in academic discourse[3] and seemed to gain popularity at the expense of *multinational* and *supranational*.[4] Compared to the three spatial terms, *postnational* is really the odd man out. Its first use can be traced back to the late 1960s, but it still has not made it into the OED.

The introduction of new terms demands semantic reflexivity. New terms lend themselves to definitions by their users. The word *transnational* first gained importance in studies on immigration. In a very successful book from 1994 three American anthropologists announced that *transnationalism* was 'an idea whose time has come'. They defined transnationalism 'as the processes by which immigrants forge and sustain multistranded social relations that link together their societies of origin and settlement' (Basch, Schiller and Blanc, 1993: 7). Transnationalism was first defined as a social process related to articulations of identity and feelings of belonging transgressing the nation-state. Because immigrants – at least mentally – kept crossing borders they were seen as archetypical transnationals. Transnationalism was proposed as an analytical term to study their transnational behaviour. In an examination of the concept, Steven Vertovec, professor of transnational anthropology at Oxford, proposed it as 'an umbrella concept' capable of grasping 'some of the most globally transformative processes and developments of our time' (Vertovec, 1999: 459). The study of migration was thus only one of several fields in which transnationalism could be analysed. Other fields included economic transactions, supranational policies and religious communities. For Vertovec, transnationalism denoted global processes of movement beyond the national space. Others have defined transnationalism as a new social space emerging out of these processes (Faist, 2000) or have focused on the role of 'non-institutional actors from civil society' (Portes, 2001: 185). Some scholars choose to differentiate between a *transnationalization* from below and a *globalization* from above (Pries, 2002). From this rudimentary overview, we can distil a core meaning. Transnationalism is the analytic term for:

- a process (or a series of processes)
- through which people and symbols (to a lesser extent goods) are moved
- across nation-states
- by agents from below
- producing new spaces
- that challenge the nation-state

The processual meaning is emphasized by the term *transnationalization*. The transnational condition can also be conceptualized as *transnationality*. Only the verb *transnationalize* seems to be very rare. As pointed out, transnational is being semantically delimited from globalization. It is also distinguished from *international*, which denotes the interaction of states within an international system, and from *multinational* which either describes a condition of ethnic diversity within a state or cross-border activities carried out by economic actors (e.g. multinational corporations).

Semantic fields

For the most part migration scholars participated in the first clarification of the meaning of transnational. They tried to reserve the concept to cross-border activities from below. The vocabulary in which they anchored the concept was very much dominated by their own research agenda, which privileges questions concerning identity. I will now examine the use of the term transnational in a wider perspective, including other semantic fields and vocabularies. I shall concentrate on two fields both relating to community. The first revolves around the concept of political community and includes key terms such as governance, civil society and citizenship. The other links community with identity and locality. My examination will again concentrate on definitions from scholars in various disciplines.

Within a broadly conceived area of political science, *transnational* emerged slowly from the 1960s in studies of international relations. As early as 1962, Raymond Aron spoke of a transnational *society* that emerged from people, goods, beliefs and organizations crossing borders (Aron, 1962). In 1962, Stanley Hoffmann referred to various units interacting within a 'transnational net' (quoted in Kaiser, 1971: 802). Almost ten years later the term was given a forceful role in Joseph Nye's and Robert Keohane's effort to distance international relations theory from its realist foundations. They reserved the term transnational to relations and interactions across state borders 'that are not controlled by the central foreign policy organs of governments' (Nye and Keohane, 1971: 331). Transnational thus implied nongovernmental relations. For Nye and Keohane, it was important to acknowledge the existence of these forces on the world scene in order to criticize the exclusively statist approach of the realist school. In the same line of thinking, Karl Kaiser combined the idea of nongovernmental transnational *actors* with the existence of a transnational society in which these actors interacted with governments (Kaiser, 1972).

But as pointed out in the previous section, this non-state meaning of transnational has resurfaced strongly in other areas. If we stay within political science the growing efforts to conceptualize political systems such as the European Union have been important for the proliferation of the term transnational. EU's political system is often conceptualized as trans-national *governance*. Governance is a concept that has been used to cover some of the same meanings as transnational (Kjær, 2004). It is opposed to *government*, which refers to the institutional configuration of a state: '*Governance* is not political rule through responsible institutions such as parliament and bureaucracy – which amounts to *government* – but innovative practices of networks, or horizontal forms of interaction' (Eriksen and Fossum, 2002: 27). Governance is viewed as an informal and horizontal decision-making process which operates at different levels simultaneously. Eriksen and Fossum furthermore view governance as inherently transnational. The conceptual logic seems to be that the multiplicity of levels and actors only make sense in a setting not confined to the nation-state or any other known political entity. Governance has no inherent boundaries and is therefore transnational. Supranational, on the other hand, belongs to the field of government: 'Transnational action or mobilization can be distinguished from the former legal and institutional sense of the term "supranational"' (Favell and Geddes, 1999: 6). For Favell and Geddes, transnationalism operates in 'the new spaces of governance opened up by the internationalization of political structures' (1999: 6). Transnational and governance belong together. The two words seem to reinforce each other. Although both terms emphasize an actional and processual meaning, governance tends to borrow the idea of a political entity from government. The EU can thus be conceptualized as a *system* of multi-level governance.

The EU is a typical 'transnational' case. By studying the EU, many dimensions of politics can be conceptualized in transnational terms. References to a European public sphere or a European *civil society* are made in the name of the transnational (Rumsford, 2003; Eriksen, 2005). Eriksen directly links a transnational public sphere with policy networks to emphasize the flexible and non-statal: 'There are transnational public spheres emanating from the policy networks of the EU' (Eriksen, 2005: 351). Transnational certainly also pertains to European *citizenship*, which – it is claimed – has an 'obvious transnational character' (Bellamy, Castiglione and Shaw, 2006: 16).[5] Finally, transnational *democracy* is becoming prominent in discussions of how the EU is to progress (Rumsford, 2003; Köchler, 2005). In some respects, transnational democracy indicates the utopian end point in a chain of equivalences that connects governance, networks, civil society, citizenship and democracy. This chain is opposed to another chain that links government with nation-state.

Transnational also belongs to a semantic field delimited by concepts such as space, community and identity. Transnational space is used to denote a sphere of interaction which is not limited to a particular territory. It is often viewed as a social *space* in which transnational entities interact across several localities. Arjun Appadurai invented the term *translocality* to capture

the effect of what he saw as the emergence of 'postnational social formations' (Appadurai, 1996: 42).[6] Transnational is thus used to conceptualize an
understanding of space which does not fit into the older spatial vocabulary
of territory, place and locality (Patel, 2004: 16). The word *deterritorialization* is often used to denote the processes in which these new transnational
spaces take form. From the concept of social space there is but a short step
to *community* and *identity*. Migrations studies have focused on 'the transnationalization of identity' (Sørensen, 2003: 465). Geographers have made the
link between space and identity: 'the transnational . . . is a space in which
new forms of (post)national identity are constituted' (Mandaville, 2002:
204). Appadurai speaks of 'translocal affiliations' (1996: 50). Others speak
of transnational *cultures* (Hannerz, 1996) or transnational communities
(Albert, 2001) in which new identities are being constructed. As was the case
in the semantic field of governance, this semantic field includes a host of
terms that designate crossing, flexibility and multiplicity. Here it is enough
to mention such fashionable terms as *hybridity*, *melange* and *diasporic pluralism*.[7] There seems to be a tendency towards doubling or intensifying the
meaning when transnational is added.

In the following, I will restrict my examination of the meaning of
transnational to statements concerning *Europe*. I deal with two cases corresponding to the two semantic fields already mentioned. The first has to
do with constructions of a European identity.

Transnational identity – European identity

The concept of the transnational acquires meaning within a semantic
field outlined by community, identity and culture. To speak of transnational
identity makes sense. Scholars discuss different types of transnational identity: diaspora identities, immigrant identities and also European identity.
For the last 20 years, a widespread debate over European identity has been
going on (Ifversen, 2002). When scholars debate whether there is such a
thing as a European identity they involve themselves in reflections on
the possibility of conceiving of a transnational identity. Conceptualizing
transnational identity includes discussions on the concept of identity.
And to use the term identity in scholarly debates immediately involves
identity theory.[8]

I shall begin by reflecting on the role played by the concept of identity in
statements on European identity. The national matrix of identity developed
in the nineteenth century has heavily influenced any concept of collective
identity. Although other concepts of collective identity (either territorially
bounded or related to social or religious groups) certainly existed alongside

this matrix, national identity has offered a dominant model for identification. To cut a long conceptual history short, we can simply point to the three semantic coordinates that define this model of collective identity: territory, time and culture. The nation expresses itself through its culture which is linked to time by tradition and history, and which is embedded in a particular homeland. The territory of social coexistence and state rule is thus turned into a homeland for the people living in the nation.

The national matrix anchors identity in culture and tradition. The rooting of identity (with the whole metaphoric armature) in homeland and history becomes the dominant feature of identity marking. It therefore seems logical that we witness efforts to 'nationalize' European identity, that is, to articulate European identity within the national matrix. Nationalization here means searching for features of a European culture (Christianity, Enlightenment values, Roman and Greek ideas, etc.) rooted in a European homeland and history. Until recently use of the national matrix was predominant in official European identity politics. In scholarly debates we can observe similar perceptions of structural similarities between European and national identity, for instance when European identity is viewed as 'quasi-national' (Beus, 2001), which recognizes a rather 'thick' identity based on common values, history and to some extent common land. Its 'quasi' character stems from the fact that, to quote Jos de Beus, 'European identity will be composite. It will not replace national identity' (2001: 294). From this it is possible to engage in a discussion on the relative strength of the two identities. Beus chooses a rather Solomonic solution when opting for 'the domesticating interplay of European identity, national identity and minoritarian identity, such as regional identity' (2001: 294). Others speak more sceptically of a Euro-nationalism that threatens to become hegemonic and risks fortifying a cultural image of Europe to be used in exclusionary strategies. Gerard Delanty has argued for the existence of such a version of European identity:

> Today, more than ever, the discourse of Europe is taking on a strongly ideological character. In this transformation Europe becomes part of a hegemonic cultural discourse. (Delanty, 1995: 6)

Anthony Smith has dismissed any possibility of a European identity on the grounds that it does not display the same solid rooting as national identity:

> In the European context, the only way in which a truly united Europe could emerge is through the slow formation of common European memories, traditions, values, myths . . . there are no overarching shared

> memories, myths and symbols which can unite Europeans, apart from
> the unusable ideas of medieval Christendom or imperialism. (Smith,
> 1995: 142)

In Smith's view, European identity is a hollow 'fiction' that does not
contain the necessary features to be a workable collective identity. Smith
and Delanty agree about locating any reflections on European identity
within the national matrix (but obviously disagree about whether it will
be feasible). Beus chooses a less robust view on how a European identity
can be conceived of, but he still sees it as an identity with the same features as a national identity.

In recent years, scholars have gone to great lengths to 'de-nationalize'
European identity, using two strategies: engage in discussions on the
general meaning of identity, and transfer conceptualizations of European
identity from the cultural to the political field. Let us first have a look at
those efforts conducted at redefining the meaning of identity. A typical
approach is to emphasize the *processual* character of culture and consequently the flexible nature of identity. This theoretical argument is
based on a criticism of the alleged essentialist character conferred to culture
within the national matrix. The flexible nature of identity can be grasped
in various ways. Identity can be viewed as part of a cultural *practice*. When
the focus is on practice (for example, a discursive practice) any expression of identity will have to reveal its provisional status. The basic claim
is that there can be no completely fixed identity or, as Riva Kastoryano
puts it: '[identities] are refined and affirmed in action and interaction
and change with the cultural, social and political environment' (1997: 4).
One problem with this processual view on culture and identity is, however, that it has difficulties handling different degrees of flexibility and
rhythms of change. It needs at least to be supported by a structural perspective on the existence of various interrelated layers of meaning or
rhythms of change. But a processual view makes it easier to imagine a
European identity – either in the future (since identity changes) or as
one of several identities (since identities are flexible). In its most radical
form, a processual view will focus solely on identity as negotiated and
not take semantic stability into consideration. For Kastoryano, European
identity can be reduced to yet another identity that will add to a growing
multiculturalism, which is the 'ground for negotiation of multiple identities' (Kastoryano, 2000: 178). In this view, European identity becomes
an element in a constant reshuffling of identities.

The problem of differentiating between multiple identities can be
handled by distinguishing between *thick* and *thin* identities. Thickness

and thinness can be used to describe the semantic content of identities. Some identities have elaborate semantics; others are less elaborate and have a looser character. Or they might concern the effect of the identity on people. Some identities will work better than others. Cécile Laborde, a French political scientist, has proposed a model containing four layers of identity: the first is a primordial ethnic layer, the second a layer of 'broad culture', the third a layer of political culture, and the fourth consists of 'abstract, universalist political ideals and procedures' (Laborde, 2002: 598). For the moment, I shall leave out the whole problem of how these identities relate to each other and just point to the steps pursued by Laborde. A first step is to go from a robust – Laborde talks about an essentialist – view of identity (grounded in culture)[9] to a voluntaristic view (grounded in politics). Another step is to let identity become semantically thinner and more abstract as one goes from one echelon to the other. Laborde chooses the metaphor of a pyramid in her ordering. If we insert European identity into the pyramid it can be placed at the top, which indicates that it is thinner and more abstract than, for instance, national identity. At the same time, it will be de-essentialized so to speak, which means that it will be more prone to negotiations. In this way, a thin and abstract European identity might be based on a cultural semantics, albeit only in a rather loose and abstract sense. This is what we find in the traditional listing of particular European values. A definition of European identity based on adherence to values can be strengthened conceptually by linking them to a European *civilization*. In his analysis of European culture, Edgar Morin, the great French sociologist, reserved the concept of civilization to those European values that could be transferred from one culture to another (Morin, 1988). European civilization thus carries an identity, which transgresses local identities. There is, however, a risk involved in thinning out the cultural features of European identity. If European identity becomes too abstract and too universal, the particular European dimension will fade away. To avoid this, the concept of European civilization will have to include references to a recognizable cultural dimension. Morin solved the problem by perceiving of European identity as a result of the interplay between a European culture (with its history) and European civilization (with its values).

When European identity is connected to a European civilization, it can be given the status of an overarching, *supranational* identity that is able to contain all the different national identities. The problem with this neat view of European identity – with its pyramids, arches or concentric circles – is that it might not fit so neatly with other identities as claimed. It is possible, for instance, to imagine national identities with strong universalistic pretensions, such as those identities that incorporate an imperialist past (e.g. British and French national identity). If European identity is looked at from a local, national perspective it also seems reasonable to assume that there exist several interpretations of European identity. As formulated by Thomas Risse: 'it is unclear whether European Germans and European Italians mean the same thing when they identify with a common European heritage' (Risse, 2000).

Instead of turning European identity into an overarching identity within a hierarchy of identities, its composite and mixed character might be underlined. European identity might still be perceived as transgressing other identities, not because it is placed on a higher level, but because it contains elements from different national and regional cultures. Romano Prodi once talked of Europe as 'a transcultural amalgam' (Prodi, 2000: 45). This expression nicely catches the double-sided idea of transgression and mixture associated with the concept of the transnational. Long before Prodi, Morin proposed seeing European culture as essentially characterized by a permanent, dynamic mixture of various elements, or in his own words (in my translation) as 'a permanent dialogical hotbed' (Morin, 1988: 77). But we are still left with the problem of how mixture translates into a single identity. Is it enough to state, as the Swiss sociologist Martin Kohli does, that 'European identity. . . may be part of a specifically hybrid pattern where contradictions remain virulent and situational switches occur' (2000: 131). It is, of course, much easier to perceive of European identity as something that can be conceptualized independently of other identities and view mixing as a negotiation between recognizable identities. Hybridity, on the other hand, has the advantage of avoiding the problems of imagining a complete European identity, which is not either very thin or very essentialist. A problem with hybrid identity, however, is to provide it with semantics. We are often left with the option of conceptualizing European identity as 'an ample cultural multiplicity' (Habermas and Derrida, 2003) or as simply 'contested, negotiated, contextual, contradictory and shifting' (Stråth, 2000: 32). At some point, however, we have to acknowledge that expressions of a European identity also depend on available semantic resources.

Although we accept that the negotiated nature of European identity is limited by available discourses, by the communicative situations in which it is articulated and by the effect it has on people we do not have to endorse an essentialist or thick version of identity. Not every thin concept of European identity needs to be 'parasitic on a communitarian idea of unchosen belonging', as Rainer Bauböck seems to imply (2000: 5). As I have tried to show, there is room even for culturally framed concepts of

European identity that do not hinge on an idea of unchosen belonging. An identity based on a European civilization goes in the direction of the supranational. The various versions of multiple identities are closer to the idea of a transnational identity. In Figure 6.1 I summarize the different versions of European identity.

The italicized keywords conceptualize European identity within a cultural language. The points on the line indicate a progressive move towards the transnational, followed by a thinning out of the cultural semantics or by its replacement with political semantics.

Transnational citizenship – European citizenship

So far I have concentrated on the questions raised by conceiving of European identity in terms of a transnational identity. I now turn to another important community concept, namely *citizenship*, which points towards a different semantic field. Contrary to concepts like *governance*, citizenship does not contain an inherent transnational meaning. It has a long history of being rooted in a national setting. With the creation of a European citizenship in the Maastricht Treaty in 1992, the concept has entered a 'transnational' arena. The existence of this new, transnational form of citizenship has fed a whole scholarly debate on how to describe and evaluate it.

The concept of citizenship is rooted in a semantic field including the concepts of government, political community and rights. But at the same time the concept contains elements of culture. Theoretical arguments on

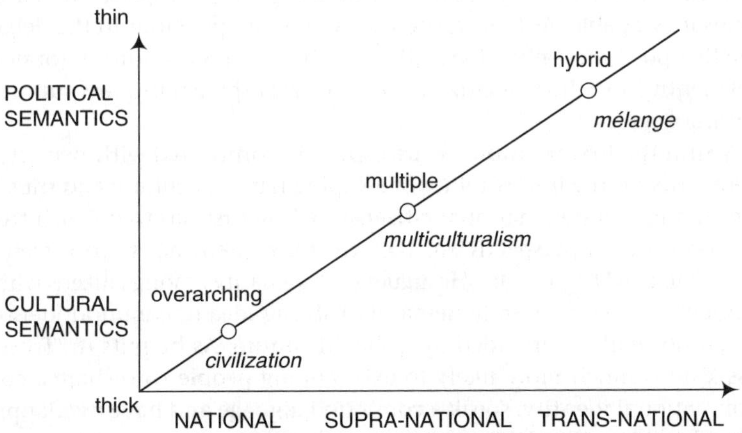

Figure 6.1   Versions of European identity

citizenship are very much about determining the balance between the cultural and the 'extra-cultural'. I shall claim that the various arguments concerning the transnational dimension of European citizenship turn around this balance. The citizenship debate thus involves the question of European identity. That is one more reason why the concept of citizenship is an excellent testing ground for conceptualizations of the transnational.

If we look at the basic meaning of citizenship it is about entitlement and membership (Pocock, 1998; Smith, 2002). Citizenship can be defined as an entitlement to be member of a state and to be part of a political community. It can furthermore be defined as a scheme through which membership activities are expressed and regulated (Wiener, 1997: 534). Normally, three elements are pointed out as constituting the core of citizenship. These are rights, access to participation and belonging (Wiener, 1997: 534). Rights based on political and moral principles concern the specific entitlements of the citizens. Access relates to the political community within which one can participate. Finally, belonging concerns both formal requirements for acquiring citizenship and broader cultural determinations related to identity. It is these latter determinations that tie citizenship to a vocabulary of culture. Any effort to transnationalize citizenship involves a reflection on how this tie can be either cut or reconceptualized. An examination of the scholarly debate over European citizenship reveals different positions in handling the link between a culture pointing toward the nation and a sphere of politics with the potential of transgressing national culture. At the core of the debate we find the notion of *political identity*. Although contributors will adhere to the different basic meanings of citizenship, the question of political identity seems inescapable. As I see it, there are four main positions in the debate. The first position claims that national culture is a precondition for political identity and thus for citizenship. The other three transgress culture to varying degrees.

Within the first position we are primarily confronted with two sets of arguments for the impossibility of escaping national culture and thus for conceiving of a transnational citizenship. The first has to do with trust, the second with perspectivism. The trust argument has been forcefully formulated by David Miller. He argues that solidarity among citizens within a modern democratic state demands a strong idea of common identity, which normally is provided by a shared culture. As he puts it: 'Trust of this kind is much more likely to exist among people who share a common national identity, speak a common language and have overlapping values' (Miller, 1998: 48). Although Miller sometimes emphasizes that nationality is only constituted through belief, he often ends up relating beliefs to 'the real differences between peoples' (Miller, 2000: 28). For Miller, citizenship demands trust. Without a basic trust, he claims, it would be difficult to expect that the duties bound to citizenship rights could be carried out (2000: 84–5). If having a common culture produces trust, the only way to imagine trust among European citizens is to imagine a corresponding supranational culture on a European scale. This is not a viable option according to Miller. His argument against European citizenship contains two elements. On the one hand it is empirical. 'For people across Europe the nation remains their primary focus of political identity and allegiance', he claims (Miller, 1998). On the other hand it is conceptual. In his view, citizenship means solidarity which can only be provided by people of the same culture. When citizenship is defined in this way, it becomes easier to place national culture at the centre.

The trust argument is often supported by what I will call the perspectivist argument. By this I mean the idea that any interpretation of values and principles must be grounded in a limited sphere of interpretation. This argument – which relies on a basic hermeneutic insight – is nicely formulated by Veit Bader for whom 'universalist "political" principles get particularized as soon as one looks at their interpretation, at their institutional translation, and at civic and political cultures, virtues, and traditions of good practice' (Bader, 1999: 384). At first hand, the argument is directed against those who ground citizenship in universalist principles. But it also includes a criticism of the idea that political principles can be cleansed of ethno-cultural references. This idea of freeing identity from culture is often expressed as a patriotism that differs from nationalism by not grounding identity and feelings of solidarity in culture. For Bader and those endorsing his version of perspectivism, any space of interpretation must include culture (or what he also calls 'legitimate ethnic particularism'; Bader, 1997: 788). Most people would probably accept a notion of interpretative particularism. Habermas, for instance, speaks of a necessary contextualization of universal political principles within the perspective of one's own particular history (Habermas, 1996: 289). But, contrary to Bader's position, Habermas makes a distinct conceptual separation between a political identity based on a shared political culture and what he terms pre-political identities. He is thus arguing for a transgression of the cultural, whereas Bader's perspectivism points in the opposite direction: the political culture is anchored in culture as such. The question that remains is how limited or how grounded one's perspective is. Bader and Miller advocate a position that ties citizenship to culture – understood solely in national terms – and thus makes transnational citizenship difficult to conceive of. They are right in emphasizing that there are obvious difficulties in lifting culture to a European level and claiming that it retains the same qualities (trust, solidarity) as national cultures. But the core of the argument – that common political action in the end depends on a common culture – is questionable.

To a large extent the discussion of a possible transnational citizenship depends on the way citizenship is understood. A liberal, rights-based understanding, more or less directly, will point toward the universal principles contained in human rights. Many would argue, however, that this move takes place at the expense of a motivational anchoring of citizenship. So-called neo-republican citizenship theory, which opens up a second position in the debate on European citizenship, marks an effort to conceptualize citizenship and political identity through classical republican arguments about the link between responsibility, public participation and identity. The main thrust of the argument is that citizenship is constituted through a political practice of participating in a constant negotiation within a public sphere. As Richard Bellamy, a leading neo-republican, phrases it, 'a polity is continually reconstituted more appropriately to recognize, respect and represent the opinion of its members. Herein lies the constitutive role of citizenship' (Bellamy, 2001: 7). Citizenship is thus neither the result of a cultural identity nor of universal principles. Causality is reversed: identity and trust are the results of political practice. Reiterating a classical argument, Bellamy notes that 'practice leads citizens to develop various dispositions of civility, tolerance, reciprocity' (Bellamy, 2001: 7). In this view, raising citizenship to the European level does not demand culture, but the development of a European *public sphere* or a European *civil society*. According to Bellamy, such a sphere is visible in a rudimentary form through the actions of various transnational organizations dealing directly with EU's institutions (Bellamy, 2001: 30). Whether this is actually so is an empirical question that I do not intend to test. At the conceptual level, we can note that the neo-republican argument reverses the relation between identity and action. Identity is not a necessary prerequisite for common action, but the outcome. This reversal is, however, open to criticism since it has difficulties answering why people choose to agree or disagree with each other in the first place (Canovan, 2000: 422). It is obvious, on the other hand, that in conceptual terms civil society is easier to transnationalize. As mentioned, a transnational civil society at a European level is certainly not inconceivable. But Bellamy's reliance on practice does not really convince that a civil society will be culture-free.[10]

As noted, a way of entirely escaping the demand of a common culture is to emphasize the universal dimension of citizenship. The universal nature of citizenship is most evident in the field of rights where citizens' rights point towards human rights. Traditionally, rights-based arguments of citizenship are part of a liberal doctrine, which primarily focuses on the autonomy of the individual. Because liberalism favours a view of rights as universal principles underpinning the political community, it encounters the problem of how to conceptualize the dynamic or political character of rights.[11] What we have here can be formulated as the standard paradox of democracy: how can the principles and rules underpinning democracy themselves be treated democratically? In general, there seems to be two answers to this question, either to favour a strong constitutionalism that emphasizes the rules or to stress the dynamic and risky character of democracy. Elisabeth Meehan has presented an interesting approach to European citizenship adding a dynamic perspective to a right-based view (Meehan, 1993). I see this approach as a third position in the debate on European citizenship. Meehan is arguing that rights claims – and particularly claims of social rights – not only focus on the autonomy of the individual, but also reveal an underlying ideal of a solidaristic moral order (Meehan, 1993: 177). This general argument is used to perceive of emerging claims of workers' rights within the EU – following the policies promoting free movement of capital, labour and goods – as revealing 'traces of the idea of a common moral order' (Meehan, 1993: 178). The development of European citizenship is furthermore viewed as an illustration of how citizenship is being reconceptualized through a decoupling of rights from nationality and hence from culture. According to Meehan, the continued focus on social and political rights within the EU shows that the creation of a European moral order and even a polity can take place through a rights-based practice. This view builds on the premise that claims for social rights are based on interests and social identities. This more classical, liberal premise of interest-seeking individuals or groups obviously makes it easier to circumvent the reference to culture. The coupling of social rights and interests and the decoupling of nationality and citizenship can lead to a definition of citizenship primarily based on residence and work.

Meehan's position is opposed to a strict republican view of citizenship. Within a republican conceptualization, citizenship has to be based on the creation of a civic bond and civic principles generated within a civil society. Meehan foresees the emergence of a solidaristic order as a combined result of top-down integration, rights-based claims and citizens pursuing their interests. All this seems to rely on the fragile presupposition that interest claims will lead to a broader understanding among Europeans. From a republican viewpoint, Meehan's social-liberal conception of citizenship reduces the polity to a community based on interests stemming from production and labour. It is also questionable whether her version of a European citizenship qualifies as transnational. The universal understanding of citizenship that she relies on tends to efface the flexibility and multiplicity associated with transnational. Although rights claims based on 'transnational interests' are part of her argument, the universality of rights – not transnationality – seems to be the magic that makes European citizenship evolve in the first place.

The last position I shall evoke is typically formulated under the heading of constitutional patriotism. This position combines the universalistic features of citizenship as they are embedded in constitutions with a republican argument on the identity-generating capacity of the political practice within civil society. In the view of Habermas, the most renowned proponent of this position, constitutional patriotism is based on a separation of a shared *political culture* from 'subcultures and prepolitical identities' (Habermas, 1996: 289). Culture is thus relegated to a sphere located outside and underneath politics. Departing from a classical liberal argument, Habermas argues that the constitutional principles of human rights make a separation from culture conceivable. He furthermore locates the identity-generating and trust-generating feature within the shared political culture.[12] Precisely how substantial this political culture has to be is debatable. Habermas admits that the modern constitutional state contains a cultural deficit that constantly endangers the identity-building capacity of its political culture. To overcome this deficit, Habermas relies on the solidarity and the benefits produced as well by the extension of social rights through the welfare state as through participation in the public sphere. Constitutional patriotism has the advantage of walking on two legs, so to speak. It can emphasize 'the reflexive moral identity' generated by allegiance to universal principles to use an expression by Jean-Marc Ferry (quoted in Schnapper, 1997: 210), or it can put the accent on the political identity evolving from participation in the public sphere.

Constitutional patriotism is often associated with a *postnational* identity, because it is intended to sever the link to the ethno-national definition of culture. Furthermore, this position is formulated as a normative response to what is seen as the growing social and cultural pluralization of societies and the transgression of state borders caused by globalization (Habermas, 1996: 291; Lehning, 2001: 257). Multiculturalism and globalization form part of the argument for circumventing culture, since they demonstrate that contemporary nations are not held together by a common culture. Due to this growing diversity, they must instead rely on a generalized and abstract trust. The disconnection of culture from the political community can furthermore be supported by a flexible concept of identity that allows for a choice among multiple identities. The idea of transgression goes hand in hand with a processual account of identity which is at the core of the transnational. Constitutional patriotism thus seems to provide the best arguments for a transnational citizenship.

Concluding remarks

The concept of the transnational belongs to a vocabulary that is summoned to capture major phenomenological changes. The concept has a transitional character in as much as it is used to describe something that is in-between. At the same time, it carries a normative load. To point out transnational phenomena involves a contestation of the two components making up the nation-state. Transnational is different from the national condition, and it is outside the realm of the state. Nor is transnational synonymous with supranational which just tends to lift the national to a higher level. To conceptualize a European identity as supranational means charging Europe with the same symbolic powers as those belonging traditionally to the nations. A transnationalization of European identity means first of all a de-nationalization. At the semantic level, this manifests itself through a shift from a cultural vocabulary to other vocabularies. In some constructions, European identity is linked to civilizational values of a universalistic nature. In others, identity shifts towards the political. But transnationalization is also evident in the conceptual doubling that takes place when the flexible and transitory meaning of the concept of identity is emphasized. When identity is always multiple and negotiable, we cannot fix it to a particular place.

Just as identity was traditionally tied to the nation, so has citizenship been linked to the state. Although citizenship belongs to a semantic field of politics (and law), it touches upon identity. Belonging is an essential part of the basic meaning of citizenship. To transnationalize citizenship means to transfer it to political systems different from nation-states. European citizenship is a case in point. The ongoing establishment of a European citizenship has spurred a lengthy debate among scholars. It is contested whether citizenship can be transferred to a non-nation-state and retain its basic meaning. Sceptics claim that citizenship is vested in culture, whereas proponents opt for a de-nationalizing move that diminishes or deconstructs the cultural baggage of citizenship. As with identity, two strategies are available, either a universalizing one which emphasizes the role of rights in European citizenship, or one that argues for the important role of participation within civil society. Whereas the first strategy resembles the civilizational reference in the field of identity, the latter is more truly transnational in that it focuses on the role of a civil society which is neither within the nation-state nor above it. As within the identity debate we can also observe a tendency of conceptual doubling when citizenship becomes linked to concepts signifying flexibility and transition such as governance and civil society.

The debates on European identity and European citizenship thus exemplify how the transnational is being conceptualized, and how this concept is also influencing perceptions of changes taking place.

Notes

1. *An Introduction to the Principles of Morals and Legislation.*
2. F. Nietzsche, 'Jenseits von Gut und Böse', *Achtes Hauptstück: Völker und Vaterländer*, No. 242.
3. It appeared five times as often in titles indexed in the *International Bibliography of Social Sciences* in the period from 2000–5 compared with 1980–90.
4. If titles in the *International Bibliography of Social Sciences* can be taken as an indicator, transnational was used three times more often than multinational in the period from 2000–5, whereas multinational was used slightly more than transnational in the previous ten years. Again judging from the number of titles, the use of supranational is far more limited.
5. Bellamy, Castiglione and Shaw do not distinguish sharply between postnational and transnational contrary to what Shaw did in an earlier work on postnational constitutionalism within the EU: 'Postnationalism articulates an idea of change and transformation in relation to the nation-state . . . and not merely an alternative use of its political forms and cultural signifiers such as identities and legal orders in another international, transnational or even subnational contexts' (Shaw, 1997: 587). Although not stated explicitly, her use of the term postnational serves to emphasize a temporal dimension. See Shaw (1997) for a conceptualization of European citizenship as postnational.
6. Appadurai defines postnational in temporal as well as spatial terms. In the latter understanding postnational indicates alternative forms for the organization of global exchanges that contest the nation-state (Appadurai, 1993).
7. Compare the following list collected by Vertovec: 'transnationalism is often associated with a fluidity of constructed styles, social institutions and everyday practices. These are often described in terms of syncretism, creolization, bricolage, cultural translation and hybridity' (Vertovec, 1999: 451).
8. Identity theory has become a separate field of scholarly interest. See the huge bibliographies at http://www.euborder.soton.ac.uk/biblio02a.htm and in Brubaker and Cooper (2000).
9. I also leave out the problems of how to determine ethnicity and distinguish it from 'broad culture'.

10. The theoretical arguments against the identity-producing effects of civil society are often combined with doubts about the actual existence of a European civil society (Closa, 2001; Deirdre and Schlesinger, 2000; Liebert, 2001).
11. The flourishing of various designations such as liberal nationalism or liberal republicanism must be seen as efforts to come to grips with this problem from within a liberal doctrine.
12. In thinner versions of constitutional patriotism, a shared political conception of justice will be enough to promote identity-building (see Lehning, 2001: 250).

References

Albert, M. (2001) 'Territoriality and Modernization'. http://www.uni-bielefeld.de/soz/iw/pdf/albert_3.pdf.

Appadurai, A. (1993) 'Patriotism and its Futures', *Public Culture*, 5(3): 411–29.

—— (1996) 'Sovereignty without Territoriality: Notes for a Postnational Geography', in P. Yager (ed.), *The Geography of Identity*. Ann Arbor, MI: The University of Michigan Press, pp. 40–58.

Aron, R. (1962) *Paix et guerre entre les nations*. Paris: Calmann-Lévy.

Bader, V. (1997) 'The Cultural Conditions of Transnational Citizenship', *Political Theory*, 26(6): 771–813.

—— (1999) 'For Love of Country', *Political Theory*, 27(3): 379–97.

Basch, L., Schiller, G. and Blanc, C. S. (1993) *Nations Unbound: Transnational Projects, Postcolonial Predicaments, and Deterritorialized Nation-States*. New York: Gorddon and Breach Publishers.

Bauböck, R. (2000) 'European Integration and the Politics of Identity', Austrian Academy of Science, ICE – *Working Papers Series* no. 8.

Bellamy, R. (2001) 'The "Rights to have Rights": Citizenship Practice and the Political Constitution of the European Union', in R. Bellamy and A. Warleigh (eds), *Citizenship and Governance in the European Union*. London: Pinter/Continuum, pp. 41–70.

—— Castiglione, D. and Shaw, J. (2006) 'Introduction: From National to Transnational Citizenship', in R. Bellamy, D. Castiglione and J. Shaw (eds), *Making European Citizens: Civic Inclusion in a Transnational Context*. London: Palgrave Macmillan, pp. 1–28.

Bentham, J. (1789) *An Introduction to the Principles of Morals and Legislation*. Ch. XVI, note 143. http://www.econlib.org/library/Bentham/bnthPML0.html.

Beus, J. de (2001) 'Quasi-national European Identity and European Democracy', *Law and Philosophy*, 20: 283–311.

Bourne, R. (1916) 'Trans-national America', *Atlantic Monthly*, 118: 86–97. http://www.swarthmore.edu/SocSci/rbannis1/AIH19th/Bourne.html.

Brubaker, R. and Cooper, F. (2000) 'Beyond "Identity"', *Theory and Society*, 29: 1–47.

Canovan, M. (2000) 'Patriotism is Not Enough', *British Journal of Political Science*, 30: 413–32.

Closa, C. (2001) 'Requirements of a European Public Sphere: Civil Society, Self, and the Institutionalization of Citizenship', in K. Eder and B. Giesen (eds), *European Citizenship between National Legacies and Postnational Projects*. Oxford: Oxford University Press, pp. 180–201.

Deirdre, K. and Schlesinger, P. (2000) 'Can the European Union become a Sphere of Publics'?, in E. O. Eriksen and J. E.Fossum (eds), *Democracy in the European Union – Integration through deliberation?* London: Routledge, pp. 206–29.

Delanty, G. (1995) *Inventing Europe – Idea, Identity, Reality.* London: Macmillan.

Eriksen, E. O. (2005) 'An Emerging Public Sphere', *European Journal of Social Theory*, 8(3): 341–63.

——— and Fossum, J. E. (2002) 'Europe at a Crossroad – Government or Transnational Governance', *Arena Working Papers* WP 02/35. http://www.arena.uio.-no/publications/wp02_35.htm.

Faist, T. (2000) 'Transnationalization in International Migration: Implications for the Study of Citizenhip and Culture', *Ethnic and Racial Studies*, 23(2): 189–222.

Favell, A. and Geddes, A. (1999) 'European Integration, Immigration and the Nation-state: Institutionalising Transnational Political Action', *EUI Working Papers* No. 99/32.

Habermas, J. (1996) 'The European Nation-state – its Achievements and its Limits: On the Past and Future of Sovereignty and Citizenship', in G. Balakrishan (ed.), *Mapping the Nation.* London: Verso.

——— and Derrida, J. (2003) 'Europe: plaidoyer pour une politique extérieure commune', *Libération*, 31.5-1.6, pp. 44–6.

Hannerz, U. (1996) 'The Withering Away of the Nation?', in U. Hannerz, *Transnational Connections: Culture, People, Places.* London: Routledge, pp. 81–90.

Ifversen, J. (2002) 'Europe and European Culture – a Conceptual Analysis', *European Societies*, 4(1): 1–27.

Kaiser, K. (1971) 'Transnational Politics: Toward a Theory of Multinational Politics', *International Organizations*, 25(4): 790–817.

Kastoryano, R. (1997) *Negotiating Identities: States and Immigrants in France and Germany.* Princeton, NJ: Princeton University Press.

——— (1998) 'Transnational Participation and Citizenship: Immigrants in the European Union'. *WPTC-98-12.* http://www.transcomm.ox.ac.uk/working%-20papers/riva.pdf.

——— (2000). 'Des multiculturalismes en Europe au multiculturalisme européen', *Politique étrangeres*, 1: 163–78.

Kjær, A. M. (2004) *Governance.* Cambridge: Polity Press.

Köchler, H. (2005) 'The European Constitution and the Imperatives of Transnational Democracy', *Singapore Year Book of International Law*, 9: 1–15.

Kohli, M. (2000) 'The Battlegrounds of European Identity', *European Societies*, 2(2): 113–37.

Koselleck, R. (1996) 'A Response to Comments on the *Geschichtliche Grundbegriffe*', in H. Lehmann and M. Richter (eds), *The Meaning of Historical Terms: New Studies on Begriffsgeschichte.* Washington, DC: German Historical Institute.

Laborde, C. (2002) 'From Constitutional to Civic Patriotism', *British Journal of Political Science*, 32: 591–612.

Lehning, P. B. (2001) 'European Citizenship: Towards a European Identity?', *Law and Philosophy*, 20: 239–82.

Liebert, U. (2001) 'New Governance and the Prospect for a European Sphere of Publics', *CEuS Working Paper* 10.

Mandaville, P. (2002) 'Reading the State from Elsewhere: Towards an Anthropology of the Postnational', *Review of International Studies*, 28: 199–207.

Meehan, E. (1993) *Citizenship and the European Community*. London: SAGE Publications.

Miller, D. (1998) 'The Left, the Nation-state, and European Citizenship', *Dissent*, 45(3): 47–51.

—— (2000) *Citizenship and National Identity*. Oxford: Polity Press.

Morin, E. (1988) *Europæisk kultur*. Copenhagen: Gyldendal.

Nye, J. S. and Keohane, R. O. (1971) 'Transnational Relations and World Politics: An Introduction', in *International Organizations*, 25(3): 329–49.

Patel, K. K. (2004) Nach der Nationalfixiertheit: Perspektiven einer transnationalen Geschichte. Antrittsvorlesung, Berlin: Humboldt Universität.

Pocock, J. G. A. (1998) 'The Ideal of Citizenship since Classical Times', in G. Shafir (ed.), *The Citizenship Debates*. Minneapolis: University of Minnesota Press, pp. 31–41.

Portes, A. (2001) 'Introduction: The Debates and Significance of Immigrant Transnationalism', *Global Networks*, 1(3): 181–93.

Pries, L. (2002) 'Transnationalisierung der sozialen Welt?', *Berliner Journal für Soziologie*, Heft 2: 263-73. http://www.ruhr-uni-bochum.de/soaps/download/-publ-2002_lp_transdsozwelt.pdf.

Prodi, R. (2000) *Europe as I See It*. Cambridge: Polity Press.

Risse, T. (2000) 'Nationalism and Collective Identities: Europe Versus the nation-State?' Draft. http://www.deutsche-aussenpolitik.de/resources/seminars/gb/euracowa/document/jonesrhodes.pdf.

Rumsford, C. (2003) 'European Civil Society or Transnational Space?', *European Journal of Social Theory*, 6(1): 25–43.

Schumacher, N. (1971) 'Evolution du vocabulaire des relations internationals', *Le Langage et l'Homme: Recherches Pluridisciplinaire sur le Langage*, 15: 48–58.

Schnapper, D. (1997) 'Extract from Dominique Schnapper, La relation à l'Autre: Au Coeur de la pensée sociologique', *Theory & Event*, 3(2): 1–21.

Shaw, J. (1997) 'Citizenship of the Union: Towards Post-National Membership', *The Jean Monnet Working Papers* No. 6. NUY School of Law.

Shore, C. (2000) *Building Europe: The Cultural Politics of European Integration*. London: Routledge.

Smith, A. D. (1995) *Nations and Nationalism in a Global Era*. Cambridge: Polity Press.

Smith, M. (1895) 'Four German Jurists', *Political Science Quarterly*, 10(4): 664–92.

Smith, R. (2002) 'Modern Citizenship', in Isin, E. F. and Turner, B. S. (eds), *Handbook of Citizenship Studies*. London: SAGE Publications, pp. 105–17.

Snow, A. H. (1912) 'The Law of Nations', *The American Journal of International Law*, 6(4): 890–900.

Sørensen, N. N. (2003) 'Review Essay: From Transnationalism to the Emergence of a New Transnational Research Field', *International Journal of Urban and Regional Research*, 27(2): 465–9.

Stråth, B. (2000) 'Multiple Europes: Integration, Identity and Demarcation to the Other', in B. Stråth (ed.), *Europe and the Other and Europe as the Other*. Brussels P.I.E.: Peter Lang, pp. 385–420.

Vertovec, S. (1999) 'Conceiving and Researching Transnationalism', *Ethnic and Racial Studies*, 22(2): 447–62.

Wiener, A. (1997) 'Making Sense of the New Geography of Citizenship: Fragmented Citizenship in the European Union', *Theory and Society*, 26: 529–60.

7
Constitutional Patriotism: Canada and the European Union

John Erik Fossum

Introduction

The purpose of this chapter is to discuss the question of allegiance in complex multinational and poly-ethnic entities, with a specific focus on the EU and Canada. Both are claimed to be multinational and poly-ethnic, with such traits also being reflected in their official doctrines. Diversity awareness is thus an explicit concern that has to figure in their policies on allegiance formation.

The particular approach to allegiance formation that I will examine here is constitutional patriotism. Both the EU and Canada have formulated institutional-constitutional and policy arrangements that have been informed by the spirit of constitutional patriotism.[1] The kind of identity we can associate with constitutional patriotism is one that is conducive to respect for and accommodation of difference and plurality.

Constitutional patriotism refers to a mode of attachment wherein citizens are bound together by subscription to democratic values and human rights, rather than through the traditional pre-political ties that nation states have appealed to (Habermas, 1994, 1996, 1998; Ingram, 1996; Eriksen and Fossum, 2000; Fossum, 2003). Constitutional patriotism is contextual; however, it also contains an inbuilt tension between general legal principles and the context within which and on which they operate. These tensions are readily available in the rapidly growing body of literature on constitutional patriotism (Calhoun, 1992, 2002; Habermas, 1994, 1996; Ingram, 1996; Booth, 1999; Michelman, 1999; Canovan, 2000; Markell, 2000; Lacroix, 2002; Cronin, 2003; Fossum, 2003; Kumm, 2005; Bohman, 2005), a body of literature with quite different positions on how constitutional patriotism can broach these tensions. How thick this form of allegiance needs to be to work in highly diverse societies is a greatly disputed matter.

To shed light on this it is useful to consider what might be understood as the minimum requirements for this form of allegiance to serve the necessary integrative needs for a community, and how accommodating of difference and diversity constitutional patriotism is. Note that this latter point is not only about the scope for voicing dissent, it is also about the prospects for exit (understood in a communal and/or territorial sense). Some claims for difference are simply very difficult to accommodate within a common framework. With exit being an available option, the conditions for fostering loyalty and effecting voice change. Constitutional patriotism, as nationalism, is a mode of attachment that is based on a particular constellation of exit, voice and loyalty.[2]

In the following I first provide a brief definition of constitutional patriotism. Thereafter I try to discern what kind of constellation(s) of exit, voice and loyalty that sits best with constitutional patriotism, including how different/similar to nationalism this is. After that I try this out on the EU and Canada. The focus is on three sets of dimensions which help shed light on each entity's particular understanding of constitutional patriotism and the underlying constellation of exit, voice and loyalty. I examine what these cases tell us about the role of rights in promoting/ fostering constitutional patriotism, through focus on each entity's Charter. Further, I look at each entity's commitment to difference/diversity through examining their respective multiculturalism policies. I seek to identify the philosophy of allegiance underpinning each entity's policy framework so as to establish whether these are informed by the spirit of constitutional patriotism. An important concern is to establish whether the policies are essentially reflective of respect for difference/diversity or are simply a more subtle form of integration. This should be considered together with the final point, that of exit options. The focus is on democratic provisions for territorial exit. Is constitutional patriotism based on an approach to territorial exit that is different from or similar to that of nationalism?

What are the minimum requirements for such a mode of allegiance to serve the necessary integrative needs for a community?

Constitutional patriotism defined

The contextualization of democratic values and human rights in a constitutional structure permits the willing acceptance of a system of authority embedded in the constitution, and this is what holds people together and makes for their constitutional patriotism. Citizens are bound to each other not by traditional pre-political ties that nation-states have appealed to but by subscription to democratic values and human rights (Habermas, 1996: 465f, 1998; Ingram, 1996). This type of identity is conducive to respect for and accommodation of difference and plurality. It is post-national and thinner than national identity. It is thin also in that its substantive content is shaped by and ultimately made subject to consistence with a set of constitutionally entrenched procedures. Habermas notes that the 'universalism of legal principles is reflected in a procedural consensus, which must be embedded in the context of a historically specific political culture through a kind of constitutional patriotism' (Habermas, 1994: 135). The procedural consensus is founded on the notions that

> the rationally based conviction that unrestrained freedom of communication in the political public sphere, a democratic process for settling conflicts, and the constitutional channeling of political power together provide a basis for checking illegitimate power and ensuring that administrative power is used in the equal interest of all. (Habermas, 1994: 135)

Rights are central to this notion of allegiance, through our recognition of other persons as holders of rights. Rights can ensure both an individual sense of self and a collective sense of membership of a community. The core of modern rights is their individual nature. Individual rights are based on a notion of reciprocal recognition that ensures personal autonomy, which is intrinsic to the medium of law (Habermas, 1996: 88). Legal relations highlight the general and universalizable aspect of the recognition relationship, so that what is recognized is the person as a holder of rights, not the particular personality traits or attributes of the person. This relationship is not universally applicable but reflects the view of law as bounded in that it applies to specific settings. The social recognition serves to underline that rights are always steeped in and shaped by a particular political culture.

Minimum requirements: Autonomy

Autonomy has two facets, private and public, associated with the constitutional state and democracy, respectively. Private autonomy presupposes protective rights that guarantee against state incursions into the affairs of individuals, whereas public autonomy presupposes rights to participation to enable the citizens to see themselves not only as subject to the law but also as the authors of the law (Habermas, 1994: 112, 1996: 120). Without fundamental rights that guarantee the private autonomy of citizens there would be no assured way to institutionalize in a body of law the conditions for future citizens to utilize their public autonomy. The public and private autonomies are interrelated because

> in the final analysis, private legal persons cannot even attain the enjoyment of equal individual liberties unless they themselves, by jointly exercising their autonomy as citizens, arrive at a clear understanding about what interests and criteria are justified and in what respect equal things will be treated equally and unequal things unequally in any particular case. (Habermas, 1994: 113)

Democracy and the rule of law, both of which are critical components of constitutional patriotism, stand in a relation of tension. Habermas has more recently noted that 'the allegedly paradoxical relation between democracy and the rule of law resolves itself in the dimension of historical time, provided one conceives of the constitution that makes the founding act into an ongoing process of constitution-making that continues across generations' (Habermas, 2001a: 768).

Claims for differential treatment must be assessed with direct reference to how they affect this internal relation between the citizens' public and private autonomy. If such claims undermine either set of autonomy, they cannot be justified. If serious enough they would undermine the foundation for constitutional patriotism.

Habermas's insistence on the primacy of individual private and public autonomy does not necessarily detract from recognition of the political salience of ethnic or other differences. Whilst the system of rights is universalistic in its content, rights are not necessarily blind to cultural differences. In fact, '[a] correctly understood theory of rights requires a politics of recognition that protects the integrity of the individual in the life contexts in which his or her identity is formed' (Habermas, 1994: 113).

How thick? Two conceptions of constitutional patriotism

Constitutional patriotism is often thought of as something of an oxymoron: simultaneously an attempt to bridge the universalism of basic rights and the particularity of a community of allegiance and identification. Built into the concept there are two seemingly opposite pulls: universalist and particularist.

I will approach thickness by examining how far we can 'stretch' the constitutive features of constitutional patriotism in either of these directions. More concretely, I measure thickness by examining different conceptions of constitutional patriotism in relation to three dimensions: exit, voice and loyalty. Every mode of allegiance is based on a particular or distinctive constellation of exit, voice and loyalty. Scope for exit (in its various dimensions – synchronic as well as diachronic) has strong bearings on diversity: for its scope, type and handling. (Ethnic) nationalism for instance largely assumes away the question of exit, as its main preoccupation is with a distinctive community and its protection. Nationalism posits a community with no real exit from its past, as nationalism 'makes us one with our past and thus fully accountable for it' (Booth, 1999: 252). Memory of the past helps sustain the sense of community and identity, whose continued protection is again premised on high thresholds against most forms of exit (through separation, and secession, that is through sub-unit exit); a strong onus on loyalty; and voice is always sought mitigated or modified whenever the issue of communal needs and protection is activated.

Thus, to understand the thickness of the mode of allegiance embedded in constitutional patriotism we need explicit attention to exit, both to understand how constitutional patriotism relates to the past – with focus on the issue of memory – as well as to properly handle the structural institutional dimension of allegiance formation and sustenance. The law is a central means of social integration (Habermas, 1996). When the law and culture are embedded within the institutions of the state, that is, when there is no real recourse for exit, their embedding in the state produces a strong system for ensuring loyalty, channelling voice and sustaining a sense of memory of the past and a sense of commitment to the common future.

Which constellation of exit, voice and loyalty best suits constitutional patriotism? Given the onus on patriotism, how strong is the communal dimension of constitutional patriotism? On this dimension, how far from the ethnic nationalist constellation is constitutional patriotism? In the following I draw on the debate on constitutional patriotism. My concern is not to provide accurate reconstructions of authors' positions; instead I draw on these positions to try to understand the particular constellation of exit, voice and loyalty that underpins constitutional patriotism.

It might be useful to start with Calhoun's criticism of Habermas, whose notion of constitutional patriotism he finds too thin and as cast too narrowly. What Calhoun thinks Habermas ignores is a broader view of the constitution: not simply as a legal-political arrangement but also as '*the creation of concrete social relationships*; of bonds of mutual commitment forged in shared action, of institutions, and of shared modalities of practical action' (Calhoun, 2002: 152–3). In my framework, Calhoun stresses loyalty more than Habermas. He also sees Habermas's notion as overly narrow, as Habermas apparently casts it as an opposite rather than as a possible complement to nationalism. Calhoun argues that this is based on a misconstrual of nationalism, as it does not simply rest on pre-political identities, but can also be a mode of fostering a form and level of 'peopleness' within the political sphere. Calhoun notes that '[t]he U.S. example could inform a different conception of constitutional patriotism, stronger than that advocated by Habermas' (2002: 152).

The question is whether Calhoun's notion stretches constitutional patriotism beyond its reasonable limits, that is, undermines constitutional patriotism's fragile balancing of different concerns. Underpinning Calhoun's conception of constitutional patriotism, we can discern a distinctive pattern or constellation of loyalty, voice and exit. Nationalism, also the kind that Calhoun argues is compatible with constitutional patriotism, necessarily has a strong element of *loyalty* built into it. Nationalism is based on a categorical type of identity: people hold such a strong allegiance to their nation that they are willing to ultimately die for it.

This position clearly makes up one definite end-scale of the identitarian dimension of constitutional patriotism. Here we can posit the presence of a positive identification with something which is designative of us; a set of mechanisms to instil a positive sense of identification; and the ability to define the other and also to exclude those that are deemed to be different – the non-us or *others*. This position is highly attentive to the patriotism component of constitutional patriotism; it is not clear that it is equally attentive to the constitutional component.

What is important to underline is that this constellation is premised on a particular role attributed to *exit*, a point that is little broached within the national frame but whose salience is raised when we look at it from the cosmopolitan angle (which is where Habermas after all locates constitutional patriotism).[3] The national community is bounded, with clear provisions on exit. When constitutional patriotism is linked to nationalism this automatically brings in the relation to the state and the states system – as also Calhoun did with his reference to the US. Doing so has deep implications for the scope for exit. Three aspects of exit are here particularly relevant, which we may label as argumentative, communal and territorial. On the first, argumentative, the legal provisions on private autonomy ensure argumentative exit through protection of silence or licence to step out of the communicative space; citizens need not partake in all forms of activities. Nor do they have to avail themselves of voice. But the onus on positive identification also likely sets social limits on the scope even for argumentative exit. On the second, communal dimension, the issue is how far individual communities can exit from the norms of the larger society. Societies generally accept various forms of 'functional exit'. We see this in relation to religious communities, which may be able to opt out of the (public) school system or military service or the like. Similarly, ethnic and other groups may be allowed partial opt-outs of the majority language community through provisions for the protection of own language and through federal arrangements. But these run up against the third and most serious case of exit: *territorial* exit: Calhoun's nationalist version of constitutional patriotism can hardly be said to be compatible with provisions for sub-unit exit through secession or separation.

Thus, when we operate within the states system and the nationalist frame is our reference, physical exit is possible for individuals and to a limited extent also for groups, but the threshold for territorial exit through secession or separation is very high and subject to strict national and international legal provisions. In today's world, states are legally ordained to and also mostly physically able to uphold sovereign territorial control. High barriers to exit can thus serve as vital mechanisms for sustaining the peculiar constellation of loyalty and voice set out above. In other words, such limited recourse to exit greatly increases the state's ability to instil a common sense of allegiance through additional provisions for socialization, disciplining and control.[4] This distinctive constellation of loyalty, voice and exit may thus have less to do with the *particular* mode of allegiance involved, and more to do with the state's ability to exercise sovereign control of a given territory. Allegiance formation takes place within a national frame, where this frame is accepted as legitimate and where the state is equipped with strong sanctioning measures to ensure compliance.

Any close association with nationalism produces a conception of constitutional patriotism whose underlying mode of allegiance ends up being too thick. I think Calhoun falls into this trap, whereas Habermas does not, precisely because he operates with a thinner conception of allegiance. In effect, drawing on Habermas rather than Calhoun, the model of constitutional patriotism that I see emanating from the patriotism end of the scale sees this as requiring a cosmopolitan orientation, with weak territorial exit provisions, and a link to the past, 'as a storehouse of lessons' (Booth, 1999: 256); a *post-national* rather than a national form of loyalty; and a communicative community with a strong onus on fostering a communal sense of allegiance.

But this is not the only conception of constitutional patriotism. Given nationalism's hankering for particularity, the obvious step would be to argue that the other end of the constitutional patriotism scale would be occupied by identification with normative universals. Apparently, Habermas's early position was precisely that, but with identity understood in postconventional terms, not in relation to concrete others but to a kind of 'anticipated . . . community of others . . .' (Markell, 2000: 42 with reference to Habermas, 1974). In later work, notably *Between Fact and Norms* (English version, 1996), Patchen Markell detects a greater emphasis on how any effort to ground normative universals, in particular structures, has to contend with the fact that any such grounding will yield an inadequate and/or weak reflection of the universal principles. This means that there is no safe anchor for affect (of such a kind as to sustain democracy) in concrete institutions. There are therefore limits to how far positive identification with a specific set of principles can go in allegiance terms. Markell (2000), in his reconstruction of the philosophical position that informs Habermas's more practical-political writings, detects a different understanding of constitutional patriotism, one that is ultimately based on reflexivity (which only rests on certain procedural preconditions). Any set of principles and institutional arrangements has to be open to deliberative challenge if their true universal potential is to be properly unleashed. The net result is not positive identification, but rather what may be termed ensuing identitarian ambivalence:

> If universal normative principles always depend on supplements of particularity that enable them to become objects of attachment and identification but that are also never quite equivalent to the principles they purport to embody, then constitutional patriotism can best be understood not as a safe and reliable identification with some pure set of already available universals, but rather as a political practice of refusing or resisting particular identifications – of insisting on and making manifest this failure of equivalence – for the sake of the ongoing, always incomplete, and often unpredictable project of universalization. (Markell, 2000: 40)

This second notion of constitutional patriotism highlights voice over loyalty and exit. Note that it also puts considerable premium on what I would label as 'negative voice'; 'citizens . . . must learn to fear, be angry at, and be ashamed of the very institutions and cultures that claim their attachment and allegiance' (Markell, 2000: 54). This is a way of establishing and enforcing standards and as such forms a vital component of democratic reflection. This can also be construed as a measure of exit from the past, certainly in positive allegiance terms, albeit not in moral terms, as the past and memories of it are central feeders of the ongoing reflexive process.

Loyalty in the conventional sense would in this understanding of constitutional patriotism play third fiddle, as it is always subject to discursive challenge and is reined in by procedures anchored in universal principles, whose very entrenchment in procedures can also be discursively challenged.

In my reading, the central role of voice in this notion of constitutional patriotism also colours the actors' conception of and relation to constitution; not as an agreed-upon frame but better thought of as a 'working agreement', i.e. 'an agreement which has come about argumentatively, but where the actors may have different but still reasonable and acceptable grounds for their support' (Eriksen, 2003: 204–5).

The critical issue here is whether not the ensuing mode of allegiance might be too thin to sustain a community. How will such a system hold together? The key to the answer in Markell's account is the constitutional democratic state: Markell does not bring in the cosmopolitan dimension. This link to the state – as the frame within which law's role of social integration is given institutional sustenance – must be considered as the key to stability and as guarantor of a measure of thickness. But this also means that the reflexive process is subject to the strong socializing mechanisms of the state; how long can such an open-ended process be carried out before it clashes with the institutional interests of the state and becomes subdued under it? In other words, the issue may not be thinness but ability to sustain the reflexive orientation.

The critical question, then, is how this notion of constitutional patriotism sits with cosmopolitanism. It seems to me that the reflexive character of this notion of constitutional patriotism ultimately presupposes a cosmopolitan frame and hence a very different relation to exit: for this to be truly reflexive, it has to have provisions not only for exit for persons and arguments but also for territorial sub-units. The reason is that citizens' allegiance to the polity is grounded on the universal principles' constant embedding in institutional form, a form of allegiance that is constantly subject to deliberative challenge and is marked by considerable ambivalence. As the character of this grounding varies, allegiance is also always necessarily conditional. Hence, citizens within a sub-unit who do not find the system to operate in line with their interests must have legal procedures available for exit, but of course ones that are consistent with universal principles.

Within this framework, the aggregate political system is only legitimate insofar as the reasons and justifications for staying together are stronger than the reasons for departure or removal through territorial exit. But since exit has profound effects not only on those who leave but equally on those who remain – the procedures for exit have to be democratic and based on reciprocity.

From this discussion what I end up with are two possible interpretations of constitutional patriotism, each of which is based on a distinctive constellation of exit, voice and loyalty. Both versions are inspired by the literature, but neither is a direct transposition because the versions presented here are framed to take exit properly into consideration. Doing so gives a peculiar twist to each constellation – including what the scope for and character of voice and loyalty imply.

In my reading, the issue of the requisite thickness of allegiance in constitutional patriotism has strong bearings on how far from the state frame and the national mode of community constitutional patriotism can be taken. Table 7.1 shows that the second version presented above takes us furthest away and represents a significant departure, dependent

Table 7.1   Two conceptions of constitutional patriotism (CP)

	Constitutional Patriotism I (CP I)	*Constitutional Patriotism II (CP II)*
Exit	• Moderate 'cosmopolitan openness' for persons and arguments • Exit provisions only from communicative community, not available to territorial entities (3)	• High 'cosmopolitan openness' for persons and arguments • Provisions for sub-unit exit from the polity, in compliance with democratic norms (2)
Voice	• Rights to ensure individual autonomy • Communication aimed at fostering agreement on common norms: pragmatic, ethical and moral • Communication to foster solidarity and sense of community (2)	• Rights to ensure individual autonomy • Communication aimed at reaching working agreements • Communication to foster trust in procedures and rights • 'Negative voice' (1)
Loyalty	• Positive endorsement of culturally embedded constitutional norms • Positive identification with the polity (1)	• Ambivalence towards any form of positive allegiance • Systemic endorsement through critique (3)

(1), (2) and (3) denote descending importance.

as it is on an explicit cosmopolitan constellation, whereas the first version essentially relies on the state form and can operate within a system of states.

Below, I apply these two versions of constitutional patriotism to selected aspects of the EU and Canada to establish how well these entities cohere with constitutional patriotism, and what this entails for diversity awareness and handling.

Constitutional patriotism in the EU and Canada

Why discuss constitutional patriotism (CP) in relation to the EU and Canada? Neither is able to rely on an agreed-upon national mode of allegiance. In recent decades, efforts to forge an alternative doctrine to nationalism have been made, most notably multiculturalism. Canada is also a pioneer in that it is the first democratic state to establish democratic conditions for territorial exit for subunits. The EU was set up as an explicit repudiation of ethnic nationalism – and as a case of possible *exit* from Europe's national past. The EU also permits territorial exit; Greenland, for instance, left the Union in 1984 (the European Constitutional Treaty has an explicit exit provision).

Both the EU and Canada are to varying degrees multi-ethnic and multi-national.[5] Precisely because they test, or better exceed, the bounds of national allegiance, there have been frequent attempts to consider the mode of allegiance they seek to elicit as evocative of CP.

Below, I look at three relevant dimensions which are central to constitutional patriotism and which can help shed light on the particular constellation of voice, loyalty and exit that informs each entity. First, charters or bills of rights are central in instilling a sense of allegiance akin to CP, as well as in helping to ensure the institutional conditions for autonomy. Individual rights are also central preconditions for voice. Second are the entities' central policy doctrines on diversity protection/promotion. Here I look at each entity's multiculturalism policy as a case of explicit recognition of diversity. An important issue is whether this policy framework is ultimately set up to foster a deeper sense of loyalty to an implicit or explicit mode or foremost respectful of different ways of life. Third, I look at territorial exit provisions. If such exist, they can be considered tests of stateness, or conversely, as indicators of each entity's degree of cosmopolitization. The question is whether these three dimensions in each case can be summed up into a coherent constellation of CP, whether along the lines of CP I or II. My initial hypothesis is that Canada will embody the constellation of CP I and the EU that of CP II.

The Canadian Charter

The federal Canadian Charter of Rights and Freedoms (1982) was a central component of the Canadian Constitution Act 1982, which patriated the constitution from Britain. The Act was intended as a core vehicle in the symbolic founding of Canada as an independent country and as one based on democratic constitutionalism. The previous constitution (the BNA Act 1867) had of course set Canada up with representative democracy, but suffered from serious constitutional shortcomings, among them the failure to evoke a common spirit of allegiance within a self-professed democratic constitutionalism (Cairns, 1988: 27).

The Charter can be understood as a central vehicle to rectify this by instilling a sense of constitutional patriotism based foremost on liberal individual rights, albeit with some allowance to the more complex notion of Canada as a 'community of communities'. The Charter contained certain group-based rights such as language rights, but they 'can be justified in terms of individual rights' (Taylor, 1993: 165). The gist of the Charter was to foster an individual rights-based patriotism that would confront and challenge the deep diversity required to fulfil the province of Quebec's collective goal of cultural and linguistic survival.

The introduction of the Charter sparked great opposition, in particular from Quebec separatists, who argued that it would not foster a viable constitutional patriotism, because the Canadian Charter was introduced without the province of Quebec's explicit consent. They therefore deemed the Constitution Act 1982 illegitimate. The province of Quebec has still not signed the Constitution Act 1982. Further, they argued that the Canadian Charter was unnecessary in Quebec, as Quebec in 1975 passed its own *Charte des droits et libertés de la personne*. A further objection was that the Canadian Charter did not offer explicit protections for Quebec's cultural or national distinctiveness, and as such would bar exit for the French-speaking language community. To them, the Canadian Charter's strong individual rights basis would prevent Quebec from instituting measures to protect and promote its cultural and linguistic uniqueness. The Charter was therefore seen as insensitive to the cultural diversity of Canada.

What this reveals is that the CP that was sought through the Canadian Charter could not be rooted in a common understanding or shared memory of the past; it was inserted into a divided community; and the core vehicle for propounding this sense of allegiance has itself created considerable conflict. Neither the setting nor the Charter is therefore reflective of CP I. The Charter was set up as a mild case of exit from Canada's past, a past that had been constructed as dominated by the two founding peoples.

CP – both versions – is intended to overcome past divisions, even through a certain distancing from the past. CP sees the past as a repertoire of lessons. The Canadian Charter could henceforth be thought of as an attempt to embody the set of minimum common denominators that the long period of co-existence had taught people to respect.

Nevertheless, the Canadian Charter was structured to be barred from doing so in line with the criterion of autonomy, which is central to both versions of CP. It is clear that the Canadian Charter contained a significantly strengthened constitutional recognition and protection of individual rights; however, and this is the crux, it also contained group-based rights and a notwithstanding clause which were communal exit provisions in the sense that they permitted governments to opt out of several Charter provisions.

Quebec's apparent opposition to the Charter might suggest that the Canadian Charter only fosters constitutional patriotism outside of Quebec. However, Quebec also has its own Charter. One question is whether a system of dual charters is compatible with CP. The two charters are quite similar in their insistence on basic rights. Such insistence could help to further a liberal rights-oriented convergence in Canada (Taylor, 1993; Norman, 1995; Schneiderman, 1998). But both charters also contain elements that may negatively affect the internal relation between private and public autonomy, in the sense that they both include group rights. The Quebec Charter offers far stronger protection of French language rights and is more conducive to the pursuit of collective goals than the Canadian Charter. The latter is therefore more conducive to CP in either version (I or II), because of its stronger focus on individual rights, its clearer cosmopolitan orientation and its more inclusive nature, in cultural terms.

When we look at Canada's development post-1982, we find that Canada has undergone a Charter revolution (Morton and Knopff, 2000; Cairns, 2003). This process has served to strengthen individual public and private autonomies and the vital links between these so that the constitutional arrangement does speak to tenets of democracy and the constitutional state. The Canadian Charter can therefore be seen as a step in the direction of founding the Canadian Constitution on some notion of CP.

The Canadian Charter has won acceptance over time, even in Quebec (Cairns, 2003). It has also fostered a constitutionally based and driven participant democratic culture which has proved to be quite hostile to political leaders and the jurisdictionally based claims of governmental actors. The Charter has expanded the public autonomy of a range of groups whose former status was marginalized. This has occurred at the same time as the traditional liberal rights of citizens have gained a stronger constitutional footing. These developments have taken place within a setting that has *not* managed to reach an agreed-upon constitutional settlement. Further, Quebec has taken language-protective measures that do not comply with the Canadian Charter. An important driver of the constitutional struggle is the presence of different, distinct and particular identitarian narratives, with conflicting communal aspirations. These have in their active engagement with the past been unable to come to terms on a constitutional settlement. Nevertheless, rather than through a working agreement we could say that they have converged on what may be considered a working arrangement: basic constitutional principles are agreed-upon together with a commitment to a peaceful and reasonable interchange on its subsequent development. We may conclude that insofar as the Canadian Charter experience can be said to comply with CP in the first place, the dynamic of contemporary and historical contestation and reflection it set in motion is closer to CP II than to CP I.

The European Charter[6]

CP is the philosophical approach to the fostering of allegiance that we can discern from the European Charter. The European Charter's approach to CP is also 'rooted' in ethical content, in particular through the commitment to social rights and social solidarity, as part of the Communities' socio-economic structure. In my previous assessment of the Charter's basic philosophy I noted that it appears thicker than that of a classical liberal statement of fundamental rights and freedoms. However, this commitment may not amount to that much, given the EU's limited competence in the social policy area (Menéndez, 2003).

The latter point has a strong bearing on how pervasive this embrace of constitutional patriotism can be, given that the Charter's provisions will be steeped in the particular legal-institutional context that makes up the Union. If we start with the provisions for ensuring *public* autonomy and for ensuring the mutually supportive interaction of citizens' private and public autonomies presupposed by CP, we find that the Charter reflects the *weakly* developed citizenship rights of the EU. Still, EU citizenship is an 'open-textured concept' with considerable transformative capacity.

The problem of weakly developed citizenship rights in the Charter is likely to be amplified by the fact that the Charter does not affect the pillar structure. Note that although there has been a gradual move of policy areas from pillars two and three to one, the ECJ is excluded from pillars two and three and Parliament's role is merely consultative.[7] Citizens' private autonomy can thus be considered as weakened in the sense that and insofar as persons are not able to appeal to the ECJ when their rights are infringed.[8] Such weakening applies even more clearly to citizens' public autonomy. Note that institutionally speaking it is only within the first pillar that the entire populace of the EU can conceive of itself as a law-maker. Within pillars two and three the citizens are represented by their respective national representative systems and here decisions are reached by unanimity. In other words, citizens' deliberations are not reflected in the decisions of one set of institutions over which the entire body of citizens can exercise control and accountability. Autonomy suffers.

A further issue pertains to the constitutional status of EC law. Treaty changes, filtered by the jurisprudence of the Court of Justice, have contributed to the forging of a material constitution at the European level. The European legal order is thus self-sufficient, with fundamental rights as a founding principle.

Nevertheless, the principled and practical status of this material constitution is controversial. It did not come about through the drafting of a formal constitution. The historic lack of a democratic constitution-making process deeply influenced the Laeken Convention, which sought to rectify this. The Charter was also touted as an important step in the efforts to bridge this gap. The Convention that drew up the Charter drafted the text *as if* it were to be incorporated in the Treaties.[9] This text is based on existing rights (from the EC treaties, the ECHR, the constitutional traditions of the member states, and other international conventions).

Koen Lenaerts, Judge of the First Instance of the European Communities, and Eddy de Smijter argue that the effects of the proclamation will be the same as if the Charter were inserted into the Treaties. They note that

> to the extent that the Charter is to be regarded as an expression of the constitutional traditions common to the Member States, the Court will be required to enforce it by virtue of Article 6(2) *juncto* Article 46(d) EU 'as general principles of Community law' . . . The Charter is thus part of the *acquis communautaire*, even if it is not part yet of the Treaties on which the Union is founded. (Lenaerts and de Smijter, 2001: 299)

The Charter could give impetus to the process of forging a *democratic* EU constitution through fostering a rights-based CP. In legal terms, the Charter is more than a declaration of intent and already in the Laeken process served as a spearhead for CP in the EU (Duff, 2000; Eckhout, 2000). The great uncertainty today appears political more than legal. The French and Dutch rejection of the Constitutional Treaty in popular referenda in June 2005 created considerable uncertainty as to the further pursuit of a formal-democratic constitution for the Union. In the absence of such a political will, the Charter's being steeped in and adapted to the Union's structure, could defang it as a significant spearhead for CP.

The European Charter is no doubt a weaker instrument for fostering CP than the Canadian Charter. Further, the prospects for CP in the EU more than even in a contested state such as Canada hinge on the Union's overall development *as polity*. The Union as a non-state entity is to a considerable extent institutionally barred from instilling CP I. Without continued constitutional commitment it may also be saddled with the negative voice of CP II but without the modifying or unifying elements that make it CP in the first place. The risk facing Europe is that the integration process unleashes voice along particular identitarian lines but without at the same time being able to ensure that these are subjected to a constitutional *working arrangement* (as we saw in Canada) that helps ensure agreement on basic rights and mutually respectful procedures of communication and interaction.

The European Union's and Canada's multiculturalism policies

Canada

The diversity of Canada has long been officially recognized. What is particularly notable is that this has given rise to a public rhetoric that is quite different from that associated with nationalism, which when provoked would always refer to some cultural symbol of unity. To illustrate, when asked in 1999 to define the Canadian identity, the then Minister of Intergovernmental Affairs, Stephane Dion said that it consisted of respect for basic rights and respect for diversity.[10] No explicit reference was made to a common heritage or common traditions.

The recognition of Canada's diversity has been propounded through minority rights and multiculturalism. The country is officially bilingual and multicultural.[11] It offers official recognition of immigrant ethnicity. As Will Kymlicka (1995, 1998) has underlined, multiculturalism as a doctrine is premised on the notion of integrating immigrants from diverse cultural backgrounds into society – without eliminating their characteristics. It seeks to avoid the twin evils of assimilation and ethnic separation or ghettoization. It is also an ideology that speaks to interethnic tolerance and the benefits that accrue to society from its diversity (Norman, 2001). This doctrine is premised on the notion that integration or incorporation of people from different backgrounds is a two-way process, which places requirements on those who integrate, but also on those who are already there. The essence is to heighten social inclusiveness as well as self-reflection on the part of both the arriving minority/ies and the receiving majority, to ensure a process of mutual accommodation and change. Analysts find that the Canadian multiculturalism programme has been informed by these notions, although it is contested how well it has done.[12] They also claim that it has contributed to heightening awareness of difference and the need for accommodating difference and diversity (Kymlicka, 1995, 1998).

Multiculturalism's approach to socialization and incorporation is clearly different from that of nationalism. In what sense is it consistent with CP? In my reading it seems to straddle the line between CP I and II. It is more focused on integration than on diversity awareness, although the onus on reciprocal adaptation speaks to a kind of reflexivity that is closer to CP II because it to some extent at least deprives the receiving community of automatic resort to a given set of norms and traditions. Traditions – this is how we do things here – do not only have to be communicated to the newcomers (with the assumption that they be adopted and emulated) but have to be explained and justified; hence they are open to deliberative challenge and change.

The European Union

The European Union's approach to diversity can be said to be based on universal principles, as well as on recognition of – notably national – difference. There is no real agreement within the Union on how to strike this balance. This also colours the academic debate. Some analysts stress that the Union should, and to some extent also does, do more than simply accommodate existing national identities. It represents an attempt at forging a distinct *post-national* mode of belonging (Habermas, 1998: 2001b). This is based on the notion of the Union as a vehicle to *exit* from central aspects of Europe's past. Efforts to invoke Europe's past and history as a resource to foster agreement on a constitutional arrangement will very likely backfire and generate negative voice. Europe is apparently confined to CP II or abandon CP altogether.

Other analysts stress that national diversity awareness is a defining feature of the Union. Joseph Weiler has argued that the Union's normative hallmark is the *principle of constitutional tolerance*, which is premised on consolidation of democracy within and among Member States and on the recognition that 'the Union . . . is to remain a union among distinct peoples, distinct political identities, distinct political communities . . . The call to bond with those very others in an ever closer union demands an internalization – individual and societal – of a very high degree of tolerance' (Weiler, 2001: 68). In this reading the national community is seen as the locus of primary and deeper attachments. The overarching European entity is equipped with some form of constitutional authority, but its authority is not entrenched in a system of strong sanctions; as it has a strong voluntaristic component. If Weiler's assessment is correct, such an entity would be closer to deep diversity (Taylor, 1993; Fossum, 2004) – that is, accepting different conceptions and visions of what the polity is, and ought to be – than to CP.

These comments suggest that the Union's handling of diversity is not reflective of CP I, as there is no common identity or sense of community, however frail. Neither is it entirely correct to say that it is marked by CP II. There are several competing efforts to develop a mode of allegiance that appears thicker than the deep ambivalence to any sense of positive identification that is reflective of CP II, but the past crops up and renders agreement difficult.

Provisions for Territorial Exit

The cosmopolitan universal dimension of CP presumes that a polity permits human rights norms and universal conceptions of justice and fairness to play a core role in the determination of its critical internal issues. In one reading of CP, this also includes provisions for territorial exit.

In Canada, in the aftermath of the 1995 Quebec referendum, the federal Canadian government sought to clarify the legal framework surrounding a possible future Quebec secession referendum. The question of Quebec separation was taken to the Supreme Court which handed down its advisory opinion in 1998.[13] It stated that Quebec has no legal right – under Canadian or international law – to unilaterally secede from Canada. But it went on to note that:

> Our democratic institutions accommodate a continuous process of discussion and evolution, which is reflected in the constitutional right of each participant in the federation to initiate constitutional change. This implies a reciprocal duty on the other participants to engage in discussions to address any legitimate initiative to change the constitutional order. A clear majority vote in Quebec on a clear question in favour of secession would confer democratic legitimacy on the secession initiative which all of the other participants in Confederation would have to recognize.[14]

In 1999, the federal government established a set of more specific procedural guidelines for how secession might proceed through the so-called

Clarity Act (An Act to give effect to the requirement for clarity as set out in the opinion of the Supreme Court of Canada in the Quebec Secession Reference).

Canada is the only country in the world to have spelled out a set of democratic procedures for separation or break-up.[15] These apply not only to Quebec, but to any province. Actual negotiations with a province would not be bilateral – between the federal government and the relevant province – but would be conducted among all the governments of the provinces and the federal government.[16]

The secession reference at least to some extent takes inspiration from a cosmopolitan conception of political community. It notes that:

> The ultimate success of [an unconstitutional declaration of secession leading to a *de facto* secession] would be dependent on recognition by the international community, which is likely to consider the legality and legitimacy of secession, having regard to, amongst other facts, the conduct of Quebec and Canada, in determining whether to grant or withhold recognition.[17]

This statement can be seen to underline the role of global public opinion as a watchdog for upholding the condition of reciprocity. The emphasis on legitimacy serves as a powerful reminder of the need to act in a manner consistent with international standards of legitimacy. The statement cannot be construed to the effect that the international community should serve as *the* source of standards of legitimacy, but it is entirely consonant with the notion that democracy is based on universal principles whose proper sustenance requires that they be globally accepted and embraced.

Whether such provisions will comply with CP hinges on the critical issue as to what counts as a viable justification for territorial exit and further that the procedures for determining whether exit can take place are consistent with autonomy: they cannot violate private and public autonomies and their co-constitutive character.

It seems to me that the Canadian provisions for territorial exit may be somewhat consonant with CP II, for two reasons. First because the Canadian provisions do highlight the principle of reciprocity (although it is not clear until tried whether this principle will be properly embedded in actual practice), and second because it speaks to the central tenet of reflexivity, which is that any system of authority must justify itself to those affected by it – even to the extent of having recourse to physical withdrawal. It is also noteworthy here that the ECT's exit clause does not contain the same level of reciprocity.

Conclusion

In the above I have tried to clarify CP's ability to handle diversity. There are several different approaches to CP in the literature. I found that once we consider the issue of exit, which had not been systematically dealt with in the literature, it was possible to identify two notions of CP, each based on a distinctive constellation of voice, loyalty and exit. When we consider CP in relation to nationalism, it is quite clear that both versions of CP are based on constellations of voice, loyalty and exit that are distinctly different from those we can discern from nationalism. The two versions of CP identified here differ foremost on the state vs. cosmopolitan dimension.

I then discussed the two versions of CP in relation to the EU and Canada. I found that both Canada and the EU were trying to draw on CP, with mixed luck. I also found that Canada did not bear out the initial hypothesis: it appears to be closer to CP II than to CP I. The Union has sought to pursue both CP I and II, but whereas it may have tried to pursue CP I more strongly than has Canada, it has not succeeded. A critical difference between the EU and Canada is that whereas deliberations in Canada take place within the framework of democratic constitutionalism as guiding norm set, the key issue in the Union is *whether* there will continue to be a commitment to further constitutionalization. The norm set is clearly present also in the Union; what is at stake is this norm set's ability to shape the Union's self-conception as a democratic constitutional entity.

In my reading, the constitutional dimension is the key; it brings to bear the integrative and sanctioning power of the law and the state. What is particularly puzzling with CP then is precisely what is and should be the relation to the state. CP after all is premised on a cosmopolitan rather than a statist frame but how far from the state can we really go? It is here that these two cases can offer new and revealing insights. I tried to argue that Canada's commitment to CP II also has an element of cosmopolitanism built into it. Canada is therefore a very interesting case to follow in allegiance terms. One critical question is how far we may stretch stateness in a cosmopolitan direction before the system starts to unravel or starts to develop stronger more traditional forms of allegiance based on a territorially reconfigured entity.

Another is the status of constitution as contractual arrangement. CP, as Habermas has noted, should be associated with an alternative conception of constitution-making, that of constitution-making as an ongoing process. The Canadian situation is closer to a notion of constitution as an ongoing reflexive process (Chambers, 1998). The constitution might here be understood as a working arrangement, wherein basic rights are recognized and respected. This helps ensure that the discussion of essential questions of identity and belonging is conducted in a peaceful and respectful manner. The interesting question that the comparison of Canada and the EU can shed light on is whether these conditions can only be ensured within the institutions of the state or whether weaker institutional arrangements can also sustain them. How far from the state can CP really go?

Notes

1. On the analysis of the European Constitutional Treaty as a case of thick constitutional patriotism, see Kumm (2005). On the Canadian Charter as a case of constitutional patriotism, see Cairns (2003) and Fossum (2001).
2. I here draw on the categories developed by Hirschman in his famous *Exit, Voice and Loyalty* (1970) although I adapt them to suit my purposes.
3. Eriksen and Weigård note that in Habermas's more recent work (from the early 1990s on) 'we see the contours of a discourse-theoretical conception of the cosmopolitan order' (Eriksen and Weigård, 2003: 232). Note that this is a complex and contingent conception of cosmopolitanism.
4. Kymlicka (1998), in his assessment of Canadian multiculturalism policy, which has been widely critiqued for fostering ethnic ghettoization, underlines the state's strong identity forming role.
5. On this see Kymlicka (1995, 1998). See also Gagnon and Tully (2001) and Fossum (forthcoming).
6. The following analysis draws on Fossum (2003) but has been updated.
7. The ECJ only has jurisdiction on what regards articles TEU 35 and 40 as specifically provided in Article TEU 35, Section 1 and Article TEU 40, Section 4, second paragraph.
8. Citizens may have recourse to other legal instruments such as the national constitutional systems and the ECHR.
9. CHARTE 4105/00. See also European Commission (2000).
10. Speech by Stephane Dion to the 7th Triennial NACS Conference, Reykjavik, Iceland, August 1999.
11. The Canadian multiculturalism policy was introduced in 1971, and in 1988 it became officially enshrined in the Multiculturalism Act.
12. It should also be noted that the very doctrine of multiculturalism is debated and challenged.
13. *Reference Re Secession of Quebec*, [1998] 2 SCR 217.
14. *Reference Re Secession of Quebec*, [1998] 2 SCR 217.
15. Note that the Draft Treaty establishing a Constitution for Europe contains a provision (Article I-60) that permits voluntary withdrawal from the Union, CIG 87/2/04.
16. Bill C-20:3.1. <http://www.canlii.org/ca/as/2000/c26/sec3%2Ehtml>.
17. Canada, Supreme Court *Reference Re Secession of Quebec*, [1998] 2 SCR 217.

References

Bohman, J. (2005) 'Reflexive Constitution-making and Transnational Governance', in E. O. Eriksen (ed.), *Making the European Polity: Reflexive Integration in the EU*. London: Routledge.

Booth, W. J. (1999) 'Communities of Memory: On Identity, Memory, and Debt', *American Political Science Review*, 93(2): 249–63.

Cairns, A. C. (1988) *Constitution, Government, and Society in Canada: Selected Essays by Alan Cairns*. Toronto: McClelland and Stewart.

_____ (2003) 'The Canadian Experience of a Charter of Rights', in E. O. Eriksen, J. E. Fossum and A. J. Menéndez (eds), *The Chartering of Europe: The European Charter of Fundamental Rights and its Constitutional Implications*. Baden-Baden: Nomos.

Calhoun, C. (1992) *Habermas and the Public Sphere*. Cambridge, MA: MIT Press.

_____ (2002) 'Imagining Solidarity: Cosmopolitanism, Constitutional Patriotism, and the Public Sphere', *Public Culture*, 14: 147–72.

Canovan (2000) 'Patriotism is Not Enough', *British Journal of Political Science*, 30: 413–32.

Chambers, S. (1998) 'Contract or Conversation? Theoretical Lessons from the Canadian Constitutional Crisis', *Politics and Society*, 26: 143–72.

CHARTE 4105/00, *Record of the first meeting of the Body to draw up a draft Charter of Fundamental Rights of the European Union (held in Brussels, 17 December 1999), Convention on the Charter of Fundamental Rights*, Brussels, 13 January 2000.

CIG 87/2/04 REV 2, *Treaty establishing a Constitution for Europe*, Brussels, 29 October 2004.

Cronin, C. (2003) 'Democracy and Collective Identity: In Defence of Constitutional Patriotism', *European Journal of Philosophy*, 11(1): 1–28.

Duff, A. (2000) 'Towards a European Federal Society', in K. Feus (ed.), *The EU Charter of Fundamental Rights*. London: Kogan Page.

Eckhout, P. (2000) 'The Proposed EU Charter of Fundamental Rights: Some Reflections on its Effects in the Legal Systems of the EU and of its Member States', in K. Feus (ed.), *The EU Charter of Fundamental Rights*. London: Kogan Page.

Eriksen, E. O. (2003) 'Integration and the Quest for Consensus. On the Microfoundation of Supranationalism', in E. O. Eriksen, C. Joerges and J. Neyer (eds), *European Governance, Deliberation and the Quest for Democratisation*. ARENA Report 2/03, Oslo: ARENA.

_____ and Fossum, J. E. (eds) (2000) *Democracy in the European Union: Integration through Deliberation?* London: Routledge.

_____ and Weigård, J. (2003) *Understanding Habermas*. London: Continuum.

European Commission (2000) 'Communication from the Commission on the legal nature of the Charter of Fundamental Rights of the European Union', *COM (2000) 644 final*, Brussels, 11 October.

Fossum, J. E. (2001) 'Deep Diversity versus Constitutional Patriotism: Taylor, Habermas and the Canadian Constitutional Crisis', *Ethnicities*, 1: 179–206.

_____ (2003) 'The European Charter – Between Deep Diversity and Constitutional Patriotism', in E. O. Eriksen, J. E. Fossum and A. J. Menéndez (eds), *The Chartering of Europe: The European Charter of Fundamental Rights and its Constitutional Implications*. Baden-Baden: Nomos.

______ (2004) 'Still a Union of Deep Diversity? The Convention and the Constitution for Europe', in E. O. Eriksen, J. E. Fossum and A. J. Menéndez (eds), *Developing a Constitution for Europe*, London: Routledge.

Fossum, J. E. (forthcoming) 'The Transformation of the Nation-state: the EU and Canada Compared', in M. Maduro and D. Halberstam (eds), *The Constitutional Challenge: People, Power and Politics in Europe and America*. Cambridge: Cambridge University Press.

Gagnon, A.-G. and Tully, J. (2001) *Multinational Democracies*. Cambridge: Cambridge University Press.

Habermas, J. (1974) *Theory and Practice*. London: Heinemann. Translated by J. Viertel.

______ (1994) 'Struggles for Recognition in the Democratic Constitutional State', in C. Taylor and A. Gutmann (eds), *Multiculturalism*. Princeton, NJ: Princeton University Press.

______ (1996) *Between Facts and Norms: Contributions to a Discourse Theory of Law and Democracy*. Cambridge, MA: MIT Press.

______ (1998) *The Inclusion of the Other*. Cambridge: Polity Press.

______ (2001a) 'Constitutional Democracy: A Paradoxical Union of Contradictory Principles', *Political Theory*, 29: 766–81.

______ (2001b) *The Postnational Constellation*. Cambridge, MA: MIT Press.

Hirschman, A. O. (1970) *Exit, Voice and Loyalty*. Harvard, MA: Harvard University Press.

Ingram, A. (1996) 'Constitutional Patriotism', *Philosophy & Social Criticism*, 22(6): 1–18.

Kumm, M. (2005) 'To be a European Citizen: Constitutional Patriotism and the Treaty Establishing a Constitution for Europe', in E. O. Eriksen, J. E. Fossum, M. Kumm and A. J. Menéndez (eds), *The European Constitution: The Rubicon Crossed?* ARENA Report No 3/05, Oslo: ARENA.

Kymlicka, W. (1995) *Multicultural Citizenship. A Liberal Theory of Minority Rights*. Oxford: Oxford University Press.

______ (1998) *Finding Our Way*. Oxford: Oxford University Press.

Lacroix, J. (2002) 'For a European Constitutional Patriotism', *Political Studies*, 50: 944–58.

Lenaerts, K. and de Smijter, E. (2001) 'A "Bill of Rights" for the European Union', *Common Market Law Review*, 38: 273–300.

Markell, P. (2000) 'Making Affect Safe for Democracy? On "Constitutional Patriotism"', *Political Theory*, 28: 38–63.

Menéndez, A. J. (2003) '"Rights to Solidarity": Balancing Solidarity and Economic Freedoms', E. O. Eriksen, J. E. Fossum and A. J. Menéndez (eds), *The Chartering of Europe: The European Charter of Fundamental Rights and its Constitutional Implications*. Baden-Baden: Nomos.

Michelman, F. I. (1999) 'Morality, Identity and "Constitutional Patriotism"', *Denver University Law Review*, 76(4): 1009–28.

Morton, F. L. (Ted) and Knopff, R. (2000) *The Charter Revolution and the Court Party*. Peterborough: Broadview Press.

Norman, W. (1995) 'The Ideology of Shared Values: A Myopic Vision of Unity in the Multi-nation State', in J. H. Carens (ed.), *Is Quebec Nationalism Just? Perspectives from Anglophone Canada*. Montreal & Kingston: McGill-Queen's University Press.

_____ (2001) 'Justice and Stability in Multinational Societies', in A.-G. Gagnon and J. Tully (eds), *Multinational Democracies*. Cambridge: Cambridge University Press.

Schneiderman, D. (1998) 'Harold Laski, Viscount Haldane, and the Law of the Canadian Constitution in the Early Twentieth Century', *University of Toronto Law Journal*, 48.

Taylor, C. (1993) *Reconciling the Solitudes: Essays on Canadian Federalism and Nationalism*. Montreal: McGill-Queen's University Press.

Weiler, J. H. H. (2001) 'Federalism without Constitutionalism: Europe's Sonderweg', in K. Nicolaidis and R. Howse (eds), *The Federal Vision*. Oxford: Oxford University Press.

8
Beyond Community and Rights: European Citizenship and the Virtues of Participation[1]

Richard Bellamy and Dario Castiglione

The return of the citizen

The revival of citizenship studies over the past 20 years has been associated with two sets of related challenges to the liberal democratic regimes of nation-states. The first set consists of the challenges to national political cultures posed by ethnic diversity and minority nationalism within the state, and globalization (often associated with commercialization and Americanization) without. These developments have prompted debates over the importance of nationality and a shared culture as sources of reciprocity and allegiance between citizens and between citizens and the state. For example, academics and policy-makers have fiercely debated such issues as the content of civic education in schools and the degree to which naturalized citizens should be obliged not just to adhere to the political norms of the host nation but also to acquire certain its social and other cultural characteristics, such as the dominant religion and language. The second set of challenges stems from the political, social and administrative problems posed by the growing electoral apathy of citizens, the fiscal crisis of the welfare system, and the transformations of the relationship between the public and private sectors induced by neo-liberal policies. These developments have also been broadly linked to market-driven global forces and a multicultural concern with recognition at the expense of the politics of redistribution. They have given rise to debates over the degree to which markets or the law prove better than democratic politics at enabling citizens to influence public and private producers and service providers and hold them accountable.

Both sets of challenges have led social and political scientists to investigate the presuppositions of citizenship and to ask whether the role of the citizen can be adapted to a context that goes beyond a form of liberal democracy linked to the nation-state. The first set of challenges is evident in the concern of sociologists, in particular with the rules of membership that give access to citizenship and in comparing the responses of different social systems to the growth in immigration (Brubacker, 1992). There has also been a related debate amongst political theorists over the degree to which liberalism and democracy either conflict with or assume some form of national political community. Both discussions are related to an earlier clash between liberals and their communitarian critics prompted by the second set of challenges. Communitarians had argued that liberals encouraged a self-defeating form of extreme individualism by concentrating on rights to the neglect of the claims of society and the common good. By offering a link between issues of entitlement and just distribution, on the one hand, and issues of membership and solidarity, on the other, the theory of democratic citizenship promised a synthesis of – but also, as Will Kymklica has remarked (Kymlicka, 2002: 284–318; Kymlicka and Norman, 1994: 352–81), a kind of 'strategic retreat' from – this argument, which it was felt had reached an *impasse*. However, the opposition between these positions resurfaced recently and connected to the debates over the first set of challenges in the current discussions surrounding cosmopolitan theories of global democracy and the claims of international justice.

In various ways, therefore, contemporary accounts of citizenship have concentrated on either a communitarian concern with belonging or a liberal concern with rights. In both cases, a more traditional focus on political participation has taken second place. For communitarians it arises only when a people or demos shares a common good and values through belonging to a relatively homogeneous and circumscribed political community. For liberals, democracy is but one, and not necessarily the best, means for individuals to exercise and secure their rights. Indeed, in a global and market-oriented society, the law and impartial regulators may be superior guarantors of individual rights. For them, citizenship is a matter of entitlement rather than political participation or civic commitment. Yet, as republicans of different hues point out, it is through participation that rights are created and defended and communities built (Oldfield, 1990; Pettit, 1999).

The debate on European citizenship draws upon, but does not entirely belong to, the recent revival of interest in the citizen's role and character. It first developed within a more juridical and administrative discourse, which had the prime aim of defining the specific, primarily economic, rights and liberties that accrue to member state nationals in relation to the nascent European juridical space. However, the often contradictory demands that lie behind criticism of EU's legitimacy have pushed this discussion beyond that early stage, leading it to take on board the current preoccupations of sociologists, political scientists, theorists, politicians and policy-makers rehearsed above – even if traces of the original legal bias remain. Consequently, the political aspects of citizenship have been understood mainly in terms of a bundle of rights that define the status of the citizen, while the social aspects have been interpreted almost exclusively in terms of criteria for admission or membership. It is our contention that this perspective offers a partial and partly misleading genealogy of the historical forms of citizenship, one that unduly reflects the dominant concern with belonging and rights of recent studies and the juridical framework within which EU citizenship initially developed. The purpose of this chapter is to offer a more adequate normative model of the citizen that fits not only with the development of the European political order, but also makes sense of its historical roots in the modern languages of democratic citizenship where participation is central.

One way of exploring the ways citizenship as participation, rights and belonging interact with each other is by seeing them as different aspects of how citizens accept the legitimacy of any organization. This acceptance depends on the congruence between four dimensions of its operation.[2] On the one hand, it must be deemed legitimate at what might be called the 'polity' level. This level involves the acceptance of its *sphere* of operation as legitimate, be that decided territorially or on the basis of particular tasks or functions, and on those who are controlled by it being legitimately considered (and considering themselves) its *subjects*. On the other hand, it must be deemed legitimate at what might be called the 'regime' level. This entails that citizens consider the political system legitimate in the sense of both the *styles* of politics it employs and their *scope*. In other words, the regime's style must be thought to be sufficiently democratic in terms of its representativeness, the operation of elections and so on, and it must be deemed not to intervene into non-political areas.

All four dimensions (the *sphere* and *subjects* of the polity, and the *style* and *scope* of the regime) can be said to have an 'external' (objective) and an 'internal' (subjective) aspect that reflect rights and belonging respectively. From a more objective perspective, all four must meet certain minimum standards of justice. Yet subjectively, citizens must also identify with them as somehow 'theirs'. After all, Britain, France, Italy and Germany all subscribe to the objective legitimacy standards set by such international rights charters as the European Convention on Human Rights. However, their citizens still identify themselves as British, French,

Italian and German and would be unhappy with a proposal suggesting, say, that we now consider the German regime as that of Europe as a whole and send our representatives to its parliament and so on. Indeed, within all these countries there are minorities, such as the Scottish in Britain, who desire a separate polity and regime of their own. In these cases, the regime and polity of Germany and Britain respectively may meet objective standards of legitimacy but they lack subjective legitimacy.

Why is identification with a regime and polity important? Part of the reason lies in the fact that agreement on the objective criteria exists at a fairly abstract level and there is considerable scope for disagreement on how they should be interpreted when applied to particular cases. All these countries recognize rights to freedom of speech and privacy, for example, yet interpret them in very different ways. Details of a politician's private life are not considered a matter of legitimate public interest in Germany, but in Britain they are with the result that British newspapers can publish matters that German papers may be prevented from revealing. To accept the validity of such differences one need not rely on some form of communitarian-based relativism, merely an acknowledgment that a plurality of reasonable views of rights is possible. Indeed, alternative positions are generally articulated by different ideological, cultural and interest groupings within any given community. Citizenship as participation comes in here; for it has traditionally been the way a people who feel they belong together have democratically decided how they should understand their rights and establish fair rules of co-operation.

The next three sections will explore how far this synthesis of belonging, rights and participation can hold together given the challenges confronting the nation-state, using the EU as an example. The next section will explore the attempt to ground European citizenship in a sense of Europeanness, while the section after that will examine the claim that the EU can offer a new form of post-national citizenship linked to rights. Both proposals are found wanting. By contrast, the subsequent section outlines the prospects of employing a form of participatory citizenship as the source of both belonging and rights not only in the EU, but also more generally in any modern complex society.

Citizenship as belonging: a European Community?

When the policy of European citizenship was first mooted, it was conceived as providing a symbol of identification with the EU. As such, it went along with such other symbolic measures as the introduction of a

European passport, anthem and flag. The hope was that as the member states pooled certain sovereign powers, so citizens would in some appropriate sense also pool their national identities. Access to EU citizenship rights would stem from and help promote identification with the EU as a polity within its given sphere.

This policy arose out of the belief that the pattern of legitimacy within the EU must mirror that of the nation-state and stem from a citizenship of belonging based on certain symmetry between sovereignty and identity. According to the ideal of the nation-state, for a people to exercise self-government they must identify with each other and with the polity and its regime, which must be sovereign within its own territory. As the demands of minority nationalities have brought to light, this match between a sovereign state and a single people was rather less common than the ideologists of the nation-state assumed. Yet sovereignty and identity in both the EU and the member states are now pulling apart in new and dramatic ways, undermining any form of citizenship that assumes a neat overlap between them.

An analysis of each of these terms reveals why. Sovereignty refers to the possession and exercise of power. It is an attribute of both the polity and the regime aspects of any organization. The polity aspect of sovereignty concerns where, over whom and by whom power is exercised, thereby connecting respectively to the sphere and subjects of politics. It involves both the domestic exercise of power over and by subjects within defined spheres, and the foreign employment of power to defend or extend the polity. The regime aspect of sovereignty concerns the ways power is exercised. As such, it connects to the scope and styles of politics, both in the domestic and the foreign arena.

With a certain degree of exaggeration, which reflects the historical origin of the idea within the context of monarchical absolutism, sovereignty is often assumed to be an absolute and unitary condition (James, 1999). A regime must possess total constitutional independence and be the supreme authority in the way it governs the territory and people of an autonomous polity. This condition entails that any dispersal of power must be vertical and hierarchically ordered. Thus, federalism standardly represents a vertical parcelling out of the polity aspect of sovereignty, with powers being delegated from the centre, which retains the final say. Likewise, the separation of powers usually consists of a vertical distribution of the regime aspect of sovereignty, with one of the branches being more decisive than the others, though which branch – the executive, legislature or judiciary – differs between political systems and even according to the issue.

Identity refers to the internal aspects of legitimacy. As we noted above, a legitimate polity requires subjects to identify with both each other and the boundaries defining the political sphere, whilst a legitimate regime involves citizens regarding their identities as adequately recognized by the prevailing styles and scope of politics. As we also remarked, a polity and its regime may meet perfectly acceptable external standards of legitimacy and yet fail to satisfy internal expectations. If a national minority do not identify with one or other aspects of the polity, then it and its regime will be unacceptable no matter how unexceptionable its procedures might be. Similarly, a regime may enshrine just principles, but the ways they are implemented can still fail to recognize the identities of certain groups. For example, the ability of linguistic minorities to participate fully in politics will be hindered if they cannot do so in their own tongue, even if the system enshrines equal voting rights for all. Legitimacy requires some congruence between sovereignty and identity, therefore, even if such an identity has more often been a matter of history and civic engagement than of ethnicity and culture.[3] In other words, where power is situated, over whom, by whom, how it is exercised and for what purpose must all match the ways people conceive of themselves and of their relationships with each other.

The ideology, if not necessarily the reality, of the Westphalian state system, assumed this fit existed within the nation-state. Its achievement was to bring together territory (sphere), functions (scope) and people (subjects) within a single political system (style). Where other political identities and units existed, these were embedded within, and so subordinate to, the larger political identity and unit. Thus, Britishness was supposed to accommodate English, Welsh, Scottish and Northern Irish identities. Each region formed a part of the United Kingdom, with their local governments feeding into the Westminster system. As this example indicates, this hierarchical and unitary organization of sovereignty and identity was never wholly uncontentious and today it clearly is not. Both the polity and the regime aspects of sovereignty have been challenged, with identity being similarly affected.

With regard to the polity aspect, greater interconnectedness at the international level and greater heterogeneity at the local and regional levels have undermined not only the functional efficacy of states to frame independent socio-economic and security policies, but also their ability to draw on or forge a national identity capable of sustaining an allegiance to either the public good or the collective institutions and decisions that define and uphold it. Externally, states have become increasingly involved in and subject to international bodies, with a concomitant loss of power.

Internally, minority nations have argued in consequence that they can be as viable as the larger political units to which they currently belong, and have demanded greater autonomy and even independence. Likewise, immigrant groups look for recognition of their ethnic identities in special rights and group representation. Meanwhile, a more diffuse and fragmented set of attachments that are both sub-national and transnational in character have developed amongst people generally. For example, the ties of family, work, ideology, religion and sport increasingly operate either below or beyond the nation-state, competing with and diluting any sense of a purely national identity.

The regime aspect of sovereignty and identity is also affected. We must now confront a situation of multiple and interacting *demoi*. This circumstance has profound consequences for where and when democratic decision-making can take place, amongst whom and about what. Increasingly, different policies will generate very different answers to each of these elements. This fact also poses challenges to how we apply democratic norms, potentially questioning the suitability of simple majority rule, formal conceptions of the rule of law and notions of equal citizenship should these fail to protect minority interests or respond to important differences of context. As a consequence, multinational states such as Britain, Belgium and Canada – but also more unitary ones such as France, Italy and Spain – are evolving new styles and scopes of politics to cope with this situation, introducing a hitherto unprecedented degree of constitutional and democratic complexity (for a survey, see Austin and O'Neill, 2000).

The EU emerges from these self-same forces, being both a mechanism whereby nation-states have responded to these changes and a challenge to their current polity and regime sovereignty and the identification their citizens have with them (Milward, 1993; Scharpf, 1999). Compared to the member states, though, the EU's nascent polity and regime are even more complex. Within the EU, function and territory are pulling apart, producing growing disjunctures between its territorial and its functional membership in core policy areas. As a result, it is developing into a poly-centric polity with a multilevel regime. This process involves the redistribution of sovereignty and the creation of multiple political identities (Ruggie, 1993: 172). For example, in monetary policy Britain, Denmark and Sweden stand aloof. Indeed, different polices tend to involve different types of territorial actors operating in different sorts of institutional settings. In many cases, the actors are sub- or transnational rather than national, with the comitology process involving private as well as public agents and agencies. Moreover, representatives in even the same body are often selected in different ways by their respective constituencies, as in elections to the EP. The jurisdictions – the spheres and subjects – of these various bodies are not clearly demarcated, they often have different powers in different parts of the EU and they employ different styles and possess different scopes of politics. Nor is there any overarching authority to decide disputes between them. Except in very restricted domains, such as certain aspects of competition policy, the EU has few exclusive competences and has not asserted its hierarchical control over the member states. Meanwhile, European citizens increasingly view their political engagement less, or not solely, as a general commitment to a particular party and system, and more as a concern with various causes and issues (Klingemann and Fuchs, 1995). Though voting is in decline, non-electoral political participation is in the ascendant. As a result, people have become members of a range of new alliances, some national, others sub-national and many of a transnational nature, and (as we noted) now operate as members of multiple *demoi*.

A standard hierarchical account would regard these different identities and their corresponding centres of decision-making either as operating at distinct levels or as components of an evermore overarching political identity and system, with the regional being nested within the national and the national within the European. However, neither of these models works entirely in either functional and institutional or personal terms. European measures are not discreet, they alter the shape of domestic politics – introducing new subjects, namely resident citizens from other member states, and new spheres, by giving economic, foreign, security and justice policy a significant European dimension; whilst altering its scope, through the need above all to ensure the freedom of capital, goods, services and labour within the Union, and its styles – from European elections and referenda, through the raising of European issues within domestic politics, to the enhancement of executive power offered by the intergovernmental aspects of EU decision-making. At the same time, national, sub-national and transnational concerns continue to shape European integration and policy-making.

A citizenship of belonging on the nation-state model will not work for the EU, therefore. We belong to too many polities – our member states, our issue and interest groups, our ideological and cultural communities, and so on. Nor are these neatly ordered in a hierarchical way. We cannot either treat belonging to the EU as an all-encompassing form of identity, enabling us to be European-British, European-Christians, European-socialists and so on. Nor can we regard these as discrete identities, so that I am British for certain purposes and a European citizen for others.

Thus, identification with the EU arises for the most part in combination with other identities, interacting and occasionally conflicting with them (Bellamy and Castiglione, 1997a). The multiplication of polities and regimes, operating at different levels of aggregation and attracting varying degrees of identification, changes the character of both the external and the internal legitimacy either of these can assert. The task is to find an account of citizenship that can make normative sense of these multiple forms of belonging.

Citizenship as rights: a European constitutional patriotism?

The weakening of national sovereign power has led some commentators to believe the answer must lie in a post-national citizenship grounded in rights. Rights have long offered the dominant approach to citizenship within the liberal tradition and inform its interpretation of the constitutional practices of liberal democracies. This liberal model conceives rights, the rule of law and constitutional democracy in largely juridical terms (Bellamy and Castiglione, 1997b). Although there are different variants of this juridical paradigm (British, American and broadly European), they all concentrate on the importance of legal mechanisms for controlling the abuse of power and protecting individuals. Their aim is to secure a just framework of rights within which citizens and the government can legitimately act. The resulting liberal constitution lays out the entitlements and obligations of citizens vis-à-vis both the state and each other. It constrains what individuals may do to or expect of others and what the state may do to or expect of them. As a consequence, rights define not only the subjects of the polity but also its sphere and the scope and styles of its regime.

Developing this liberal thesis, John Rawls has argued that citizens of a liberal democracy share an overlapping consensus on political rights (Rawls, 1993). The citizens of a state that upholds these principles of political justice not only should be obliged to obey it, but also, because they share these rights, will actually feel an allegiance to it. Thus, a polity possessing a just regime will be stable over time. In a similar spirit, Habermas maintains that it is the just political culture of a state that binds us to it, rather than nationality or some other social, religious or ethnic cultural force (Habermas, 1996). We identify with a polity because of a constitutional patriotism stemming from the justice of its regime. In the Rawlsian scenario, if EU institutions embody standard liberal democratic rights to which all adult members have access through being citizens, they should give substantial and permanent support to them.

Habermas concurs, but suggests, at least on some occasions, a partial thickening of the Rawlsian consensus. He shares Rawls's belief that European citizens should identify with EU institutions if they are just, but adds they also do so because they reflect a distinctly European (as opposed to American, say) political tradition that results from a particular historical process. Nevertheless, this European political culture is fundamentally political rather than cultural. For instance, it is characterized by a commitment to a welfare state and the abolition of the death penalty (the main contrasts Habermas draws between Europe and the US in this regard). Like Rawls's overlapping consensus, therefore, Habermas's constitutional patriotism ultimately issues from the rights presupposed by democracy.

There are two problems with the Rawlsian and Habermasian arguments. First, as we noted in the last section, rights may provide a source of objective legitimation for an organization, but they are at best a necessary rather than a sufficient condition for subjective legitimation. In part, this arises because Rawls and Habermas elide the legitimacy of a regime with that of its polity. However, a regime may be objectively legitimate yet fail to attract the subjective allegiance of all its citizens because they question the legitimacy of the polity within which it operates. By contrast, citizens of an objectively illegitimate regime often offer it tacit support because they subjectively identify with the polity – presumably many Iraqis felt like this under Saddam. Likewise, a polity may be objectively legitimate, in the sense of not being the result of recent conquest or colonization, but still lack subjective polity legitimacy among a cultural minority. Moreover, this absence of subjective polity legitimacy may lead citizens to question the legitimacy of the regime, even if it meets fairly abstract democratic criteria. For example, few if any Quebec nationalists would deny that Canada is democratic *per se*. Their own view of rights and democracy are more or less the same as Canadian federalists in abstract terms. But they do feel that in the context of the existing Canadian polity its political regime lacks democratic legitimacy because, in their view, the French territories cannot deploy these rights in ways that reflect their cultural interests.

The second problem kicks in here. As we noted, in the liberal tradition rights supposedly define politics. Consequently, they cannot themselves be matters of normal political debate. In fact, the rationale behind constitutional bills of rights is to allow their judicial protectors to overturn or constrain political decisions that offer supposedly illegitimate interpretations of rights or appear to neglect them altogether. In Rawls's theory, the potential tension between democracy and rights is resolved by arguing that liberal democracy assumes a consensus on certain political, civil and social rights. Habermas approaches the same issue from the opposite direction, as it were. In his view, a consensus on rights is both the endpoint and the presupposition or rationale of democratic deliberation. We discuss with others in order to (and because we can) agree on rights. The difficulty with both theories is that beyond the most abstract level, and sometimes even here, there is considerable disagreement about the foundations and character of rights, and how they apply to particular issues. Moreover, debates about rights not only provide the substance of many political debates, they also produce different accounts of the nature of the political.

Take the main ideological divide within liberal democracies between libertarians and social democrats. As Table 8.1 shows, these two positions generate contrasting views of rights. These different conceptions lie behind the main contemporary political divisions, animating debates about the welfare state, the regulation of the market economy and so on. Moreover, there can be no overarching theory of rights that encompasses both positions. For these, views conflict in often incompatible ways.

Table 8.1

	Libertarian	*Social Democrat*
Legal Rights (liberties and immunities)	Formally equal -ve liberties	Formally equal -ve liberties through certain immunities for reasons of substantive equality and linked to social rights to defend their equal worth
Political Rights (powers)	Protective, limited	Protective and informative, limited
Social Rights (claims)	Few (mainly insurance and compensatory) or none	Broad range: including enabling and distributive as well as insurance and compensatory
Civic Rights (powers)	Few (consumer) or none Strict divide between state/civil society, public/private	Workers and consumer Need for state to regulate and balance civil society
Duties	Of respect, with duties subordinate to rights	Of concern and respect, with duties being corollary of rights

Part of the reason for the intractable character of their conflict arises from the fact that, as Table 8.2 reveals, each offers a different view of all four of the dimensions of politics.

Thus, debates between libertarians and social democrats are not within a political framework of rights, they are about that framework.

The same goes for citizenship. It too is not constructed by a set of political rights. Rather, citizenship has been about the claiming of rights and the constitution of the political realm. Thus, workers in the nineteenth century did not just seek to become subjects (by obtaining the vote) in an otherwise unchanged political system. They sought to extend the sphere of politics through the introduction of industrial democracy, to change its scope by allowing greater regulation of the economy, including public ownership of certain industries, and to alter its styles, through such measures as recognizing the right to strike. Women campaigners made similarly broad demands when claiming the franchise that likewise aspired to change both polity and regime. In the late twentieth and early twenty-first centuries, the political demands of cultural minorities have been if anything even more dramatic. For example, Britain has

Table 8.2

	Libertarian	*Social Democrat*
Subjects	All autonomous agents capable of entering legally recognized contracts, particularly in the economic sphere	All autonomous agents capable of entering legally recognized contracts, including social and political sphere
Spheres	Political a narrowly defined public framework for social interaction. Political discussion and intervention, if not regulation, inappropriate within a broad private sector.	Political a more broadly defined public framework for social interaction. Political discussion and intervention, if not regulation, inappropriate within a narrower private sector.
Scope	To protect the natural -ve freedom and formal equality of individuals	To foster autonomy by preserving the broader -ve freedom and more substantive equality of individuals and classes
Styles	Constrained maximization to achieve mutual advantage via market trading	Constrained maximization to achieve mutual benefit via pluralist bargaining

introduced new devolutionary structures to accommodate the demands of Scottish, Welsh and Northern Irish communities, with potentially new regional assemblies for parts of England as well. These have changed all four dimensions of politics within the UK – possibly rather more so than was initially foreseen. However, it cannot be argued that these various challenges will give rise to an ever-expanding set of com-possible rights, as Habermas appears to suggest. For these challenges often clash with each other, are both regressive and progressive, and set up tensions that give rise to fresh demands as part of an ongoing process through which citizens continuously reconstitute both polity and regime.

Needless to say, the EU represents a major change to the nature of politics within all the member states. There has been a tendency to view EU citizenship as simply a grant of rights by the member states that legitimates, but does not change, the existing EU structures. In other words, rights offer an objective form of legitimacy that citizens should embrace and identify with. Yet citizens are clearly ambivalent about the EU. Most may welcome it, but their identification with it is qualified in numerous ways. In particular, there are endless debates over both its polity dimensions – does it do too much or too little – and the character of its regime – too intergovernmental and insufficiently federal, or vice versa. Consequently, European citizens have not been mere passive recipients of rights.

For example, in a rather fragmented way, reflecting both the lack of a common European public sphere and the non-hierarchical structure of decision-making, citizens' pressure has forced onto the political agenda environmental, food safety and other risk-related issues. By so doing, they have redefined the sphere and the subjects of democratic politics by appealing to an enlarged conception of affectedness cutting across national boundaries. Although this is not an exclusively European phenomenon, the integration process is an ideal terrain for addressing many of the concerns citizens have with regard to the risks they face as consumers in a more global and integrated network of production and distribution. The same applies to the new patterns of mobility and communication that the integration process has both reflected and encouraged. Just as these have contributed to the creation of the new status of European citizenship for member state nationals, so they have also posed the problem of equal treatment for third-country nationals and the extension of their rights of residence. Similarly, the formation of a European juridical space has facilitated struggles and demands for the extension of civil rights at a national and sub-national level, altering in the process the style and scope of local politics. Finally, the EU has simultaneously encouraged the homogenization of citizenship rights at the transnational level while encouraging their differentiation at a local level by fostering demands for the recognition of certain forms of cultural, ethnic and linguistic diversity, which previously had been denied within national regimes. In sum, rights do not constitute and cannot of their own accord legitimately constrain politics or citizenship. Rather, they are themselves constituted through citizenship activity. If the EU is to be seen as a remaking of the politics of the nation-state, then we need a language of citizenship that mirrors their part in this process.

Citizenship as participation: the role of civic engagement

The rights and belonging paradigms offer rather 'passive' and mainly 'vertical' views of citizenship. The former tends to establish citizenship either as a series of individual and mainly 'private' entitlements (in the liberal version) or as 'clientelistic' claims against the administrative state (in the social democratic version). The latter treats the acquisition of citizenship as the product of natural bonding, acculturation and socialization. These processes supposedly define the citizen's sense of identity, determining how he or she acts and thereby qualifying him or her for this status. Both views posit a relationship between the individual and a larger, superordinate entity – the state or the community – as the essence of what being a citizen is about. Moreover, as we have seen in the previous sections, both views tend to reduce the role and importance of disagreement as an essential component of politics.

However, disagreement is an inherent feature of coexistence and cooperation in societies operating in the normal 'circumstances of justice', with relative scarcity and limited altruism (Rawls, 1971).[4] Its origins lie as much in the imperfections of human character and social arrangements (bad faith, self-interest, entrenched forms of injustice) as in the plurality of values, conditions and lifestyles of modern societies; besides reflecting the sheer complexity of political issues and social cooperation. The resulting disagreements give rise to what Jeremy Waldron has described as the 'circumstances of politics': the condition of having to reach agreement on collective policies (including the constitution of the polity and its regime) in the face of disagreements about the right and the good (Waldron, 1999: 102). Citizenship-as-participation comes in here, as the way in which citizens, as equal and full members of a political community (a 'horizontal' as well as a 'vertical' bond), actively engage with each other in order to create and re-create the conditions in which they can address the 'circumstances of politics'. They do so by trying to agree on the more objective and universalistic aspects of legitimacy (norms, values, rights, duties), and by establishing the more subjective and local forms of legitimacy (affiliation, identity and solidarity) that can sustain them.

Disagreement enters into politics, therefore, producing an ongoing political constitutionalism whereby a polity and its regime is continually reconstituted more appropriately to recognize, respect and represent the values, opinions and vital interests of its members. The side-lining of the participation paradigm in the process of European integration, and the almost exclusive focus on rights and identity issues, has resulted in timidity in recognizing the legitimate role citizens have in the constitutionalization of the EU. This is also due to a misunderstanding of the nature of citizens' participation in modern, complex societies. We shall examine this timidity and the misunderstanding in turn.

If few theorists share our belief that citizens' actions and struggles do and should play a continuous constitutive role in establishing rights, obligations and political practices, many are willing to grant them a part in rare moments of exceptional constitutional change. Though we have disputed the implied distinction between normal and constitutional politics (see Bellamy and Castiglione, 1997b), believing momentous change often and more readily occurs as the result of cumulative and incremental shifts in people's opinions, values and institutional practices, it is nonetheless true that in many democracies some kind of formal popular consultation and debate is deemed necessary for a major reform of the constitution. How far Europe is going through such a constitutional moment remains a moot point. The failed ratification of the proposed Constitutional Treaty suggests there is at best little enthusiasm and at worst considerable antagonism for such a step. Yet, in spite of the indeterminacy of the pace and direction of the constitutionalization process, it remains true that over the past few years the EU has embarked upon a self-conscious constitution-building exercise that has attempted to rationalize the EU's institutional architecture and define its scope, values and legal personality (Castiglione et al., 2007).

In the EU context, supporters of both the rights and the belonging views of citizenship have put great store by these 'constitutional moments', since they regard the formal declaration of the Charter and/or the Constitutional Treaty as an essential condition for fixing the rights and political identity of EU citizens. Liberals of different shades consistently argued for the Charter to be both legally binding and fully incorporated into the constitutional text. For they consider incorporation essential to establish a conception of personhood based on equal dignity and a certain degree of security in one's liberties. Besides, from a democratic perspective, they regard the proclamation of the fundamental rights of European citizens as a way of giving legal substance to the European *demos* and the creation of a public communicative sphere for opinion formation (Eriksen, 2001; Habermas, 2001; Rodotà, 2001). For their part, communitarians, who wish Europe to become a new civic nation, have clamoured (albeit with less success) for the introduction of core substantive values into the constitutional document. They argue that what holds Europeans together is their common historical, religious and cultural heritage. Giscard d'Estaing's claim that Turkey is ethnically and culturally too different to be allowed to join is illustrative of this position.

Yet, in spite of the importance that advocates of the rights and belonging paradigms put on formal constitutionalization, they have paid little attention to the role that citizens might play in it. Both camps seem satisfied with the very indirect way in which citizens were represented in the two conventions, through a low-key self-selecting process occurring within current institutions. There has been little concern over the conspicuous lack of public interest in these proceedings or the minimal press coverage it has received. Some of the initiatives organized to give public visibility to the convention proceedings have been rather perfunctory, as in the case of the Youth convention, while the attempt to involve citizens more directly through the participation of civil society organizations has been largely symbolic and not thoroughly thought out. Indeed, at the 2002 Social Forum in Florence denunciations were made of the aloofness of the convention process from the debate about Europe and its geopolitical place in a globalized world – the issue that truly concerns the peoples of Europe.[5] The only formal role that citizens have been assigned, and only in those few cases where a member state's domestic procedures require it, is to vote in referenda in the final phase of the ratification process. After the experiences of the Danish referendum on Maastricht and the Irish on Nice, however, even such limited involvement is considered problematic. There seems to have been a presumption that popular consent should only serve to rubberstamp whatever agreements had already been made between governments and the Commission. It remains to be seen whether the French and Dutch 'No' will alter this attitude. Certainly, the natural reaction of the EU elite, as it appears from the way in which they are trying to avoid popular involvement in the approval of the new Treaty instead of the Constitution, does not appear to be encouraging (Castiglione, 2006; Castiglione et al., 2007: 244–51).

The extremely limited role allowed for citizens' direct participation is sometimes attributed to the relative lack of urgency and momentousness with which institutional reform is seen by the European citizens and the difficulty of arousing popular interest in rather complicated issues of institutional engineering that seem to have no direct or tangible impact on policy. But this is clearly not true of the series of crucial decisions taken by the EU and the member states over the past few years that have precipitated the present round of constitution-building. Enlargement and monetary union are constitution-making events with clear policy implications, and yet public discussion at European level has been carefully managed and often curtailed. Where it has surfaced at national level, as in the British case about the Euro, it has been due more to the presence of a strong popular opposition (often opportunistically manipulated by part of the elite opposed to any form of integration) than to a genuine openness to a considered and well-informed public debate. Indeed, the full social and political implications of some of the policy and institutional decisions taken as part of the establishment of a European common currency, such as the 'stability pact', the role of the European Central Bank, and the price-stability criteria, have only just begun to be publicly debated. The rigidity of some of the structures and policies put in place has given rise to calls for reform from many, often quite disparate, quarters. However, these calls have met with strong resistance – not just from the institutional centre of the EU, but also from many member states, who fear that any change may undermine the whole structure of macro-economic policy put together in the wake of monetary union, whose legitimacy it is felt rests more on the painstaking way in which administrative decisions were arrived at than any clear popular support.

It is evident that at a macro-political level, Europeanization has resulted in a timid approach to the virtues of democratic debate and democratic decision-making. This timidity is largely due to the difficulty of imagining democracy in conditions where there seems to be no unified *demos* capable of speaking with a single voice. It also reflects a very narrow interpretation of what is meant by citizenship as 'the right to have rights' (Lefort, 1998). On the Aristotelian view, the *right* to have rights is what makes citizens' participation not just possible but essential to their very role. However, this expression can also be interpreted in a very different way, to mean simply the already given *set of rights* that come with the right of citizenship. This alternative view belongs to the juridified conception of politics propounded by modern liberalism and typifies postwar constitutionalism. Indeed, many American authors, citing the use of this phrase by the US Supreme Court, treat it as a summary of the more 'passive' and 'private' view of citizenship-as-rights (Kymlicka, 2002: 288, 322–3, n6).[6] Yet, we doubt that the participatory implications of this expression can be entirely jettisoned (Waldron, 1999; Bellamy, 2001). If there are reasonable disagreements about rights, so that they fall within the 'circumstances of politics', then there can be no justification for favouring elite over democratic-based procedures for their settlement. In a society where citizens are presumed to be equal, the ideal of 'comparative justice' proves the most suitable norm for distributing the political authority to make decisions concerning not only policies but also principles.[7] Participation, seen as citizens sharing in political power with other citizens, is the right that makes it possible for them to establish the nature and extent of the set of rights they should all enjoy. Such participation should be understood as an *equal* and *reciprocal* right to have an *effective* voice in making the collective decisions on which all citizens' life-chances depend (Bellamy, 2000: 155–9, 177–83).

This argument returns us to the original ideal of citizenship-as-participation that we find in the classical injunction that the citizens of a republic are those who are both *rulers* and *ruled*. However, it is often argued that this understanding of citizenship does not apply to the conditions of modern politics and society, where the individual citizen's input is no longer necessary for the polity to both function and survive. This claim proves misplaced. As John Stuart Mill observed in his *Considerations on Representative Government*, 'political machinery does not act of itself . . . [it] has to be worked by men and women, and even by ordinary men and women. It needs not their simple acquiescence, but their active participation, and must be adjusted to the capacities and qualities of such people as are available' (Mill, 1861: 5). Active participation is therefore as important an ingredient of modern as it was of ancient democratic government, though the particular form that it takes, and the institutional machinery through which is channelled, must, as Mill says, be 'adjusted to the capacities and qualities' of the people available in the modern world. It is in this sense that, besides being looked at as a right, participation needs to be seen as a quality of the institutions and the virtues of the citizen.

In this regard, the timorous view of citizen participation often rests on a misunderstanding of the preconditions of the classical conception of citizenship that leads to the assumption that it cannot be adapted to modern complex societies. Both liberals and communitarians tend to assume it presupposed a homogeneous and simple society, in which public matters were strictly separated from private ones. Homogeneity ensured there was little disagreement on basic values while simplicity meant that the policies to be decided were few. The strict public/private split arose from citizenship being restricted to those whose property was sufficient for them to be free to engage in public service without any desire for a reward, with public matters in any case excluding the management of private affairs. As a result, there was little scope for a clash of interests. In these circumstances, all those qualified to do so had the time to deliberate on the public good and were likely to reach an impartial and consensual agreement on it.

These conditions hardly hold in the modern world. Liberals and communitarians react differently to this state of affairs. Liberals argue that politics has degenerated in being largely about the pursuit of private interests by public means. What were to become the twin evils of later republicans, factionalism and rent-seeking, they claim are now the norm. This fact provides the main reason for taking rights out of the political arena altogether and handing their protection to the courts. The most that can be expected of citizens in the way of civic virtue is to be law-abiding and have a passive toleration of others. The difficulty with this analysis is that the restricted account of politics and its virtues it proposes is itself only likely to be adequate in relatively homogeneous and simple societies motivated by the public good. People will only be happy to trust in others and abide by the law, keeping participation to a minimum, where there are shared interests and values. However, if everyone is self-seeking, why should we expect judges, public servants or politicians to be any more disinterested than anybody else? *Sed quis custodiet ipsos custodes* becomes the central question, to which no satisfactory answer has yet been given. Communitarians accept this diagnosis of modern liberal politics, but advocate a return to the ancient virtues within more localized settings, where homogeneity and simplicity prevail. Yet this solution appears hopelessly anachronistic, and could only be established and sustained by a decidedly illiberal degree of moral policing and interference with individual choice. Such a policy seems unsustainable and unacceptable even at the local level, let alone at that of entire nations. Moreover, it too succumbs to the very problems it seeks to overcome. The emphasis on our communal and familial ties risks further dividing and factionalizing society, creating barriers between included and excluded groups and individuals.

Fortunately, we believe things are not as bad as these accounts suggest. The classical view has Roman as well as Greek antecedents, and was developed by later thinkers well aware of the modern predicament. In the neo-Roman account, class and ideological conflict were taken as givens. The spur to participate was precisely to avoid a rival faction taking power so that they could use public means to pursue private ends. The solution to these struggles was to find ways of balancing the various groups within a system of mixed government – thereby obliging them to co-operate with each other. As the American Federalists presciently saw, complexity and size aided this process (Bellamy, 1996). The one produced a plurality of interests, so that any faction would always have to contend with other factions. The second allowed power to be dispersed territorially, so that any polity always had to contend with the claims of various sub-polities, thereby preventing central government dominating all. As we noted above, the EU is evolving in the direction of a poly-centric polity with a multilevel regime. It is our contention that this is producing mixed forms governance that offer an opportunity for developing such a neo-republican conception while avoiding the dangers of factionalized and rent-seeking participation its critics fear.

Although multilevel governance undermines the sense of unity that characterizes traditional forms of democratic power, and so apparently multiplies the occasions for factionalism and rent-seeking, it does not necessarily exclude the introduction of other forms of more diffuse democratic participation and deliberation, thereby giving the citizens more of a say on what matters most to them in relation to their life-chances. In comparison to the national level, Europe offers opportunities as well as apparent losses. European politics is undeniably often characterized by log-rolling and horse-trading between national governments in defence of sectoral interests of various degrees of legitimacy. However, it also offers forums for a more deliberative style of politics – one that is partly detached from the constraints imposed by modern-day party politics, and sometimes better able to combine individual and democratic perspectives with those advanced by expert bodies. For example, the Commission, or some of the agencies and committees under it, can often assume a more general view of the Union's and its citizens' common good, countering some of the more particularistic and partial positions advanced by the national governments (Craig, 1997; Joerges, 1997). Thus, certain aspects of the BSE crisis testify to the ability of European institutions to defend the interests of European consumers against the entrenched power of certain sectors within national communities. But, the reverse also holds true. For intergovernmentalism has also allowed some particular interests to be successfully defended against the force of simple majoritarianism within a given national community. From such a perspective, it should also be possible to find and develop modes and instruments of transnational governance that, along with efficiency, also value citizens' more direct input (see Cohen and Sabel, 1997).

The encouragement of such forms of governance at the European level may also be able to compensate for the more populist and executive-centred tendencies in national democracies, which tend to stifle proper democratic debate and deliberation and occasionally show worryingly authoritarian inclinations. Indeed, for all its lack of effective power, or perhaps because of it, the European Parliament may some times be able to reflect European public opinion better than the sum of the national parliaments or governments could, as arguably it was the case in the Iraq crisis. Certainly, it's highly representative character and the need to reach decisions by a majority of all MEPs and not just of those who vote, encourages a deliberative and consensual form of politics. The complexity of European decision-making is often criticized. Yet it is arguably the very diversity and mutually balancing character of the various policy-making polities and regimes comprising the European Union that places it in a better situation than the more hierarchically organized national systems to represent the variety of rights, interests and identities that characterize citizenship in modern societies.

As for the practical problems raised by active participation, the typical concerns about citizens' willingness to engage in decision making are partly misplaced. In modern complex societies, citizens no longer participate solely in a narrowly defined public political domain. It has become increasingly evident that people live in overlapping networks of decision-making that are not organized in a simple hierarchy. An increasing number of decisions affecting individuals as private persons, but also as citizens, are made in ways and places that escape direct political control. The burgeoning of the regulatory function of the state (and of the European institutions) through independent or semi-independent agencies, which often operate in the field of privatized public utilities, poses, for instance, the problem of how to organize and give representation to the interests of the citizen-consumers, balancing the growing power of corporate enterprises in semi-monopolistic economic sectors. Similarly, the globalization and internationalization of capital and labour markets have weakened the connection between territory and economic activities, thus sapping the vital sources of industrial and work-based democracy, while making large groups of economic agents powerless. European-wide territorial policies should aim both to protect the vital interests of local populations and to foster institutional and associative forms that re-empower them.

To have meaning, participation must apply as much to civil society as to the state. There is nothing entirely new in this, since most conceptions of democracy recognize the supporting role played by civil society and associational life in general. Involvement in civil society, however, should not be seen simply as an education for politics, or as the seedbed for the virtues of political citizenship. In many cases, though not in all, participation in civil society is no different from participation in politics, and the virtues required in both are mutually sustaining, if not the same. There are important ways in which the political virtues of *civicness*, which entails acquiring a sense of what the public interest is, can at times be fostered or even coincide with the cultivation of the more *civil* forms of virtue, consisting in the development of generalized trust, a sense of fairness, reciprocity, and a general civility in the relation to others. Modern participation requires these virtues to be actively exercised in the practices of citizenship and collective decision making, in which individuals may engage through forms of traditional political participation, but also more directly either at the local level or in social settings. These different levels and forms of collective decision-making increasingly form part of a more global interlocking system of governance, in which we continuously dip in and out following personal patterns of engagement and activism. Therefore, the problem is not that of sustaining any single or uniform pattern of civic engagement (electoral turn-out, for instance; or party membership), but of recognizing that engagement takes very different forms and that citizens should have the opportunity to have their say in a variety of settings, which may better express the intensity of their opinions or the proximity of their interests.

From such a perspective, the virtues of the modern citizens are more varied and in less need of being exercised to the utmost at all times and circumstances. Moreover, if voice and participation are important aspects of the liberty of citizens, so is 'exit' as an option that modern citizens may want to be able to exercise in various contexts of contemporary society. As Herman van Gunsteren suggests, 'people who . . . take the option of exit provide important signals on the road of peaceful change in a free society' (1998: 123). Such a change is eventually supported by the 'loyal' citizen, but neither absolute loyalty nor complete disinterest work. What is needed is a healthy and variable mix of the two options across society, people and issues (see Castiglione, 2000). Nonetheless, the virtues that characterize the cyclical involvement of the average citizen cannot be sustained in their purely procedural sense, nor can they be paternalistically imposed on them. Modern participation requires a certain amount of virtue across the polity, or to be precise, it requires a mixture between civic and civil virtues, and their practice by a substantial number of citizens. It is, after all, from the encounter with other citizens in the process of collective deliberation that the civic bond is established and cemented – in Europe no less than in other places.

Conclusion

The belonging and rights accounts of citizenship fail to be genuine accounts of citizenship at all. For different reasons, both sideline the main rationale for citizenship – namely, participation in making collective decisions in the face of disagreements over values and conflicting interests. It is the fact that these disagreements and conflicts exist that makes democratic politics necessary to resolve them in ways that avoid tyranny or domination. For there can be no expert or impartial decision-maker in such circumstances, and the only way to ensure one's views and interests are fairly considered in the final decision is to play a part in making them. Once the necessity of civic participation is acknowledged, it remains to be seen whether it is possible. Again the belonging and rights-based accounts assume it is not. Here too we have challenged their arguments, suggesting that the very processes they assume have undermined such political agency may well be promoting it. Indeed, the rejection of the Constitutional Treaty by France and Holland could be seen as underlining this point. The impossibility of a civic Europe lies more in a failure of political will and imagination than any limits of modern societies as such.[8]

Notes

1. This is a revised version of an article that first appeared in *Quaderni Fiorentini: Per la storia del pensiero giuridico moderno* 31 (2002) Tomo I, pp. 349–80.
2. For a discussion of this, see Bellamy and Castiglione (2003).
3. The assumption that identification with a polity requires strong ethnic and cultural ties – e.g. A. D. Smith, *The Ethnic Origins of Nations* (1986) – appears unrealistic for most states, let alone multi-state entities such as the EU. Multiculturalism is the norm rather than the exception. As Will Kymlicka (1995: 1) notes, 'the world's 184 independent states contain over 600 living language groups and 5000 ethnic groups'. We discuss this issue more fully in Bellamy and Castiglione (1997a: 254–84).
4. As remarked by Rawls following Hume: J. Rawls, *A Theory of Justice* (1971: 126–30).
5. See also the anti-global demonstrations that have started accompanying some of the IGC meetings.
6. Cf. Kymklicka (2002: 288, 322–3, 3, note 6, which refers to *Trop v. Dulles* 356 US 86, 102 (1958)).
7. Waldron (1999: p. 238, and note 21) for reference to Joel Feinberg's understanding of 'comparative justice'.
8. For an elaboration of this point, see Bellamy (2006).

References

Austin, D. and O'Neill, M. (2000) *Democracy and Cultural Diversity*. Oxford: Oxford University Press.
Bellamy, R. (1996) 'The Political Form of the Constitution: the Separation of Powers, Rights and Representative Democracy', in R. Bellamy and D. Castiglione (eds), *Constitutionalism in Transformation. Theoretical and European Perspectives*. Oxford: Blackwell.

_____ (2000) *Rethinking Liberalism*. London: Continuum.

_____ (2001) 'The Right to have Rights': Citizenship Practice and the Political Constitution of the EU', in R. Bellamy and A. Warleigh (eds), *Citizenship and Governance in the EU*. London: Continuum, Ch. 3.

_____ (2006) 'Between Past and Future: The Democratic Limits of EU Citizenship', in R. Bellamy, D. Castiglione and J. Shaw (eds), *Making European Citizens: Civic Inclusion in a Transnational Context*. Basingstoke: Palgrave Macmillan, pp. 238–65.

_____ and Castiglione, D. (1997a) 'The Normative Challenge of a European Polity: Cosmopolitan and Communitarian Models Compared, Criticised and Combined', in A. Føllesdal and P. Koslowski (eds), *Democracy and the European Union*. Berlin: Springer-Verlag, pp. 254–84.

_____ and Castiglione, D. (1997b) 'Constitutionalism and Democracy – Political Theory and The American Constitution', *The British Journal of Political Science*, 27: 595–618.

_____ and Castiglione, D. (2003) 'Legitimising the Euro-Polity and its Regime: The Normative Turn in EU Studies', *European Journal of Political theory*, 2(1): 7–34.

Bellamy, R. and Warleigh, A. (eds) (2001) *Citizenship and Governance in the EU*. London: Continuum, ch. 3.

Brubacker, R. (1992) *Citizenship and Nationhood in France and Germany*. Cambridge, MA: Harvard University Press.

Castiglione, D. (2000) 'Public Reason, Private Citizenship', in M. Passerin d'Entreves and U. Vogel (eds), *Public and Private: Legal, Political and Philosophical Perspectives*. London: Routledge, pp. 28–50.

_____ (2006) ' "We the Citizens?" Representation and Participation in EU Constitutional Politics', in R. Bellamy, D. Castiglione and J. Shaw (eds), *Making European Citizens: Civic Inclusion in a Transnational Context*. Basingstoke: Palgrave Macmillan.

_____ et al. (2007) *Constitutional Politics in the European Union: The Convention Moment and its Aftermath*. Basingstoke: Palgrave Macmillan.

Cohen, J. and Sabel, C. (1997) 'Directly-Deliberative Polyarchy', *European Law Journal*, 3: 313–42.

Craig, P. (1997) 'Democracy and Rule-making within the EC: An Empirical and Normative Assessment', *European Law Journal*, 3(2): 105–30.

Eriksen, E. O. (2001) 'Why a Charter of Fundamental Human Rights', in E. O. Eriksen, J. E. Fossum and A. J. Menéndez (eds), *The Chartering of Europe*, ARENA Report No. 8/2001.

Habermas, J. (1996) *Between Facts and Norms*. Cambridge: Polity Press, *Appendix II: Citizenship and National Identity*.

_____ (2001) *The Postnational Constellation*. Cambridge: Polity Press.

James, A. (1999) 'The Practice of Sovereign Statehood in Contemporary International Society', in R. Jackson (ed.), *Sovereignty at the Millenium*, Special Issue 'Political Studies', 47: 457–73.

Joerges, C. (1997) 'The Impact of European Integration on Private Law: Reductionist Perceptions, True Conflicts and a New Constitutional Perspective', *European Law Journal*, 3: 378–406.

Klingemann, H-D. and Fuchs, D. (eds) (1995) *Citizens and the State: Beliefs in Government Vol. 1*. Oxford: Oxford University Press.

Kymlicka, W. (1995) *Multicultural Citizenship: A Liberal Theory of Minority Rights*. Oxford: Oxford University Press.

_____ (ed.) (2002) *Contemporary Political Philosophy*, 2nd edition. Oxford: Oxford University Press.

_____ and Norman, W. (1994) 'Return of the Citizen', *Ethics*, 104(2): 352–81.

Lefort, C. (1998) *Democracy and Political Theory*. Cambridge: Polity Press.

Mill, J. S. (1861) *Considerations on Representative Government*. London: Parker, Son & Bourn.

Milward, A. (1993) *The European Rescue of the Nation State*. London: Routledge.

Oldfield, A. (1990) *Citizenship and Community: Civic Republicanism and the Modern World*. London: Routledge.

Pettit, P. (1999) *Republicanism: A Theory of Freedom and Government*, 2nd edition. Oxford: Clarendon Press.

Rawls, J. (1971) *A Theory of Justice*. Cambridge, MA: Harvard University Press.

_____ (1993) *Political Liberalism*. New York: Columbia University Press.

Rodotà, S. (2001) 'Ma l'Europa già applica la nuova Carta dei diritti', *La Repubblica*, 8 January.

Ruggie, J. G (1993) 'Territoriality and Beyond: Problematizing Modernity in International Relations', *International Organisation*, 47(1): 139–74.

Scharpf, F. (1999) *Governing in Europe: Effective and Democratic?* Oxford: Oxford University Press.

Smith, A. D. (1986) *The Ethnic Origins of Nations*. Oxford: Blackwell.

Van Gunsteren, H. (1998) *A Theory of Citizenship. Organizing Plurality in Contemporary Democracies*. Boulder, CO: Westview.

Waldron, J. (1999) *Law and Disagreement*. Oxford: Clarendon Press.

9
Constitutional Patriotism or Neo-republican Citizenship: A Way Forward for the EU?[1]

John Maynor

Introduction

The recent difficulties to establish a Constitution for Europe[2] highlight several critical issues facing the member states of the European Union and, importantly, their respective citizens. These endeavours to clarify and codify the rights and duties of EU citizens in the proposed CT seem, among other things, to signal a move towards a richer and more robust notion of citizenship and its relation to the larger political community. Curiously, a document that is meant, among other things, to enhance the democratic nature of the Union has failed to be endorsed democratically by its citizens.[3] Putting aside these difficulties, the main purpose of this chapter is to focus on a group of theorists who believe that the Constitutional process signals a decisive shift towards a *post-national* political community with a rich cosmopolitan conception of citizenship.

For many, the EU is best understood as a post-national entity comprised of complex networks of institutions and agencies that are above those of its member states (Fossum, 2003: 322). With respect to fostering a rich version of citizenship that corresponds to its unique political community, the EU seems to be on the horns of a dilemma: how can a plural supranational entity foster and cultivate a single identity of citizenship when its overriding characteristic is its pluralism and diversity? Not surprisingly, the task of reconciling this dilemma is no small task as the EU is currently made up of 27 states with approximately 490 million inhabitants (Olsen, 2004: 468–9). To most, the key to resolving this dilemma is through the development of democratic practices and institutions which can help reconcile and lessen the difficult challenges in the face of this post-national form of institutional and popular diversity (Bellamy and Castiglione, 1998; Preuß, 1998; Habermas, 2003; Olsen, 2004: 464).

Democracy serves two main functions in this manner. First, it legitimizes the power of the polity, be it in the traditional model of the nation-state or some type of post-national polity like the EU. Second, it unites diverse individuals through self-government by enlisting them in a common project with a shared future. Thus, a focal point of any democratic polity becomes not only its forums and institutions, but also the common practices of citizenship that support them and build community.

This issue is further complicated by the understanding that citizenship has traditionally been located in the culture, traditions and experiences of the nation-state within the specific confines of its narrow community. Because the EU is a unique political entity in that it is not a nation-state and yet has certain characteristics of one since it has exclusive and dominant powers over its members, it may be that these traditional notions of citizenship do not apply. Recent debates surrounding this issue have pointed to two main philosophical accounts to help understand the development of EU citizenship. For some it has become *de rigueur* to hold up constitutional patriotism and its corresponding cosmopolitan conception of citizenship as the EU's ideal philosophical model.[4] Popularized by Jürgen Habermas (1996), constitutional patriotism represents that idea that patriotic attachments and their corresponding obligations and duties are derived from universal basic rights and not pre-political values and ideals such as culture, nationality or tradition. Alternatively, Richard Bellamy (and his frequent collaborator Dario Castiglione) has argued for a neo-republican model of EU governance that seeks to combine 'a communitarian sense of attachment with the cosmopolitan respect for diversity' (Bellamy, 1999: 197). In doing so, they argue for cosmopolitan communitarianism, a 'bottom-up approach whereby European and national identities interact' (Bellamy, 1999; Bellamy and Castiglione, 2000; Bellamy and Warleigh, 2001; Bellamy and Castiglione, 2004). The purpose of this chapter is to explore these two rival approaches to discover what, if any, significant differences there are between them with respect to the important issue of European citizenship. I will argue that while there are some similarities, the neo-republican approach is more convincing, especially when considering the form and content of citizenship developing within the EU presently.

The structure of my argument is straightforward. In the first section I briefly outline how, within the context of the EU, both these approaches can be loosely described as originating from a more or less republican perspective. In the next section I turn my attention to constitutional patriotism and its corresponding cosmopolitan conception of citizenship and argue that it overly stresses a status and rights based point of view. Next

I develop the neo-republican conception of citizenship and argue that it better reflects a balance between both status-based and practice-based notions of citizenship. I also argue that the neo-republican approach does not fall victim to the same kind of criticism levelled at constitutional patriotism since its conception of citizenship is constitutive in nature. Finally, I offer some concluding remarks and argue that given the current state of EU citizenship, the neo-republican conception of citizenship developed here is better equipped to transform traditional notions of citizenship to combat domination.

I now turn to my argument.[5]

A republican Europe?

Interestingly, as Heidrun Friese and Peter Wagner have pointed out, two of the most prominent approaches to theorizing the European polity reflect a more or less republican perspective (Friese and Wagner, 2002: 355–6). In this sense Habermas's constitutional patriotism is read as advocating a republican Europe that is at once drawn from existing socio-political structures while also being constructed as a response to the forces of cultural, economic and political globalization. For these writers, although not explicitly acknowledged as such by Habermas himself, this approach is republican insofar as it focuses on the founding of a polity and thus connects with the political philosophy of Machiavelli and others who were concerned about such things (Friese and Wagner, 2002: 355). However, constitutional patriotism is at most only minimally a republican account, and thus it may be more accurate to locate Habermas's project within the broad school of cosmopolitan liberalism since it stresses a negative conception of liberty; an emphasis on deliberation; and the fostering of both post-national structures and the accompanying notions of identity that must support them.[6] Alternatively, Bellamy's approach draws more readily from existing notions of republicanism and relies on a reading of the neo-Roman republican tradition, most recently put forward by Quentin Skinner and Philip Pettit.[7] As its guiding principle, this approach takes the view that the polity should minimize the level of domination present in society. This view sees the EU's multilayered and quasi-federalist structures as agencies ideally suited to combat domination by both strengthening certain Union level competences while retaining other elements more suited to the particularism of the nation-state.

In support of Friese and Wagner's contention, there are some commonalities between these two approaches. In a more or less consistent manner both approaches have a similar interpretation of constitutional-ism within the EU.[8] Both approaches recognize the threats brought on by the increasing pressures of globalization on the ability of the nation-state to prevent arbitrary interference within their borders. Both also recognize that certain principles that support democratic institutions, such as human rights and the rule of law must be vested in the European Union as one way in which to combat arbitrary interference. Both approaches favour some kind of notion of citizenship that can be described as at least containing some cosmopolitan elements. As Bellamy and Castiglione (2004: 189) admit, there is something of an *air de famille* with their approach and constitutional patriotism. There are, however, some important differences. One very significant difference is that each approach has a differing viewpoint on the endgame of the EU's recent moves. Constitutional patriots are far more likely to favour the continued restructuring of the polity along cosmopolitan lines and to favour the continued growth of post-national governance (Lacroix, 2002, 2004; Habermas, 2003; Eriksen, 2005). It is, of course, conceivable that neo-republicans might too favour these moves if they meant that arbitrary interference could be effectively countered.[9] However, I believe that neo-republicans are far more likely to favour moves that pursue a dual-track course that calls for the strengthening of certain aspects of the EU's multilayered model of governance, while at the same time favouring other solutions that are best dealt with at the national level (Bellamy and Castiglione, 2004: 190–1).

Although this last point is very interesting and important to an over-all understanding of both these approaches, I believe that pursuing this line would take me away from my central argument, which is to focus on the issue of citizenship. I want instead to try to isolate an important difference between these two approaches with respect to citizenship and the central theme of this volume, namely that of community and how best to foster and nurture it in the face of a plurality of cultures, nation-alities, practices, that all reside within the EU. In particular I want now to focus on how constitutional patriotism fails in this area, and point out that neo-republicanism does not. It is my belief that the neo-republican conception of citizenship is a far more robust and vibrant account than that found within constitutional patriotism, and thus it can strengthen community in the face of increasing competition between rival values and ways of life. In the next section I take up this argument by looking at just how constitutional patriotism views the EU before having a critical look at the conception of citizenship inherent within this approach.

Constitutional patriotism and cosmopolitan citizenship

For constitutional patriots, recent developments in the EU's constitutional history represent a unique opportunity to formalize and foster a post-national political community characterized by a clear conception of *European* citizenship that transcends traditional categories rooted in the experiences and borders of the nation-state. These developments seem to offer the EU the opportunity to develop a new cosmopolitan political community which signals a move towards a pan-European idea of just what it means to be a citizen of the Union with its concomitant notions of identity. For Habermas, the traditional territorial, national and social nature of the nation-state has become '*ensnared* in the interdependencies of a global economy and society' leading to the forfeiture of the state's capacity for autonomous action (Habermas, 2003: 89–90). Another problem can be seen in certain legitimation deficits in decision-making processes that can be seen in instances where agents are exposed to certain actions or decision in which they have no capacity to influence through the existing networks of democratic participation. These deficits, as I pointed out above, represent a serious problem to the liberty of individuals since these interferences are arbitrary in nature and thus signal a situation of domination. Finally, Habermas maintains that the forces of globalization have threatened the nation-state's ability to draft and implement certain social policies due to the interconnected and interdependent nature of global markets (Habermas, 2003: 89–90). The upshot of the disempowerment of the nation-state, and the corresponding community that constitutes it, is that individuals are left at a distinct disadvantage with respect to the democratic control of their lives.

Insofar as there are no well-developed global models of democracy, for many constitutional patriots, the development of the European Union is an example of an initial attempt at democracy beyond the nation-state. It is this development that has become the focus of these writers as they seek to advocate a wide-ranging cosmopolitan framework with its own specific conception of citizenship. Habermas maintains that 'cosmopolitans see a federal European state as a point of departure for the development of a transnational network of regimes that together could pursue a world domestic policy, even in the absence of a world government' (Habermas, 2003: 96). Accompanying these new forms of democracy must be measures allowing citizens access to, and accountability from, the social, economic and political processes that cut across national borders transforming traditional community boundaries. For Held and McGrew (2002: 107–8) individuals must learn to become cosmopolitan citizens who can mediate between national traditions and alternative ways of life in overlapping communities of fate. It is these overlapping communities of fate that are the key to creating the glue that holds together any type of post-national political community. Once again, citizenship plays a key role in helping to bind these communities together into one that is both viable and can support the institutional structures of the EU. Thus, in the context of the EU, citizenship becomes a key feature in officially establishing a recognized notion of 'Europeanness', but not one that is based on any type of pre-political values. However, once again we are left to ponder just how to achieve this notion without any 'thick' account of just what will bind European citizens together if the main thing they share are the EU's institutional structures, many of which seem alien to the rank-and-file citizenry as it is. A closer look at citizenship will help illuminate just how these writers view this issue and how it can serve as something that can help to constitute a community. I turn to this issue next.

At its most fundamental, citizenship defines those who are, and those who are not, members of a particular political community. It implies membership of a specific political community that extends an individual's loyalty beyond certain close ties such as family or clan. This membership allows agents to participate in the wider community that points to a political organization whose subject is a type of polity (Preuß, 1998: 139–42). For Aristotle, in the strictest sense, a citizen was one who shared in the administration of justice, was able to take office and was able to take part in the deliberative forums of the state (Aristotle, 1996: 61–3). However, modern notions of citizenship are not just about membership of this or that political community, but rather also focus on questions surrounding entitlement and responsibility. While citizenship is most easily understood as a type of status, its real significance is derived from the rights and responsibilities that accompany this status. It follows that not only must any serious theory of citizenship specify who becomes a citizen, it must also outline what rights and entitlements these citizens get and, importantly, what obligations and responsibilities are expected of them in return for their membership in this or that political community (Patten, 2000: 193). However, the significance of this last point is sometimes ignored or at least played down in some liberal theories of citizenship, which are usually deontological in nature and concentrate on the status of citizenship and not its practices.

As mentioned above, having citizenship denotes a certain status that entitles the holder to certain rights or entitlements. However, having this status also places certain duties and responsibilities on the holder such as certain norms of behaviour like civility and a contribution to the political life of the community. Where liberal citizenship is often thought of as a status-based conception of citizenship, there is a richer and more robust conception of citizenship that is often associated with the classical republicans. In this conception, citizenship is thought to focus more on the practices of being a citizen such as the active engagement and participation in political life and the civic virtues necessary to support the common good (Beiner, 2003: 198). This practice-based conception sees citizens as deliberators engaged in serving the political community by participating in a shared vision of the common good (Kostakopoulou, 2001: 87). Moreover, in this view it is only in a self-governing polity that individuals can find excellence and flourish as political animals. The upshot of having a rich practice-based conception of citizenship is that in sharing and participating in the governance of a political community that controls its own fate, certain specialized and distinct virtues are cultivated and nurtured (Sandel, 1996: 26). For these writers being a good citizen of a self-governing democratic polity not only helps to provide individuals with access to a high degree of self-mastery, it also contributes to a rich formative project of identity that can only be realized within a particular kind of community (Maynor, 2003: 11). The thought is that the act of participation itself helps to constitute certain ultimate goods, such as civility, solidarity and trust, which contribute to an individual's autonomy while at the same time allowing them direct input into the direction and content of their community (Kymlicka, 2002: 295).

Not surprisingly, a rich notion of patriotism accompanies this conception of citizenship as citizens devote themselves wholeheartedly to the common good of the community that helps provide them with a sense of attachment and well-being that otherwise they would be without. It also provides them with a particular and familiar context, which in turn allows them to flourish. Considered in this manner, patriotism is firmly fused with cultural or ethnic social unity or solidarity and is seen as a necessary component of civic virtue and citizenship. Such moves favour the particular traits and characteristics of the majority and offer scant hope to cultural or political minorities. The patriot found in this type of republic is loyal to the shared morality epitomized by the values that constitute a certain political community's or nation's ideals and norms (Viroli, 1995: 170–6). It is this last point, however, that many object to since they believe the practice-based conception of citizenship to be overly burdensome since it contains rich strands of patriotic identity that may be at odds with personal autonomy and it is this type of patriotism that

Habermas is trying to avoid (Habermas, 1996: 497–8). Habermas decries the particularism inherent in this 'communitarian' view of citizen practices and attachments and declares it unfit for the realities of modern politics (Habermas, 1996: 505).[10] The view that individuals are 'encumbered' with certain characteristics drawn from being embedded within distinct communities with rich or 'thick' narratives of culture and society has proved controversial to many and something to be avoided (Kymlicka, 1989; Rawls, 1996). To counter this claim, supporters of the practice-based citizenship approach argue that it is only in these types of communities that individuals can realize themselves by acquiring certain necessary civic virtues such as solidarity, trust and cooperation through the practices of good citizenship.

However, as I have argued elsewhere, it is wrongheaded to maintain that these two positions are necessarily antithetical (Maynor, 2003: 10–32). Any status-based conception of citizenship will have to promote certain practices aimed at perpetuating the polity and cultivating certain virtues that make it more likely that individuals will fulfil their obligations to social justice. These virtues will also help to ensure the liberal democratic polity's stability in the face of 'the fact of pluralism' (Rawls, 1996: 205). Also, both conceptions have to contain an articulation of a particular political identity to support certain preferred practices that reflect that identity (Stokes, 2002: 24). There certainly may be differences in the content and intensity of that identity, but both conceptions presuppose certain ideals and practices that help to sustain citizens' ways of life and the political community that supports them. It is on this point that I believe neo-republicanism can be clearly distinguished from constitutional patriotism. By trying to extract any pre-political notions from their conception of citizenship, constitutional patriots are in danger of leaning too far towards a strict, status-based conception of citizenship that cannot be maintained because it contains an overly 'thin' account of political identity based around rights. The result is an impoverished conception of citizenship that fails to bind the people together into a community.

This reading of constitutional patriotism status-based conception of citizenship can be clearly identified in the work of Jan Erik Fossum (2003). The thought is that constitutional patriotism fosters a sense of allegiance that is aimed not at the nation-state, the traditional locus of allegiance, but rather at broader more abstract ideals which are more 'juridical, moral, and political [and not] cultural, geographical, and historical' (Ferry and Thidbaud, 1992: 174). Seen in this way, particularistic values and norms of nationality as defined by the dominant national culture give way to more universalistic values of democracy and basic rights. It is hoped that these principles, enshrined within constitutional structures and embedded into the political culture, become the locus of attachment and support for individuals and thus become the 'shared values' necessary to the establishment of a community. These shared values centre on the image of individuals as holders of rights as opposed to individuals with this or that particular personality traits or attributes. This understanding of constitutional patriotism points to a notion of citizenship that favours the status-based conception outlined above since it is grounded in a rights-based point of view and its primary aim is to serve individual autonomy, not build and maintain rich notions of community. In this way, rights become the primary characteristic of citizens in civil society as they attempt to deliberate a common future. But it is only those rights that bind the people together since an individual's particularistic characteristics must be bracketed off if they are based on pre-political sources. We are left with the question of whether or not rights are enough to constitute a community, especially since rights are often used by citizens against each other in an antagonistic manner. In addressing this question in the next section, I will sketch out the main critique of constitutional patriotism. I then focus on just how neo-republicans conceptualize citizenship and then argue that this same kind of critique cannot be applied to their view of citizenship.

Combating domination: neo-republican citizenship

The above outlined view of constitutional patriotism's status-based conception of citizenship ties into an objection by supporters of the broad school of civic nationalists. For these writers, a political identity is a complex affair that is deeply rooted within the historical and traditional experiences of a national culture (Canovan, 2000; Miller, 2000: Bellamy and Castiglione, 2000: 163). It is only at a national level that the 'values of liberty, civic responsibility and political justice acquire their true meaning (Lacroix, 2002: 947). In other words, even though these values may attain some level of universal acceptance, they only become meaningful to individuals when mediated through the more particular experiences of a nation-state within a specific context. It is through the shared experiences of tradition and national culture that individuals build certain necessary values and norms, such as trust and solidarity, which allow them to engage in the common enterprise of self-government. These experiences bestow a level of legitimacy on a polity's ideals and institutions that are accepted by the citizenry who in turn conform to the dominant norms.

In unpacking this critique, several key issues arise surrounding questions of identity, collective engagement and the motivation necessary to encourage individuals to participate in the political process. Linked to this are questions surrounding patriotism and allegiance. For their part, critics of the civic nationalist position argue that for the EU to adopt the particularistic attachments of any of its member states would amount to a cultural tyranny in the face of its intrinsic plural nature (Lacroix, 2002). Instead, an individual's political allegiance should be dedicated to constitutional principles that support the universalistic abstract values of democracy, autonomy, the rule of law and human rights. The fear for constitutional patriots is that any form of identity that is firmly embedded within the mythology of the nation is likely to reflect notions of blind loyalty based on pre-political cultural or blood ties that can lead to insidious forms of nationalism. Thus, forms of patriotism and allegiance that are too closely tied to the images, myths and identities of the nation-state are to be avoided, especially with respect to the EU. Instead, these writers stress procedures over substance, culture-blind attachments to institutions, and citizenship without national allegiances.

It is on this point, however, that neo-republican accounts can be clearly distinguished from their rivals. Maurizo Viroli has argued that what motivates republican citizens is their deep love of liberty. Viewed in this manner it follows that a citizen's commitment to neo-republican liberty need not be intrinsically connected to the type of social, cultural, religious or ethnic homogeneity that many believe fuels nationalism (Viroli, 1995: 184). An example of this sentiment can be seen in the image of citizens readily sacrificing their lives for the republic. What motivates these citizens is the defence of their liberty and the realization that if the republic fails they not only lose their freedom, but they also lose their way of life. In republican speak, as the freedom of the city goes, so too goes the freedom of the citizen.

As mentioned earlier, the type of liberty contained in these republican accounts is inspired by neo-Roman thought and has recently been the focus of several contemporary theorists (Pettit, 1997, 2001; Skinner, 1997, 2002). According to Pettit, 'the condition of liberty is explicated as the status of someone who . . . is not subject to the arbitrary power of another' (Pettit, 1997: 31). Central to this idea is the relationship between interference and domination. Interference is thought to be when an agent's activities or choices are subject to some form of intentional intervention by another agent, whereas domination is understood to occur when an agent's activities or choices are subject to arbitrary interference by other agents (Pettit, 1997: 52–3). In seeking to minimize arbitrary interference, neo-republicans stress inclusiveness, democratic contestation and engagement, properly constituted institutions, checks and balances, and the dispersion of power across a range of legislative, administrative and judicial levels (Maynor, 2003). In order to minimize arbitrary interference, neo-republicans rely on democratic contestation and institutional structures to bring interests into the political forums so they can be accounted for and tracked (Maynor, 2005). It does this by stressing two interdependent powers: one that is more formal and works on a constitutional level and seeks to minimize arbitrary interference through the processes and institutions of governance; the other, which stresses the virtues associated with reciprocity, is more informal in nature and works on a personal level. As such, it plays a role in not only how agents relate to government institutions, but also in how they relate to one another in civil society (Maynor, 2003). Importantly, the neo-republican conception of citizenship is a central feature that links these two forms of power together because it focuses on both the status of citizenship and the practices that support and maintain that status.

Thus, for these republicans whether or not the EU can effectively minimize domination is tied to the degree to which citizens of the Union will be able to effectively influence its political decisions. If the EU is to track the interests of its citizens properly, then there must not only be the ways and means for citizens to voice their interests, there must also be a sufficient amount of virtue and participation in those ways and means to register accurately just what those interests are (Pettit, 1997: 87). In this way, the necessary virtues that make up the neo-republican version of citizenship help individuals explore and then articulate their own interests to the state and to others who must account for and track them if they are to live truly non-dominated lives. By promoting access to a common language of citizenship, the neo-republican approach prepares citizens to play the necessary active role in minimizing domination. Citizens will stand eye to eye with others knowing that they are secure in their freedom and that they have the ways and means to have their interests tracked. The neo-republican emphasis on communication and accommodation helps to foster civility, trust and solidarity within the political community as citizens collectively address their common problems.

This point ties into my earlier discussion of how neo-republican citizenship links both the status and practice based conceptions together. This point is reflected in Alexis de Tocqueville's conceptualization of two distinct forms patriotism. The first was derived from the 'instinctive, disinterested, and indefinable feeling which connects the affections of man with his birthplace'. This kind of patriotism ties allegiance to certain traditional customs and contains a healthy reverence for the past. Tocqueville believes that this kind of patriotism is 'itself a kind of religion: it does not reason, but it acts from the impulse of faith and sentiment' (de Tocqueville, 2001: 102). In many ways, this is just the kind of sentiment that constitutional patriotism is trying to avoid. Alternatively, the other kind of patriotism identified by Tocqueville is more rationally based and thus has more depth and longevity than the first. For Tocqueville, a 'man comprehends the influence which the well-being of his country has upon his own; he is aware that the laws permit him to contribute to that prosperity, and he labors to promote it, first because it benefits him, and secondly because it is in part his own work' (de Tocqueville, 2001: 103).

It is important to note that Tocqueville ties this second kind of patriotism to three key components. First, it is tied to an acknowledgement of the rule of law and certain rights and obligations. Second, it is tied intrinsically to the well-being of both individuals and the political community they constitute. Finally, there is a sense that this form of patriotism is tied to the very practices it encourages and allows citizens to view their contribution to the maintenance of the political community as being part of a common endeavour that they share with others and one in which they have part ownership. Put simply, contributing to the maintenance of the republic binds citizens together in a common enterprise, which fosters certain virtues associated with reciprocity such as civility, solidarity and trust. It also bestows on them a sense of ownership in their government, as it is a result of their own work. Thus, these citizens can have allegiance to the republic not only out of self-interest, but also for proprietary reasons. It is in this respect that the practices of good citizenship have a constitutive relationship to the maintenance of the republic, the preservation of liberty and a citizen's own well-being. It is also in this way that the building blocks of a strong political community can be laid in a firm foundation of civility, solidarity, trust and cooperation.

Viewed in this fashion, this type of patriotism and allegiance are not necessarily tied to any pre-political values, although there may be some benign overlap. Moreover, it does not follow that they will necessarily lead to a type of blind loyalty feared by constitutional patriots. Instead, it is hoped that they lead to a type of critical patriotic attachment in which citizens can view their government with both affection and a healthy dose of suspicion. Thus, patriotism considered in this sense is not singularly about the love of country, but is about the love of liberty and about supporting and participating in the ideals and institutions that support it even if that means taking a critical viewpoint (Viroli,

1995; also see Canovan, 2000: 288). This points to a type of *political* allegiance that opens up the possibility that individuals can be patriots without having to buy into the negative aspects of nationalism and particularism feared by constitutional patriots. It also points to a conception of citizenship that combines both status and practice-based elements in a constitutive manner.

In viewing citizenship in this way, some will argue that given the complexity of the European project, such a conception fails to acknowledge an inherent degree of pluralism found within the polity. To be sure, modern European society is made up of conflicting classes and social groups that often harbour incompatible but equally legitimate ways of life. Traditionally, when faced with these types of problems within a nation-state, the neo-republican solution was, as mentioned above, to disperse power to balance out competing interests. In seeking to tame and control this conflict, as Bellamy has pointed out, 'multiple spheres, subjects, scopes and styles of politics are employed to secure the mutual recognition of diverse groups'. Moreover, these conflicting interests and differences of opinion are considered the norm and highlight the importance that neo-republicans place on dialogue and conversation to solve problems and overcome difficulties (Bellamy, 2001: 56; Maynor, 2003, 115–45).[11] A central feature of deliberative models is the capacity of the deliberative process itself to enlarge agents' understanding of themselves and their community. The upshot of this form of republicanism is that it opens up the possibility that a deliberative community can develop across the European Union to minimize the amount of arbitrary interference present at both the national and supranational level. Importantly, it also follows that this European-wide deliberative community can coexist with similar ones based at the level of the nation-state. To this end, the multilayered nature of the EU can become the key to mediating the various demands from both member-states and the individuals and groups that constitute them with an eye to minimizing domination.[12] In the final section, I offer a brief analysis of the type of citizenship presently found in the EU and argue that the neo-republican conception defended above is ideally placed to help minimize domination within the Union and its member states.

Concluding remarks: neo-republican citizenship within the EU

In the above analysis, I have argued that the neo-republican conception of citizenship is more vibrant and robust than the one put forward by constitutional patriots. Moreover, I have argued that this republican conception of citizenship is better equipped to deal with domination within society because it is more than a status-based conception that only has rights to bind the political community together. It is able to combine elements from both the status and practice–based conceptions, but not in a manner that would increase domination since it views citizenship in a constitutive manner. As a final point about the superiority of the neo-republican conception of citizenship I now want to have a brief look at just what kind of citizenship is presently found within the EU and tie in my earlier argument about the neo-republican conception of citizenship and its suitability as a model for the EU.

Originally included as a provision in the 1992 Maastricht Treaty, recent developments have served to bring EU citizenship into clearer focus. Clues to both the status and practices of this European conception of citizenship can be found in the recent efforts to formalize a Constitution for Europe.[13] Article I-2 states that the 'Union is founded on the values of respect for human dignity, liberty, democracy, equality, the rule of law and respect for human rights'. Article I-10 outlines in detail the key elements of Union citizenship and states that 'every national of a Member State shall be a citizen of the Union'. Importantly, it goes on to say that 'citizenship of the Union shall be additional to national citizenship; it shall not replace it'. Other key points found here are the right to freedom of movement and residence within the territory of member states; the right to stand for and vote in European parliamentary and local elections; the right of diplomatic and consular privileges when in the territory of a third country; and the right to petition the Parliament and the Ombudsman and to use any of the Unions languages in addressing its institutions or advisory bodies. The CT also formalizes the Charter of Fundamental Rights by including it in Part II. The Charter focuses on ensuring the dignity of individuals; guaranteeing a comprehensive set of fundamental freedoms; securing equality and justice; protecting workers rights; and promoting solidarity. The CT also provides for the future accession of the Union to the European Convention on Human Rights. Another stated aim of the CT is to enhance the democratic nature of the Union by raising the status of the European Parliament, the only directly elected institution; allowing for citizen initiatives to the European Commission that hold out the promise of some form of direct citizen input into the policies of the Union; reforming certain decision making processes by introducing qualified majority voting; and specifying certain obligations regarding the consultation of civil society and the transparency of the decision-making process. These broad moves to enhance democracy within the Union are drawn from three main sources: The Charter of Fundamental Rights, the European Convention for the Protection of Human Rights and Fundamental Freedoms; and from the constitutional traditions of the member states.

An important point to mention here is that EU citizenship does not seek to replace the national identities of its member states. The preamble to the Charter of Fundamental Rights states that 'the Union contributes to the preservation and to the development of these common values while respecting the diversity of the cultures and traditions of the peoples of Europe as well as the national identities of the Member States and the organization of their public authorities at national, regional and local levels'. As Preuß (1998: 147) points out, EU 'citizenship is not likely to supersede national citizenship or to make it a status of minor importance frequently verging on mere irrelevance; rather, both statuses will coexists, representing two different principles of political organization'. And, as Bellamy and Castiglione (1998: 163) have pointed out, universal abstract principles, such as those supported by constitutional patriots, must be fleshed out by thicker concepts that arise out of specific ways of life. This points to a characterization of citizenship that is dual in nature and draws its content from both national and European sources.

This kind of differentiated citizenship is possible, even if there is considerable tension between the sources of identity contained in both EU and national citizenship. It may well be that the tension between these sources of identity can contribute to the minimization of domination. As Joseph Carens has pointed out,

> While it is true that the individual's claim to membership in the EU is mediated through citizenship in a member state and that the depth and meaning of European citizenship are in dispute, we should not overlook the fact that individuals who are members of the EU can advance legal claims before European courts apart from and even in opposition to the legislation and court rulings of the state in which they are citizens. (Carens, 2000: 165)

For neo-republicans the hope must be that over time these dual influences on citizenship – citizen of a member-state and citizen of the European Union – fit together in a complimentary, if still potentially antagonistic, manner. This enlarged notion of citizenship will still be primarily informed by the ideals and values of the national-state, but will contain a robust notion of just what it means to be a citizen of the EU since there will be opportunities to appeal to and petition agencies and courts at the EU level. The thought is that over time these thicker nation-state based notions of citizenship will evolve and converge into ones that take account of the rights and duties of European citizenship. In this way being a citizen of a member-state will also explicitly mean being a citizen of the Union and holders of this status will be committed to both entities by their practices. Of course, this means that existing notions of citizenship within the member-states must also be transformed, namely into ones that take account of the rights and duties of European citizenship. The subject of this fused notion of citizenship will be both the political organs of the member states and those of the Union, which must teach people how to use the institutions and agencies of the Union and how to effectuate change both at the national and European level.

This last idea of fused notions of citizenship interacting with each other within a specific context may seem both far fetched and counter-intuitive at first glance. However, I do not believe that this is the case, especially with reference to the neo-republican conception that I have been defending above. By having a brief look at T.H. Marshall's analysis of citizenship this final point will become clear. In his classic study *Citizenship and Social Class*, Marshall identified three distinct elements of modern citizenship: civil, political and social (Marshall, 1950). Marshall's study focused on the rights given to citizens and the social and political institutions through which they came to reside and be practiced. The rule of law and the administration of justice, in both civil and criminal matters, was the focal point of the civil elements of citizenship associated with the rights of individual freedom. The second of Marshall's elements, political rights, corresponds to the right to participate in the exercise of political power. Finally, the rights of citizenship realized through the state's educational system and through its social welfare services correspond to the social rights held by citizens. There are two key points to mention in support of my argument here.

The first is that Marshall demonstrated the importance of the institutional context in which the rights of citizenship were expressed. He maintained that it was only in these specific contexts that these rights could be realized and have meaning (Barbalet, 1988: 6). These specific contexts become an essential feature of citizenship since they are how individuals come to know and understand their political community and their role within in it. With respect to the EU, any notion of citizenship must be embedded within a particular context that is both intelligible and familiar to the citizenry if they are to understand and take advantage of their rights and develop the kind of practices to maintain their way of life. Such a move may indeed involve the very pre-political ideals or institutions shunned by constitutional patriots. The second point to mention in support of my argument is that a key feature of Marshall's analysis was his belief that citizenship rights have a transformative quality. Since these rights are independent of each other, it is possible for them to be in conflict. For example, in the context of Marshall's analysis he argued that political, social, and civil rights in a capitalist system may seem to be conflictual since there are clearly different advantages and disadvantages depending on which social class the rights holder belongs. On the one hand political and civil rights ensure that all have an equal status before the law while on the other hand social rights in a capitalist system often reinforce inequalities, especially within the class system. There is, however, a possibility that political and legal rights can transform social rights to at least minimize inequalities through the social welfare state.

It follows, then, that citizenship, and the rights and duties that accompany it, can have a transformative capacity. This is especially important since we all live in a particular or specific social context that is subjected to heavy regulation and interference from authoritative political structures (Beiner, 2003: 198–9). While Marshall's argument was aimed specifically at the conflictual nature of citizenship rights as they related to class inequality, it is important to point out the potential transformative nature of citizenship rights in light of the efforts to further formalize the status and practices of citizenship within the European Union. By giving citizens of the Union rights that exist, at least in certain respects, distinct from the rights they enjoy as members of their respective member-states, the potential for transformative changes in status and practice occurs on at least three different levels. The first is in the agents' relationship with the institutions of the EU; the second is in their relationship with their respective member-state; and the third is in their relationship with the wider structures of a European-wide civil society where they can relate to others as fellow citizens of a large and diverse political community that is distinct from the traditional one in which they have normally enjoyed their rights. In each of these areas, there is the potential that citizens can play the necessary role in helping to minimize domination. And with its focus on providing the essential tools to help citizens play this role, the neo-republican conception of citizenship outlined above is better equipped than that found within constitutional patriotism, especially within the context of the EU and the present state of citizenship found within the Union.

Notes

1. Originally presented to 'Constituting Communities – Political Solutions to Cultural Differences in Europe', convened by the Danish Research Group on Cultural Encounters, University of Copenhagen, 23–25 October 2003. I would like to thank the participants of that conference and the editors of this volume for their helpful critique. I would like to thank the Faculty Research and Creative Activity Committee of Middle Tennessee State University for their generous support in helping me complete this project.
2. All references to the Constitutional Treaty (hereafter *CT*) refer to the copy published by the European Union in the Official Journal C 310 of 16 December 2004.
3. At the time of this writing, both French and Dutch voters have rejected referenda on the CT and the UK has cancelled its planned vote.
4. For two recent attempts in this area, see Fossum (2003) and Lacroix (2002).
5. I do not intend to put forth any grand theory of citizenship or break new ground in putting forth an analysis of EU governance. Instead, my aim is more modest. What I intend to do is suggest that given the current fluctuating state of EU citizenship, the most sure-fire way to ensure that domination within the Union is minimized, the neo-republican conception of citizenship is necessary.
6. Although Fiese and Wagner contend that the position occupied by Habermas represents a strong republican perspective and Bellamy represents a weak republican perspective I believe that this is categorization is counter-intuitive. Habermas (1996: 505) specifically rejects the republican label and Bellamy (2001: 42) embraces it.
7. Although I have described this kind republicanism elsewhere (Maynor, 2003) as representing a modern republican approach, for the sake of consistency within this volume I will adopt Bellamy's term neo-republicanism since I believe that they are consistent with one another.
8. Admittedly both differ on the scope and intensity of the EU's institutions and constitutional mechanisms, but there is no fundamental opposition here.
9. For a neo-republican attempt to address this question in a broader context, see Bohman (2004).
10. This sentiment mirrors one found in John Rawls (1996: 205) who maintains that there is a fundamental opposition between this kind of communitarian republicanism and the kind of liberalism he favours.
11. For more on this point, see also Sunstein (1988) and Skinner (1996).
12. Please see Bellamy's contribution to this volume for an extended discussion of this aspect of neo-republicanism.
13. At the present time, the future of the CT is very much unknown. However, this should not affect my arguments since European citizenship is already a feature of current EU policy.

References

Archibugi, D., Held, D. and Köhler, D. (eds) (1998) *Re-imagining Political Community*. Cambridge: Polity Press.

Aristotle (1996) *The Politics*, ed. S. Everson. Cambridge: Cambridge University Press.

Barbalet, J. M. (1988) *Citizenship*. Minneapolis: University of Minnesota Press.

Beiner, R. (2003) *Liberalism, Nationalism, Citizenship: Essays on the Problem of Political Community*. Vancover: UBC Press.

Bellamy, R. (1999) *Liberalism and Pluralism: Towards a Politics of Compromise*. London: Routledge.

—————— (2001) 'The "Right to Have Rights": Citizenship Practice and the Political Constitution of the EU', in R. Bellamy and A. Warleigh (eds), *Citizenship and Governance in the European Union*. London: Continuum, pp. 41–70.

—————— and Castiglione, D. (1998) 'Between Cosmopolis and Community: Three Models of Rights and Democracy within the European Union', in D. Archibugi, D. Held and D. Köhler (eds), *Re-imagining Political Community*. Cambridge: Polity Press.

—————— and Castiglione, D. (2000) 'Democracy, Sovereignty and the Constitution of the European Union: The Republican Alternative to Liberalism', in Bańkowski, Z and Scott, A. (eds), The European Union and its Order. Oxford: Blackwell.

—————— and Castiglione, D. (2004) 'Lacroix's European Constituional Patriotism: A Response', *Political Studies*, 52: 187–93.

—————— and Warleigh, A. (eds) (2001) *Citizenship and Governance in the European Union*. London: Continuum.

Bohman, J. (2004) 'Republican Cosmopolitanism', *The Journal of Political Philosophy*, 12(3): 336–52.

Canovan, M. (2000) 'Patriotism is Not Enough', in C. McKinnon and I. Hampshire-Monk (eds), *The Demands of Citizenship*. London, Continuum, pp. 276–97.

Carens, J. (2000) *Culture, Citizenship and Community: A Contextual Exploration of Justice as Evenhandedness*. Oxford: Oxford University Press.

Carter, A. and Stokes, G. (eds) (2002) *Democratic Theory Today*. Cambridge: Polity Press.

Constant, B. (1988) *Political Writings*, ed. B. Fontana. Cambridge: Cambridge University Press.

de Tocqueville, A. (2001) *Democracy in America*, ed. R. Heffner. New York: Signet.

Eriksen, E.O. (2005) 'Towards a Cosmopolitan EU?', *Arena Working Paper No. 9*, www.arena.uio.no.

Ferry, J.-M. and Thidbaud, J. (1992) *Discussion sur l'Europe*. Paris: Calmann-Lévy.

Fossum, J. E. (2003) 'The European Union in Search of an Identity', *European Journal of Political Theory*, 2(3): 319–40.

Friese, H. and Wagner, P. (2002) 'Survey Article: The Nascent Political Philosophy of the European Polity', *The Journal of Political Philosophy*, 10(3): 342–64.

Habermas, J. (1996) 'Citizenship and National Identity', in *Between Facts and Norms: Contributions to a Discourse Theory of Law and Democracy*. Cambridge: Polity Press.

—————— (2003) 'Towards a Cosmopolitan Europe', *Journal of Democracy*, 14: 86–100.

Held, D. and McGrew, A. (2002) *Globalization/Anti-Globalization*. Cambridge: Polity Press.

Honohan, H. and Jennings, J. (eds) (2005) *Republicanism in Theory and Practice*. London: Routledge.

Kostakopoulou, T. (2001) *Citizenship, Identity, and Immigration in the European Union*. Manchester: Manchester University Press.

Kymlicka, W. (1989) *Liberalism, Community, and Culture*. Oxford: Oxford University Press.

—— (2002) *Contemporary Political Philosophy*, 2nd edition. Oxford: Oxford University Press.

Lacroix, J. (2002) 'For a European Constitutional Patriotism', *Political Studies*, 50: 944–58.

—— (2004) 'A Reply to Bellamy and Castiglione', *Political Studies*, 52: 194–6.

Lukes, S. (ed.) (1986) *Power*. Oxford: Blackwell.

Marshall, T.H. (1950) *Citizenship and Social Class*. Cambridge: Cambridge University Press.

Maynor, J. (2003) *Republicanism in the Modern World*. Cambridge: Polity Press.

—— (2005) 'Modern Republican Democratic Contestation: A Model of Deliberative Democracy', in H. Honohan and J. Jennings (eds), *Republicanism in Theory and Practice*. London: Routledge.

McKinnon, C. and Hampshire-Monk, I. (eds) (2000) *The Demands of Citizenship*. London, Continuum.

Miller, D. (1995) 'Citizenship and Pluralism', *Political Studies*, 43: 432–50.

Miller, D. (2000) *Citizenship and National Identity*. Cambridge: Polity Press.

Mouffe, C. (1993) *The Return of the Political*. London: Verso.

Oldfield, A. (1990) *Citizenship and Community: Civic Republicanism and the Modern World*. London: Routledge.

Olsen, J. P. (2004) 'Unity, Diversity and Democratic Institutions: Lessons from the European Union', *The Journal of Political Philosophy*, 12(4): 461–95.

Patten, A. (2000) 'Equality of Recognition and the Liberal Theory of Citizenship', in C. McKinnon and I. Hampshire-Monk (eds), *The Demands of Citizenship*. London, Continuum.

Pettit, P. (1997) *Republicanism: A Theory of Freedom and Government*. Oxford: Oxford University Press.

—— (2001) *A Theory of Freedom: From the Psychology of the Politics of Agency*. Cambridge: Polity Press.

Phillips, A. (2000) 'Survey Article: Feminism and Republicanism: Is This a Plausible Alliance', *The Journal of Political Philosophy*, 8(2): 279–93.

Preuß, U. (1998) 'Citizenship in the European Union: a Paradigm for Transnational Democracy?' in D. Archibugi, D. Held and D. Köhler (eds), *Re-imagining Political Community*. Cambridge: Polity Press, pp. 138–51.

Rawls, J. (1996) *Political Liberalism*. New York: Columbia University Press.

Rorty, R., Schneewind, J. and Skinner, Q. (eds) (1984) *Philosophy in History*. Cambridge: Cambridge University Press.

Sandel, M. (1996) *Democracy's Discontent: America in Search of a Public Philosophy*. Cambridge: Belknap Press of Harvard University Press.

Skinner, Q. (1984) 'The Idea of Negative Liberty: Philosophical and Historical Perspectives', in R. Rorty, J. Schneewind and Q. Skinner (eds), *Philosophy in History*. Cambridge: Cambridge University Press, pp. 193–221.

—— (1996) *Reason and Rhetoric in the Philosophy of Hobbes*. Cambridge: Cambridge University Press.

—— (1997) *Liberty before Liberalism*. Cambridge: Cambridge University Press.

—— (2002) 'A Third Concept of Liberty', *Proceedings of the British Academy*, 117: 237–68.

Stokes, G. (2002) 'Democracy and Citizenship', in A. Carter and G. Stokes (eds), *Democratic Theory Today*. Cambridge: Polity Press.
Sunstein, C. (1988) 'Beyond the Republican Revival', *Yale Law Review*, 97: 8.
Taylor, C. (1995) *Philosophical Arguments*. Cambridge, MA: Harvard University Press.
Viroli, M. (1995) *For Love of Country: An Essay on Patriotism and Nationalism*. Oxford: Clarendon Press.

10
World Conflict over Religion: Secularism as a Flawed Solution[1]

Ole Wæver

'Political solutions to cultural conflict' is the unifying theme of this book. 'The security problems of a political "solution" to cultural/religious conflict' could have been the title of this chapter.

A global outburst of anger and violence triggered by 12 cartoons of the Prophet Mohammed published in a Danish newspaper showed in 2005–6 how religion can generate political conflicts that follow particularly easily the globalized patterns linking local struggles in one place to local action in distant parts of the world (Wæver, 2006). This specific incident clearly gained such momentum because it was both fed by and fed back into a pattern of global conflict where Muslims and Western publics cumulate mutual grievances and concerns. The present chapter analyses the nature and dynamics of this wider conflict and its implications for political concepts to guide interaction within and among societies. As an aside, the analysis argues that it was far from a coincidence that this crisis started in a country like Denmark, and that it was so thoroughly mishandled there. Beyond that, the chapter will not analyse the specific cartoon crisis as such, but the reader is welcome to think about this case periodically, and I am certain the analysis and the case will illustrate each other nicely.

The main emphasis of the chapter is the global conflict between 'the West' and radical Islamists. However, this is not a purely 'international' issue, but a transnational one involving domestic politics in Islamic countries and within the West. At both levels, the political principle of *secularism* is argued to be at the heart of the conflicts.

Conflict analysis and security theory will be used to analyse the global level, while political theory and the role of religion in politics will be the main focus when discussing the domestic arena in the West.

The first section looks at the way religion has become part of global security affairs. A central argument is that we routinely misrepresent this through the historically inspired term 'wars of religion', although most of the conflicts take place between secularists on one side and actors who want a stronger role for religion in politics on the other. This points to the centrality of the principle of secularism. The next section problematizes the way the concept is treated as both simple and given. The third section then looks at where in the global conflict constellation the principle of secularism is most importantly at stake. This section serves to explain how the internal arrangements in Europe influence the global conflict relating to Islam. The following two sections address the practice of secularism in Europe – first discussing tensions and restrictions produced by the current, increasingly militant form of secularism as a 'European value', and then exploring the possibility of a more pragmatic approach to religion/politics. The conclusion turns the discussion back on the terms of the question: are we looking for political solution to cultural conflicts, or is this question part of the problem?

Wars of religion or wars against religion?

The word 'religion' appears increasingly frequently in contemporary security affairs. Many conflicts are interpreted as being 'about religion' or driven by groups of strong faith – whether *in* the Middle East, in the relationship *between* Middle Eastern actors and the West, as well as domestically within a number of countries, which happen to include the four most populated countries in the world: China, India, the United States and Indonesia.

Religion is on the verge of becoming the common denominator in world politics, which is why it is all the more important to understand it correctly. The quick and expedient categorization is *wars of religion*. This categorization is not only evident, it is also wrong.

However, it is hardly surprising that it is seen in this way when we recall Europe's history of crusades, wars and civil wars fought over religion. The words 'religion' and 'conflict' appearing in the same sentence instantaneously trigger an image of two groups pitted against each other, motivated by the force of their respective strong convictions – a *war of religion*, or to use a more modern expression, 'the clash of civilizations'. However, this is a quite misleading image today (Juergensmeyer, 1993). We rarely witness one deeply religious group engaged in conflict with another; rather, the battle is between those who want more religion in politics, and their adversaries, the secularists, who insist on a strict separation of religion and politics.

My focus is on secularism rather than secularization. Secularization is a societal process in which the influence of religion on society is weakened.[2]

Secularism is an *-ism*, a doctrine for how society *ought to be*. Religion and politics ought to be separated – and be protected against one another in order to ensure freedom of religion as well as religion-free politics. Ultimately, the aim is to ensure peace. For – the argument goes – faith is, naturally, a matter of faith; it is not rationally determinable. And if fighting is permitted over such questions, we will never have peace because there is no rational way to reach an agreement on matters of faith (Hobbes, 1969). Such is the credo of secularism and it is the justification for the *crusade to end all crusades*. To foreshadow my argument, here lies the risk of our contributing to a new cold war in which we – as in the former cold war – clearly perceive the threat against us, but are unable to see how our counterpart can perceive us as being dangerous, thus rendering us unable to understand the dynamic of the conflict.

Radical Muslims are engaged in a war, not with another religion, but against 'anti-religion'. They fear that faith is about to be quashed by modernity. The neutral, Western-style state does not set limits on sin and decadence, which Western culture, science and economics actually encourage. True practice and life conduct cannot survive in such a world. A good society, for them as for anti-secularists across the world, requires a political order that is *value-able*; fundamental values must be built into a political order. Conversely, this understanding is perceived as exceptionally threatening by the representatives of the worldly, secular order. Since the Peace of Westphalia, 1648, rule 1 has been: 'no encroachment in the name of religion in international politics'. The most dangerous of all is the coupling of religion and politics. Conversely, it is secularism itself which religious political actors fear. Here are two parties, both extremely afraid of what the other stands for. They perceive one another as a mortal threat, and the conflict can therefore escalate out of control. One party feels threatened by religion, while the other feels that their religion is threatened. Both *lead security policy*. Both believe that something fundamental is being threatened and therefore feel justified in doing whatever they deem necessary. This is brought out most clearly by drawing on the theory of securitization (also known as 'the Copenhagen School') (Wæver, 1995; Buzan et al., 1998). This theory does not define security by the use or threat of force, but more generically as a move that takes an issue beyond normal politics and places it as an issue of survival and necessary defence; a *securitizing actor* declares a given *referent object* (state, nation, the environment, economic welfare) existentially threatened and gains acceptance by the relevant *audience* of the ensuing legitimacy of *extraordinary measures* (violence, secrecy) to ward off the threat. In this way, the theory highlights how an issue and its social dynamics are transformed when reconstituted as an existential threat; securitization removes otherwise binding constraints and justifies extraordinary measures, such as the use of force or secrecy. Applying this theory helps us understand the escalatory dynamics of securitized religion (Laustsen and Wæver, 2000; Kjølberg, 2003; Madsen and Ottosen, 2003; Sheikh, 2005).[3] The theory can also be used for a relatively straightforward empirical investigation into what kinds of religion/security links dominate. There are three main types of securitizations in relation to religion: the secular state fears religious politics; religio-political movements fears the secular state; and religion fears religion. While the third occurs,[4] the two first are much more common (Juergensmeyer, 1993; 2000), and it becomes clear how they are two sides of the same conflict, as mutual security fears.

Conflicts are often exacerbated by what has become known as the security dilemma. We find it hard to understand how others can fear us, since we think we know our own motives, while we find it similarly difficult to be reassured about the intentions of others (Butterfield, 1950). Our own fear is easy for us to see. The worldly society fears religious politics; al-Qaeda represents an external threat to the West; and the secular elites in, for example, Turkey and Algeria, regard Islamists as a domestic threat.

The other side is more difficult to understand. What drives the people we refer to as fundamentalists? It is crucial to understand the degree to which *fundamentalism is security policy*. They act because they feel threatened, indeed, under attack.[5]

Both parties in the secularist-religiopolitical macro-conflict regard one another as a threat. Both are thinking in terms of security policy. Both hold religion to be the core of the conflict – the one threatened by politicizing religion, the other because their religion is threatened. Both regard secularism as the pivotal point, i.e. the principle at stake. When the religious actors lead security policy, it is called fundamentalism. When secularists lead security policy, we call it defence of freedom or something similarly heroic.

Mark Juergensmeyer, professor of sociology and religious studies, has interviewed a vast number of activists from militant religious groups representing various faiths (unsurprisingly, often in prisons). A recurring statement he heard was: 'We are already at war'. In February 1998, Osama bin Laden issued a 'fatwa' a few months prior to the embassy bombings in Kenya and Tanzania. 'The world is at war', he declared; and the point was to explain that he was not to blame for starting it. US Middle East policies constituted 'a clear declaration of war against God, his messenger and Muslims', he said (bin Laden et al., 1998; bin Laden, 2005: 60; cf. Juergensmeyer, 2000).

This is the significant difference between being a traditionalist or a fundamentalist. If one believes that one's faith is threatened; that people are not faithful enough or following the correct path, the natural response is to pore over one's holy scriptures, attend church/mosque more often, pray or appeal to others to do so. It is not to fly a plane into a tall building, but instead to seek a purely religious remedy. But fundamentalists argue that this amounts to betrayal. Why? Because, we are *so* threatened, the attack on our faith is *so* serious, that we must venture out in the world and act in defence of our faith. A purely religious answer is unable to succeed when the enemy is so powerful. Thereby, a strange hybrid emerges whereby the fundamentalists work to *defend the traditional*, but via *the means of the modern world* (cf. Marty and Appleby, 1995; Almond et al., 2003). Whether piloting planes into skyscrapers or disseminating messages via video and satellite television, bin Laden & Co. reportedly want in some respects to re-establish the Muslim world as in Mohammed's day, but they are hardly Luddites. Karl von Clausewitz said: in war, the two sides write the law for one another,[6] i.e. in war one cannot choose to do what one prefers; rather, one must do what is necessary. The logic of war leads to a focus on the efficiency of the means.

Fundamentalists and militant Islamists thus do not constitute a 'religious awakening' as such. They are no more 'religious' than many others. They do not possess an original theology; rather, they are political activists in a struggle for an alternative relationship between religion and politics.

The micro-dynamics of mobilization go a long way to explaining the shift from religion vs. religion to religion vs. secularism. During the crusades and the early modern period, the struggles were over spreading (or protecting) the right faith, and the social and political power tied to these related primarily to overall hierarchies in society, including the legitimacy of state power. This was promoted by mobilizing against an external enemy in religious terms. In today's world, the main social and power issues at stake, gender in particular, are to a larger extent local and societal. Fundamentalist movements can reasonably be seen as 'radical patriarchalism' (Riesebrodt, 1993; cf. Ruthven, 2002) and are often involved in conserving social structure and social privileges. Therefore, the threat is secularization, not another (conservative) religion. What is at stake politically and socially helps to explain how the threat is articulated.

The level of macro-explanation, on the other hand, looks at the larger historical forces and patterns. Allow me to put this in the form of a basic macro-historical periodization:

- World History, Part I, before secularization and secularism: All societies were permeated with what we today call 'religion'. Political struggles would regularly make appeals to religion, often in terms of one creed against another. The motives of these struggles would mix 'genuinely religious' ones with political and other interests, as thoroughly as religion, politics, society and law were intertwined in general.

- World History, Part II: Secularism was a disciplinary project closely linked to state-building (Asad, 2003). Gradually, the most politically salient expressions of religion shifted towards indirect presence as 'civil religion' (Burleigh, 2005). Action directly in the name of religion mostly occurred as rearguard resistance to increasing immorality.
- World History, Part III: Secularism became hegemonic in Europe's intellectual avant-garde from at least the mid-nineteenth century, within broader European society and politics during the first half of the twentieth century, in the US when the court imposed legal secularism after World War II and in the decolonizing Third World as an ideology of the first-generation state-building, typically Western-trained elites.
- World History, Part IV: With 'the return of religion' (or 'the revenge of God'; Keppel, 1995), it became possible to articulate conflict religion vs. religion or secularism vs. religion, but the micro-dynamics push towards mostly secularism as a threat to religion (and religious mobilization as a threat to the secular state).

Against my argument about secularism, not Christianity, being one side of an escalating conflict spiral, it may be pointed out that some Islamists perceive the threat as a *Christian crusade*. Bin Laden systematically refers to the 'Zionist–crusader alliance'. But even they do not depict an attack in the form of proselytization, i.e. that there is *too much religion* among us. Instead, the Christian crusade is proceeding in a more devious manner *in the form of secularism* and *moral decay* aimed at destroying Islam. (For a more complex analysis, see Wæver, 2006.)

The Pew Global Project Attitudes has conducted global surveys on, among other things, the view of the US in different parts of the world. Apparently, Muslim countries do not share the Western European image of George W. Bush as a Christian crusader. Massive majorities in Islamic countries see the US as 'not religious enough', as Americans do to a lesser extent, while a majority of Europeans see the US as 'too religious' (Pew, 2005). The predominant view of the US among the people in Muslim countries is the one the founding fathers of militant Islamism, most notably Sayyid Qutb, built on. Not only is the US degenerate, licentious, but it has more generally sacrificed morality and values to science, technology and efficiency. During a visit to the US in the late 1940s, Qutb wrote: 'I wish I could find somebody to talk with about human affairs, morality and spirit – not just dollars, movie stars, and cars' (quoted in

Gerges, 2006: 151).[7] His book *The America I Have Seen* (2000[1949]) is still widely seen as an analysis that captures the view shared by the broad population and strongly motivates the extremists (Gerges, 2006: 145). The main reproach against the US is moral depravity rather than missionary zeal.

The fact that Westerners tend to overlook how religio-political activists can feel threatened by 'the anti-religious' owes to media images of *wars of religion*. At the sight of a new conflict in the contemporary world, one of the first things a journalist will typically check is whether the parties have opposing religious convictions – because, if so, that must be the cause of the conflict – just as journalists in the 1990s looked for ethnic differences between parties in wars in order to label them 'ethnic conflicts' as if this necessarily explained what people were fighting for and against. Quite comfortable indeed to the secular West – the nature of the problem is that some people 'have too much religion'. *Secularists,* on the other hand, have apparently found the solution: the separation of religion and politics. The image of bitter wars of religion confirms the righteousness of the Western model, and places secularists in the privileged position of waiting for everyone else to catch up and end their conflicts once they learn to keep politics and religion separate. Conversely, if the majority of conflicts are actually between the religiously political vs. the secular, then Western secularists are not above the conflict but one half of it.

This party to the conflict even goes so far as to promote secularism as the framework for conflict resolution, as neutral rules of play within which it is possible to maintain religious freedom, pluralism and a place for everyone. What we promote as the neutral framework – as the solution – is the very same one part of the conflict is afraid of.

There is a significant risk of contributing to a vicious circle of mutual fear and conflict escalation if the West continues its self-assured – even self-righteous – promotion of secularism as a doctrine, raised above politics, as a precondition for politics, as the path to a peaceful, free and successful society – as something the others simply must learn.

One possible misunderstanding must be avoided. While it may appear that I objectify 'religion' and 'secularism' and treat them as homogeneous and given, I really study the processes whereby they become constituted and operate *as if* homogeneous and given objects (cf. Wæver et al., forthcoming). In line with securitization theory, the issue is not 'religion' as such as a causal factor, but what can powerfully be invoked as a basis for extreme action. Therefore, the important point here is the power of the idea of religion – as an object to be defended and as an object of fear.[8] Likewise with secularism: I can easily be misunderstood as saying that there is such a thing as an important principle of secularism. Quite the contrary – I shall argue that most suffer from the *illusion* that there is such a principle – the *idea of it* is strong, but the actual consistency of any doctrine is much weaker, as we shall see. Consequently, it is important to specify the powerful effects of two parties building a conflict on the shared assumption that there is a strict principle.

Secularism, the principle

All too often the doctrine of the separation of religion and politics is taken for granted as though 'religion' and 'politics' are given entities. Their separation in the sixteenth/seventeenth centuries is often claimed to be the premise for modernity's success in Europe, from societal peace over science, well-functioning markets and democracy to individual freedom. The problem is that there is no entity called religion. The abstract, general concept 'religion' was not widespread before that point. People were religious, but 'religion' as an abstract and distinct entity was only invented when the separation was made (Smith, 1991; Asad, 1993; McCutcheon, 2003). The same is the case with politics – it is not a stable entity either. At the same historical moment, the idea was forged of politics as free rational discussion, without reference to metaphysical and religious arguments (Berg-Sørensen, 2004). 'Religion' and 'politics' do not *simply exist*; what is more, they can be mixed or separated. Indeed, early modern Europe created a specific construction, invented entities such as religion and politics (and economics, the public and law), as a way of organizing society. It might well be a good way – but it is not a given. It is highly *political* to do so. Secularism is treated as being apolitical, but it might just be the most political of all, the most significant, most fundamental decision.[9]

And it is a form of politics that is more compatible with some religions than with others. It is more compatible with Protestantism, because the very point is that one defines religion in a *specific* manner. Religion is defined as private. For this is the other aspect of secularism: politics is to be free of religion, but religion must be kept away from the political. Where? Within the individual person. It is more difficult for religions in which the outer trappings – the external and often collective practices and social organization – are a far more constitutive aspect of the religion. This, of course, is not to say that all Protestants agree with secularism, nor that secularism is somehow a natural product of Protestantism, as is often argued. All religions are malleable and at any given time they are what their practitioners make of them. Still, it might be vaguely asserted that the move to secularism as we know it was shorter for Protestants than for some other religions – not surprising given that the secularism we are measuring up against is the one that emerged from a Protestant starting point.

Debates between religious politics and secular politics are between two competing worldviews, and it is a secularist illusion to assume that one is a neutral framework, which the other should accommodate to. Even Jürgen Habermas (2006) acknowledges that one has to take the challenges each worldview poses seriously.

Parallelism in contrast to the hierarchy – or radical incomparability – assumed by secularists is also visible in the paradoxical dependence of secularism on religion. Because secularism is defined in relation to religion, religion is always present in secularist arguments (Sørensen, 2004). Ironically, secularism does not mark an 'absence' of religion in politics – it constantly imports religion into politics in order to oppose it. This is not the secularist self-conception because it focuses on an ideal, ongoing religion-free process, but whenever secularism needs to be justified or defined to manage its boundary, the principle cannot be defined without reference to religion, or rather a specific concept of religion.

To follow Talal Asad (2006), secularism is not just a separation between religion and politics, it is a more general project shaping subjectivity to enable given kinds of society; it is a productive practice, not meaningfully understood only as an absence ('no mixing of religion and politics').

Another way to show how secularism is not a simple principle is through the comparative study of *secularisms*. Simultaneous 'headscarf debates' as well as the EU countries' attempts to draft a common constitution revealed that even though France, England, Poland and Turkey refer to themselves as secular, it actually means something very different. A distinction *has* been drawn between religion and politics – but it has been drawn in different places and according to different principles. Every country historically arranged itself with its own distinction, which could take the status of *the* general principle, as long as only one country was observed at a time. Globalization and Europeanization are in the process of coupling secularisms that require isolation to maintain their innocence. Secularism can no longer be regarded as though it is raised above politics as an obvious principle. A real-historic process is in play that positions 'comparative secularism' as a privileged object of study with political potential. Comparative secularism *reveals* how differently the limits are drawn instead of philosophically *demonstrating* that these constructions are contingent.

In real-world practices, secularism is a complex field of political-cultural constellations, but in contemporary struggles and especially in the escalating Cold War between the West and radical Islamism this complexity is reduced to a binary question. Conflicts are organized around the *idea of* (some kind of) separation, despite the fact that its concrete meaning varies drastically. The idea has become the focal point for struggles.

Where is secularism at stake?

Secularism is politically on the agenda in numerous places in the world and for different reasons:

- Failure of the postcolonial state in much of the Third World. Secularism was part of the ideology for the first postcolonial state-building elite, because it struggled to weaken local and traditional authorities and to find a path to Western-style modernization (Juergensmeyer, 1993). Anti-secularist movements have defined local politics in many places, but primarily in the Middle East it spilled over into transnational and international action.
- In the US due to domestic dialectics of the 'church/state' question. Domestic securitization has generated the pattern of 'culture wars', where the religious Right has mobilized against a perceived destruction of tradition and virtue by a secularist elite who (according to the Right) upset the balance of politics especially through the post-1945 Supreme Court concept of total neutrality. Liberals in turn have seen this revolt as a threat to the separation of church and state (Gunn, 2004; Feldman, 2005).
- In Europe, secularism has become an issue due to the pressures of globalization, first, migration (Islam), second, Europeanization (cf. above about comparative secularisms). Only as a weak third comes the limited 'religious revival' in Europe, which does not in itself put much pressure on secularism, because it generally stays off limits in relation to politics – and in Northern Europe often even reinforces secularism because secularism is seen as part of Protestantism and (thereby) part of national identity (cf. Sheikh and Wæver, 2005; Mouritsen, 2006).

So secularism is at stake politically in many places. Most important, however, is where it intersects with the 'new cold war' between the West and militant Islamism. When does secularism/religion become a security issue domestically, internationally and transnationally? And how does securitization in one place tie in to other parts of the world?

- The securitizing discourse of the militant Islamists is an obvious, though complicated, starting point. Traditionally, the main threat according to both mainstream (non-violent Islamists, for example the Muslim Brotherhood today) and violent 'jihadists' have been the apostate (in their view) secular regimes. The strategic aim is to gain political power in their home countries. But from the late 1990s some (the 'transnationalist Jihadis', spearheaded by Osama bin Laden; Scheuer, 2002; Gerges, 2005; 2006; bin Laden, 2005; 2005; Sheikh, 2005) shifted the 'centre of gravity' from 'the near enemy' (domestic regimes) to 'the far enemy' (the US and Israel). Basically, this is still justified on regional (Middle Eastern) grounds and the conflict is not global in that sense (Buzan and Wæver, 2003: 206–10). The reason why they focus on 'the far enemy' is that the 'Jewish–crusader alliance' will not allow Islamists to gain power in Muslim countries, and therefore they have to be dealt with first (Gerges, 2005: 31f, 144–50; 2006; bin Laden, 2005; Wæver, 2006). In addition this is seen as a way to mobilize and unify the *Ummah*, especially if the US assists by fighting back. One might argue that this pulls the rug from under the argument about the Jihadists fighting Western secularism, because their quarrel is not with what the West *is*, but with its military presence in the Middle East and its support of Israel. However, their understanding of Western policy is anchored in the image of what the West is – and the defining trait here is neither economic imperialism nor religious expansionism, but moral decadence, materialism and anti-Islamist hostility. The ultimate enemy is secularism – at home.

- Conversely, Western policy towards Islamic countries is part of the constellation, including US policy towards Israel/Palestine, Afghanistan and Iraq, but also EU's reaction to Turkey's infidelity law (more on this below), and the place of religion/secularism in Iraq's constitution. Most interesting in order to tie the combined conflict constellation is the general discourse about 'what is wrong with Islam' and 'what is wrong with the Arab world', and thus the overarching attitude towards the region. Here, revealingly, any role of religion in politics is treated as a problem and carefully weighed in terms of an occasionally necessary, but by definition wrong concession (Gerges, 1999; Hurd, 2004). This is ironic given the unstable balance between secular and religious politics in the US. But vis-à-vis the Muslim world, the US appears and acts like a distinct representative of international secularism.

- Since the general perception of the Muslim world is one of Western hostility towards Muslims and Islam, Europe becomes important, as witnessed in the conflict over the Mohammed cartoons. In Europe, migration and religion have become two sides of the same coin, because the largest immigrant groups are Muslims, and religious controversies focus on Islam. This in contrast to the US, where the two issues are largely separate – migration being mostly about Hispanics, and religious controversies mostly about the Christian Right (Casanova, 2005). *Europe is the best place for Muslims to observe what place for religion in society the West offers.* This chapter will now concentrate on how secularism is practised in Europe, followed by a discussion on how it could be done.

One way to view the larger constellation is as a triangle, where the US is central in terms of foreign policy, but the most complicated part as concerns religious/secularist action (Wæver, 2006). In contrast, Europe and the Islamists mirror each other more evenly.

The radicalization of secularism in twenty-first-century Europe

Instead of self-critically examining the political dogma of secularism, the tendency in contemporary Western society is the very opposite, particularly since 9/11. European politicians especially insist on secularism in an increasingly doctrinaire manner. Those who want to be inclusive, open and pluralistic say: 'Religion is all right, as long as it is private', 'all religions are acceptable, as long as they don't play an active role', 'people must give their word that democracy comes before religion' and 'you have to swear that the constitution comes before the Quran'. This sounds tolerant, but one is actually solidly planted in the most sensitive spot while uttering these otherwise friendly words. The central challenge in Europe in the years to come is to be innovative regarding the relationship between religion and politics – to fulfil the values of secularism more discreetly. Security policy therefore cannot simply be handled as a question about what to do about distant countries and peoples. It also accentuates a difficult question among Europeans.

Reacting to the challenge of religion's increasing visibility, the European debate has become more reflective, and this makes things worse. The dominant approach has changed from a vague sense that religion does not belong in politics, (back) to the *principle* of 'secularism'. By being formulated as a principle, the arguments against religion become self-reinforcing.

Secularism appears to be a clear principle; apparently simple, tolerant and equal for everyone. It therefore serves as the *line in the sand* for many Europeans: 'We must stand our ground, we must defend a fundamental principle that our society is built upon'. Upon closer examination, however, this *line in the sand* turns out to be a *line drawn in water* (Sheikh and Wæver, 2005). There is no simple principle, nor a given place to draw the line – and it is anything but innocent or neutral. Nor is it necessary to operate a strict principle.

A frequent argument is that if we give in here, the foundations of the Western democratic order disappear. The imagery is almost invariably modelled on time travel: giving in will send us back to the Middle Ages. This is because we do not *concretely* discuss what would happen if religious arguments were in play together with the many others in the democratic debate. Instead, we see 'a principle' at stake, and so regard any single, small 'violation' as the first domino capable of toppling the entire arrangement. 'Secularism' is at stake. The rhetoric of 'values' and especially 'principles' tends to support securitization, because instead of a given case carrying its own intrinsic importance, it becomes loaded with long-term implications (Buzan et al., 1998: 148f, 154, 161f). Principles do exist, and sometimes single instances should be treated according to their role as a barrier against general chance, but the politics of the 'principlification' of issues is usually treated too lightly given the power of such framing.

The image of a return to a world of religion-against-religion (World History, part I; cf. above) seems deeply implausible. In any conflict with two religions, a powerful third – and often the main opponent of both – is secularism. There is no way to get back to a pre-secularist situation, where the world will consist of only different religions.

In much of Northern Europe, it is widely observed that religious faith is gaining ground. In TV and magazines, celebrities talk about their belief in something or other – in striking contrast to say ten years ago. Faith is *in*. It has generally been treated as a good thing, a welcome and innocent spice – with politics as the big exception. In politics, the ideal to keep religion and politics separate remains. A possibly increasing role of faith in politics is playing out in inverse form: faith is having an increasing impact on European politics for the very reason that *the fear of faith* has become more acute. Religious arguments are not received into a pragmatic tussle of various religious, economic, society-ideal and self-interest arguments; instead, there is a strong, reflex-like reaction when religion is brought into politics. If a local Imam defends the stoning of women in Nigeria, there are few who explain why stoning is wrong. The majority simply say: 'That just goes to show how crazy things get when they base their arguments on religion.' They attack the form instead of arguing for their own viewpoint.

Is this wise? Those who draw their political conclusions on a partly religious foundation face the message that they must find other arguments in the public sphere. When arguing, you must use other reasons than your actual motives. It is not self-evident how this is supposed to provide for a particularly rich democratic conversation.

Would it be possible simply to drop this manner of treating religion in politics? Is it not better if the secular voices in the debate openly express what they want and what they don't want instead of telling others that they are not allowed to argue 'their way'?

Rendering religion private is simple, as seen from the secularist side, but for many people of faith it is both an amputation of religion (because a full religious life cannot be private only) and an artificial requirement about assuming political positions without including significant elements of what matter most (Habermas, 2006). The secular state boasts about treating all religions equally. However, the system is anything but equal and neutral in the relationship *between the religious and the secular*. Nor are the *different religions* treated equally in practice. To varying degrees, the dominant conceptions about justice, guilt, human values, etc. have religious roots in all societies. But this form of influence merely seeps into the debate when values cannot be justified without drawing on tradition. Religious arguments are not noted in Western politics when they stem from majority groups; they are only conspicuous when they are rare – when they stem from the minority (or a radical fraction within the majority population). The idea of 'secularism' as a limiting principle is so problematic in Europe today because it is an impossible ideal, which the majority group has no problem breaking most of the time, and then use to belabour specific groups with.

The main problem with secularism is the notion that it is a principled either/or – should we separate or mix religion and politics? Ironically, framing the matter in this way unites ardent secularists and Islamists (Hurd, 2001). Both talk about abstract separation/non-separation and in either/or terms – one group simply chooses one, 'either' (separation), and the other group 'or' (non-separation). Both Western and Islamic traditions contain complicated discussions about the relationship between religion and politics, but today's hard-line secularists and Islamists dodge difficult questions with reference to an apparently simple principle about 'separation'. Contemporary Islamists avoid living up to the Islamic traditions of engaging in reasoned debate regarding the relationship between religion and politics by replacing the debate with a simple negation of the Western position – 'we reject the Western, un-Islamic distinction between religion and politics'. And the contemporary Western debate (particularly in Europe) regards this distinction as the proverbial 'line in the sand' the West must draw in relation to Islamism, presenting it as a 'yes/no question' as opposed to a 'how question'. The respective parties reflect themselves in one another and use a one-dimensional 'secularism' to do so.

Western declarations of war in defence of the holy principles of secularism render it unnecessarily provocative, threatening and intolerant internationally, and they legitimize genuine discrimination in the name of tolerance in domestic politics. Ironically, this entails a particularly aggressive politicization of religion as opposed to the limited effects it would have if religious arguments became yet another dimension in the diversity of the political debate. By warring with those instances, secularists create a more problematic mix-up, a suspicious politicization of certain groups' religion and the possible influence of this religion on their political opinions.

Recent years have offered a number of examples, particularly in Europe, of an increasingly heavy-handed campaign against religion in politics. Since 9/11, terrorism has been interpreted as the ultimate expression of religious politics, and any coupling of religion and politics thus becomes demonized on account of the relation to terror that has been imposed on it. In cases like the Turkish infidelity law and Buttiglione's candidacy as EU Commissioner, the secularists effected a coupling of religion and politics because they believed they saw a religious influence, which they took upon themselves to expel from people who themselves claimed to be able to distinguish it. Let me use the Turkish case to illustrate this.

In 2004, the ruling post(?)-Islamist party in Turkey proposed a law against adultery. The reaction was unified condemnation in Europe and Turkey's application for EU membership was jeopardized. Interestingly, this reaction was at the same time unanimous and assumed not to need any justification. It raises the question of whether adultery is defining for European identity. Many Americans will probably answer yes, not only because adultery is illegal in 24 states, but because Europe is seen as too immoral, relativist and godless. To illustrate, the closest European politicians came to arguing their case was that the law 'gave an impression of' Turkey heading towards Sharia. There is nothing Islamic about the law as such, except that – as *New York Times* remarked (14 September 2004) – 'adultery is forbidden in Islam, as it is in most religions'. There is nothing in the law about granting religious authorities any competences. Why, then, wasn't it a domestic issue? When legitimizing international criticism and even sanctions, such as denial of EU membership, one should think the law violated clear criteria, such as the Copenhagen Criteria for membership. However, this is not the case, and the right to adultery is not mentioned in the European convention of human rights either. Also, it is unlikely that the reaction can be explained by the law being regarded as inappropriate state intervention in family matters; many countries have laws proscribing parents' physical punishment of children, and the state generally regulates laws about marriage. The Turkish law did not even equip an external actor with powers of intervention – only the parties to the marriage could present cases. Therefore, the problem seems to be 'the impression of' this relating to religion, maybe even to Sharia law. But family law in general, as in European countries, is in one way or other inspired by religion. Rules about marriage, adoption, artificial insemination and divorce are not based on abstract political reason, but come from dominant conceptions in a given society about human beings, life and love. The fact that family law draws on ideas with religious antecedents can hardly be the issue. Instead, it appears that Europeans link the ruling AKP party, due to its Islamic roots, to the dreaded Sharia law, and want to monitor this party, even if there is no clear connection or a violation of international rules. It is very likely that feminists were right in believing that the law would have had negative effects, and Turks were well advised to join the demonstrations against it. But the fact that European politicians drew heavy political implications without any legal or principled basis (and almost without critical commentary in the domestic press) reveals how strong the dogma of banishing religion from politics has become. This episode clearly contributed to polishing the enemy image in the Muslim world of Europe as crusadingly anti-religious and in favour of all kinds of decadence.

These cases probably relate to the issue of European identity. A search has been on for a while for values which define Europe and can carry future integration after the completion of projects like the internal market and monetary union. Not that adultery is the new candidate, but an influential article by Jürgen Habermas and Jacques Derrida (2003) is representative of ideas that circulate among intellectuals around the EU Commission. The three most recurrent ideas are the welfare state, international law (in contrast to power politics) and secularism. They all seem selected with the criteria of demarcating Europe vis-à-vis the US. Secularism goes well with the widespread perception in Europe that Bush and bin Laden are two religious fundamentalists dragging the world into a dangerous confrontation. Hereby, the process where secularism hardens through reflectivity and self-reference attains a third layer. First, it goes from being a preference as such to becoming a principle, and therefore defended 'as such' and not only according to the specifics of the case. When this principle then becomes a value for wider purposes, it becomes increasingly entrenched and objectified. A specific question at the first level (e.g. should schools accommodate Muslim demands for separation of the sexes in swimming classes?) is answered not concretely but in terms of defending (at the second level) the *principle* of secularism, and defending this principle becomes even more important at the third level, when it is seen as a defining European value that helps to give Europe its identity.

A particular version of this layering has been seen in Denmark and goes quite a long way to explaining the crisis in connection with the cartoons. As argued by Karen Wren and Per Mouritsen, liberal values have increasingly become the anchor for national identity in Denmark, and immigrants are faced with difficult demands based on criteria that in the Danes' self-conception are universalistic and inclusive, but de facto are presented in particularistic and often inaccessible ways (Wren, 2001; Mouritsen, 2006). More specifically, it was suggested – before the cartoon crisis – that Denmark was constructing a particularly militant secularism as part of a crisis over national identity (Sheikh and Wæver, 2005). Denmark's self-image was historically constructed against its neighbours, Germany/Prussia and Sweden, who were defined as hierarchical, humourless, authoritarian and elitist, while the Danish were egalitarian, easygoing, liberal, pragmatic and tolerant. However, the increasingly restrictive policy towards immigrants has been difficult to square with this self-image. Dialectically, this tension has been resolved by metonymically redefining liberal and enlightenment values as expressed in two areas: gender equality and secularism. A particularly intolerant tolerance emerged from this defensive upgrading of these particular values as essential to fight for. In the case of the cartoons, this attitude explained the widespread perception in Denmark that it was necessary to take even quite provocative steps to defend crucial principles, where many others would be worried about *other* liberal enlightenment values that Danes have recently downplayed and therefore removed from the relevant criteria.

Religious democratization of democracy

Lifting the exclusion of religion from politics could promote democratization and integration in Western society. The dangerous thing about the pseudo-rule is that it is selectively employed to attack some and thereby exclude them instead of engaging them in debate. This distinguishing between those who are part of the 'reasonable conversation' and those who aren't is far less constructive in relation to forging an inclusive political community as opposed to a continued democratization in which we include a greater number and greater variation in the common conversation.

As argued by William Connolly (1995; 1999), this is about a paradox deep within liberalism. A pluralistic society must necessarily draw limits.

Whom is this pluralism and influence in effect for? Roughly speaking, debates about who is included are less relevant in an authoritarian regime, because the people have no influence or rights anyway. The more pluralistic the society, the stronger the pressure to draw a line. This limit is typically defined in terms of who is *reasonable* enough to qualify. Can participation include women, the poor, the mentally ill? Over time, the limit has expanded. Connolly therefore depicts a process demanding both pluralism and pluralization. Pluralism must not coagulate and form a closed circle; instead, it must be constantly challenged so that new identities are allowed to form and become a part of the community. It is precisely because this delineation is conceived in terms of reasonable/ unreasonable that religion becomes the primary Other for politics. Pluralizing pluralism so that it includes religious arguments is therefore a particularly daunting challenge.

Some of the explanations and justifications for secularism turn into a mechanism of further hardening and further insult. The most common argument for keeping religion out of politics is that political conversation suffers when we plant our positions in something beyond discussion. The debate would die. This is a pseudo-justification. It assumes an infinitely high ideal for politics as the rational conversation. This ideal is not ordinarily maintained and implemented. In debates, justifications tussle on the basis of such different sources as self-interest, tradition, societal philosophy and which politician to trust. Not only could one part find the other part's argumentation quite 'unreasonable', but the interplay itself between different 'reasonable' arguments does not proceed as the rational testing of justifications, for the disagreement is often precisely about where the question begins and what it is about. In practice, however, these contrasting forms of argumentation in democracy interact, and one occasionally finds oneself slowly shifting from one position to another – albeit rarely because the other's argumentation 'forces' one to do so (cf. Rorty, 1989). The others' arguments are not dismissed as disqualifying the speaker. Rather, they are compared and weighed against other types of arguments. We do not generally lead a hyper-rational conversation in which we test the foundations of one another's political positions. Arguments are not deemed unacceptable on the grounds of being 'too illogical' – but a justification with a religious basis *will* precisely be rejected as a matter of principle. This reveals that *we are not dealing with an ordinary, high standard that faith arguments fail to live up to – we are dealing with a special ban against religious justifications in politics*. To pretend that political debate generally operates from this high standard – and only religious arguments fail the test – is to add injury to insult; it is to brand religion as particularly irrational. It would be more fair and honest to openly discuss the special rule against religion. It probably was justified and progressive 400 years ago, but today it ought to be reassessed openly.

In the secularists' horror scenario, reasonable conversation is positioned up against the literalist dogmatism. Debate stalls because one part merely points at a holy book. Does it? In practice, it is far from unequivocal what one ought to think on the basis of a given religious point of departure. A good example is Jim Wallis's book, *God's Politics: Why the Right Gets it Wrong and the Left Doesn't Get It* (2005). Here, a progressive American minister attempts to convince Democrats that Christianity can be mobilized for their benefit. As he writes: 'How did Jesus become pro-rich, pro-war, and only pro-American?' Who is to say that 'value politics' are supposed to mean opposition to homosexual marriage, when it can alternatively mean peace, equality and social justice? Religion is not necessarily a 'debate stopper'. First, this makes for new debates within the religious community; second, it can give an interesting interplay between secular and religious participants. The American political scientist Thomas Banchoff (forthcoming) has recently pointed out that there are endless writings about what would happen if religion were to come into play in politics. However, there is hardly any research concerning actual courses of events where the religious and the secular interact. Drawing on the example of stem cell research in the US and France, he demonstrates how this can provide a satisfactory course of events. Even secular participants can benefit from inspiration from religious debate partners once the limit has been reached for what the current rationalistic language can handle, as seen most clearly in connection with bio-ethical questions (cf. Habermas, 2006).

These examples illustrate that the contrast between a rational secular conversation modelled on an inquiry amongst philosophers against rigid doctrinaire religious believers is problematic on both sides: the existing political debate is very different from this ideal (and this much more trivial reality, which we all take for granted on all other occasions, than the contrast to religion) and religion can be involved without closing the debate.

This does not mean that dropping the ban on religion in politics is an easy solution. The religion/politics will continue to raise thorny questions. The main question is whether they should be addressed through the ordinary, ongoing political process or through special limitations on religion in politics. Do we need a special ban (formal or informal) on religion in politics, or should religious activists be met with exactly the same requirements and bans as everyone else? They are not allowed to use violence in politics and we do not allow democracy to be used to abolish democracy, i.e. 'overthrow the public order'. Or must we – as a weakened special rule – make an explicit requirement about accepting contradiction? And how do we permit faith-related arguments while simultaneously preventing religious institutions from gaining power and undermining democratic institutions? Such questions are difficult and must be handled as such – not regarded as simple and solvable via a declaratory 'separation' of religion and politics.

Especially in situations where religious politics on behalf of a majority population wins influence, it will be important to protect: 1) freedom of belief including that of atheists; 2) protection of the supremacy of democracy's institutions (i.e. no 'Council of the Guardians'); and 3) protection of human rights, not least those related to gender. These are mostly relevant in connection with the risk of a majority imposing their religiously based decision on a minority and building them into state structures. However, the early American experience was that with societal pluralism (in that case different Protestant denominations; today different religions), such models become less and less feasible (Feldman, 2005). Globalization means that we will all be Americanized, and this is a good thing (in this context).

Going beyond these standard demands on all political actors means raising problematic limitations. If put up against a majority, it tends to be anti-democratic and elitist; if in relation to a minority, it becomes a repressive lack of pluralism. One can, for instance, not demand of religious activists an 'openness' to the argument of others, because that is something that most politicians already fail to deliver. Nor should we demand that religious actors assume the principled fallibility of their own positions because the secularists typically combine the demand for this by insisting on certain 'unnegotiable' human rights and political values. We should stick to demands that are actually abided by (or are attainable), such as following decisions made by the majority, even when voted down.

But aren't high ideals always good? If good rules are ignored by secular politicians, why not just strengthen efforts in demanding it of both secular and religious actors? No, because demands that are out of touch with reality become an instrument used disproportionally against minorities. It is more conspicuous when Muslims use religious arguments than when a 'native' politician draws on widespread, religiously rooted perceptions. The majority also has greater access to political resources and are better able to use the political opportunity offered by nonconformity to rules by others.

The idea that political theorists should promote ideals if they are philosophically justifiable rests on a specific model of the relationship between theory/philosophy and practical politics. Theory is assumed to be able to arrive at general conclusions independent of any specific society, and these principles are later introduced to actual politics without consideration of the forces at play and their likely effect on political constellations. As universally valid, they are above such considerations. With a more political view – an emphasis on politics as action, interaction and constant creativity, not problem resolution – the truth in any given political situation depends on what the other actors are doing and saying (Arendt, 1968). The dominant view of the relationship between theory and politics is indebted to secularism, because it assumes supremacy of independent reason as pure authority – the structure that was installed to replace religion as justification for political authority. In contrast, I think theoretical interventions have to be calibrated with an eye on the existing political struggles and power relations in the relevant arena.

I therefore neither agree with those demanding that we must 'get religion back into politics' nor with the 'normal' European argument that we must maintain the distinction between politics and religion. It is not an objective – not an unequivocal gain – to introduce more religion into the political life; it would have advantages as well as disadvantages. Among the advantages is a greater capacity for dealing with difficult ethical and existential questions, where the narrowest understanding of politics falls short, and we can benefit from drawing on more diverse experiences and traditions. Among the disadvantages is increased fragmentation of the public into groups that do not acknowledge each other's fundamental views. But when the goal is not 'more religion in politics', then what is the point? It is to avoid a ban on religious arguments in politics, to stop beating people with a 'principle', a criterion for access. Those who might want to argue on the basis of religion have the right to try to do so. They will undoubtedly often find that it is not the most efficient approach in Europe, and it will therefore not make a significant difference in terms of the outcome of the respective debates; conversely, it wreaks considerable havoc to prohibit them from doing so.

The 'negative' effects of allowing religion will be limited, simply because the use of religion as form of argumentation is self-limiting due to the nature of politics. It is rarely wise to use arguments that only make sense to a limited section of the population. At the same time, there could be great advantages, not least because this would weaken the militantly anti-religious image of the West.

Conclusion

Naturally, reckoning with secularism is not *the* solution to terrorism, but only a small piece in the puzzle. Terrorism has many causes – economic, geopolitical, social, gender policy. Correspondingly, there must be many elements in the campaign, including the military, because the leadership cannot be affected. The image of the West influences recruitment to militant groups, which possibly is the most important in the long run. For this purpose, it makes sense to listen to how terrorists formulate their arguments and with reference to what/whom they justify their actions. Particularly important is the point at which security and religion meet – religion defended and religion feared.

This point can be influenced by how Europe deals with secularism. It affects the conflict in two ways: by modifying the images of an amoral society and its suppression and persecution of Muslims. As a bonus, Europe gains further development and expansion of its own democracy as well as its concepts of reason and rationality.[10]

Removing the superfluous, heavy-handed 'rule' – informal but strictly enforced – would serve to muffle conflict. First, internationally, we can help break the spiralling conflict between secularists and religious politics. Second, removing the special ban can promote democratization and integration in our own society. The pseudo-rule is selectively used against certain people and thereby excludes them instead of engaging in debate with them. Drawing the dividing line between those who are part of the 'reasonable conversation' and those who are excluded is less constructive than a continued democratization that includes a greater number.

The degree to which 'the West' constitutes an enemy for the Islamic world is not merely a question of 'what we directly do to them', but also a matter of 'how things are done at home'. The more we fortify ourselves in a self-satisfied manner with secularism as a glossy non-debatable principle, the more we confirm the enemy image. Conversely, if we engage in debates amongst ourselves that are not necessarily about *them*, but merely the way we debate politics, it would show that we too are struggling with difficult, as yet unanswered questions. By thus permitting 'value-full' access to political debate, we would appear less threatening.

This chapter's focus on problematizing a political principle in one sense fits into the format of the book, the idea of 'political solutions to cultural conflict'. It is a critical discussion of the current political solution and points towards a refashioned form of (post-)secularism; a new 'political solution'. However, the argument also raises questions about the general format of 'political solutions to cultural conflict'. To ask and answer a question, one must grant it terms. The terms of this question imply that (subpolitical) society is the source of conflict and divisions, and the role of politics is to regulate and contain these conflicts. The present chapter illustrates why this is a problematic, overarching approach. The subjects and subjectivities constituted in a given time and place are the product of large-scale practices and disciplinary patterns – such as secularism (cf. Asad, 1993; 2003; 2006) – that have to be recognized as political. There is no such thing as purely 'cultural' conflicts, they are already political, long before the political 'solutions' enter the frame. Correspondingly, political solutions will be indebted to and shaped by particular cultural or religious roots.

This might sound like the trivial 'everything is connected to everything' spoiler, but the argument is more precise than that. The strategy of 'political solutions to cultural conflict' is not only impossible, but also part of the problem. It draws on the basic secularist, Hobbesian narrative of the modern state and state system: differences among people are the problem; and if not contained by politics, will generate war. The role of politics, in turn, is to organize and constrain these subterranean forces and establish order. But today, most of the important conflicts derive from the inadequacies of this Hobbesian, Westphalian (secularist) model. It is not differences as such that generate conflict, but rather the blurring of differences and distinctions in a globalizing world and the ensuing, desperate attempts to mark out new differences through ethno-nationalism, fundamentalism and violence (Appadurai, 2006). The conflicts are political through and through – they are about the delineation and organization of communities and states, not about inter-human, local relations as such. Maybe the next volume should be on 'cultural solutions to political conflict' or even 'religious solutions to political conflict'.

Notes

1. This chapter is partly based on a lecture given at the University of Copenhagen Annual Awards Ceremony 2004, together with excerpts from articles printed in *Weekendavisen* (no. 52, 24–30 December 2004), *Berlingske Tidende* (24 July 2005) and *Salt* (Vol. 14, September–October 2005, pp. 14–18). In addition, I have held variations of this text as lectures numerous times in recent years, and I thank the many, many insightful critics who have contributed to the sharpening and development of the argumentation. Thanks to Jon Jay Neufeld for translating the Danish texts and to Per Mouritsen for unusually helpful questions and suggestions.
2. Secularization is obviously the object of an extensive literature. A recent and useful status on a part of the debate is Davie et al. (2003, especially Casanova's chapter). See also Asad (2006).
3. The theory of securitization is particularly useful for the current project for two reasons. First, it is an 'open' theory in the sense that it does not try on theoretical grounds to decide what is security or is not, as done by both traditional ones (the answer being military state security) and critical security theory (answer: human needs). Securitization theory defines security as form, as the lifting of issues above normal politics to a sphere of urgency and necessity.

This theoretical openness allows empirical studies of variation in security both over time and across places (Buzan and Wæver, 2003), and in this case to make it an empirical question how religion enters the security picture: what is deemed threatened by what? The second reason to choose this theory is that it seems to be able to link up constructively with the main theories of fundamentalism and religious radicalism (more on this below), and thus foster the necessary interdisciplinary synergy.

4. Two of the most important examples today of religion-against-religion conflicts is the competition between Islam and Christianity (both expanding in many places) in parts of sub-Saharan Africa, and the increasingly emerging shape of the Israeli-Palestinian conflict, which originally was run by secular actors on both sides, but now is kept confrontational by religious fundamentalists on both sides (although it is still only a partial shift in this direction, because even the religious groups on both sides define the conflict in terms of territory more than faith).

5. Many analysts have given good arguments for avoiding the term 'fundamentalism': it is misleading to extend a term originating with a specific early twentieth-century American Protestant movement to other religions; the similarities across religions are not strong enough; it is a political tool more than an analytical one; and most of the movements labelled this way do not use the term themselves. Most important in the present context is to note that using the label 'fundamentalism' is in itself a securitizing speech act: To label a movement 'fundamentalist' is to say 'they are instances of a known syndrome, and we know they can't be included in normal politics – they should be eradicated' (Juergensemeyer, 1993; Laustsen and Wæver, 2000). Juergensmeyer has pointed to the widespread political misuse of the label by governments to crack down on oppositions and limit democracy. However, I continue to use the term here while observing critically its political usage, because it is the most widespread term in the West, and it is therefore helpful to be able to discuss directly how to interpret 'the phenomenon known as fundamentalism'.

6. '[W]ar is an act of violence pushed to its utmost bounds; as one side dictates the law to the other, there arises a sort of reciprocal action, which logically must lead to an extreme' (Clausewitz, 1982 [1832]: Book 1, Ch. 1, p. 103).

7. A Gallup World Poll conducted in 2005 among 8000 women in eight predominantly Muslim countries found that the most frequent response to 'What do you admire least about the West?' was 'the general perception of moral decay, promiscuity and pornography that pollsters called the "Hollywood image" that is regarded as degrading to women' (*New York Times*, 8 June 2006: A5). According to the majority, the best aspect of their own societies was 'attachment to moral and spiritual values'.

8. Although the argument here is not substantialist in itself, in the sense that religion is ascribed specific powers, I cannot resign myself to a total abstention from using the concept of religion as demarcation, or nominalistically stick to when the actors call things 'religion'. Since I make a distinction between security in the 'religious sector' in contrast to, say, political security or environmental security, this has to draw on some criteria, and I use here a relatively standard definition that religion involves a belief in (and some add: a communication or interaction with) supernatural beings or objects. This, however, means that 'religion talk' can be distinguished from, say, 'identity talk', not that the definition captures 'what religion is' or 'the essence of religion'.

9. Political twice: first, because 'secularism' as a general aspiration or idea has far-reaching implications through its general organizing principles of rationality/superstition, political/non-political, public/private, and this-worldly/other-worldly. Second, because, as I show later, there is not one standard form of secularism but numerous versions, and thus a choice of 'secularism' is always also a choice of one specific model to the exclusion of other ones.

10. My argument is not a plea to compromise on fundamental Western principles in order to dismantle a conflict. The West will gain too, because we in the West have imposed a limitation upon ourselves by cultivating a particularly narrow form of political rationality. In order to drive out religion from politics, everything with a hint of the existential or metaphysical has gone too. Most people experience in unofficial (e.g. private) political discussions that if pursued long enough, a big political issue engenders reflections or arguments of a general, principled or personal nature that cannot be articulated in e.g. a Parliament. The West could gain a richer and more productive political life by problematizing secularism, which, ironically, is the most sacred of all political principles in contemporary society.

References

Almond, G. A., Appleby, R. S. and Sivan, E. (2003) *Strong Religion: The Rise of Fundamentalisms around the World.* Chicago: University of Chicago Press.

Anonymous [Scheuer, M.] (2002) *Through Our Enemies' Eyes: Osama bin Laden, Radical Islam, and the Future of America.* Washington: Brasseys.

Appadurai, A. (2006) *Fear of Small Numbers: An Essay on the Geography of Anger.* Durham, NC: Duke University Press.

Arendt, H. (1968) *Men in Dark Times.* New York: Hartcourt.

Asad, T. (1993) *Genealogies of Religion: Discipline and Reasons of Power in Christianity and Islam.* Baltimore, MD: Johns Hopkins University Press.

—— (2003) *Formations of the Secular: Christianity, Islam, Modernity.* Stanford, CA: Stanford University Press.

—— (2006) 'Responses', in D. Scott and C. Hirschkind (eds), *Powers of the Secular Modern: Talal Asad and His Interlocutors.* Stanford, CA: Stanford University Press, pp. 206–41.

Banchoff, T. (forthcoming) *Embryo Politics: Debating Life in a Global Era.*

Berg-Sørensen, A. (2004) 'Paradiso – Diaspora: Reframing the Question of Religion in Politics'. PhD Dissertation, Institute of Political Science, University of Copenhagen.

Burleigh, M. (2005) *Earthly Powers: The Clash of Religion and Politics in Europe, from the French Revolution to the Great War.* New York: Harper Collins.

Butterfield, H. (1950) 'The Tragic Element in Modern International Conflict', *The Review of Politics,* 12(2): 147–64.

Buzan, B. and Wæver, O. (2003) *Regions and Powers: The Structure of International Security.* Cambridge: Cambridge University Press.

—— and de Wilde, J. (1998) *Security. A New Framework for Analysis.* Boulder: Lynne Rienner Publishers.

Casanova, J. (2003) 'Beyond European and American Exceptionalisms: Towards a Global Perspective', in G. Davie, P. Heelas and L. Woodhead (eds), *Predicting Religion: Christian, Secular and Alternative Futures*. Aldershot: Ashgate, pp. 17–29.

—— (2005) 'Immigration and the New Religious Pluralism: A EU/US Comparison', discussion draft for conference on 'The New Religious Pluralism and Democracy', 21–22 April 2005, sponsored by Georgetown University's Initiative on Religion, Politics, and Peace. http://irpp.georgetown.edu/conference.htm.

Clausewitz, C. von (1982 [1832]) *On War*. London: Penguin Books.

Connolly, W. E. (1995) *The Ethos of Pluralization*. Minneapolis, MN: University of Minnesota Press.

—— (1999) *Why I Am Not a Secularist*. Minneapolis, MN: University of Minnesota Press.

Davie, G., Heelas, P. and Woodhead, L. (eds) (2003) *Predicting Religion: Christian, Secular and Alternative Futures*. Aldershot: Ashgate.

Feldman, N. (2005) *Divided by God: America's Church – State Problem – and What We Should Do About It*. New York: Farrar, Strauss and Giroux.

Gerges, F. A. (1999) *America and Political Islam: Clash of Cultures or Clash of Interests?* Cambridge: Cambridge University Press.

—— (2005) *The Far Enemy: Why Jihad went Global*. Cambridge: Cambridge University Press.

—— (2006) *Journey of the Jihadis: Inside Muslim Militancy*. Orlando, FL: Harcourt.

Gunn, T. J. (2004) 'Religious Freedom and La: A Comparison of the United States and France', *Brigham Young University Law Review*, 2: 419–506.

Habermas, J. (2006) 'Religion in the Public Sphere', *European Journal of Philosophy*, 14(1): 1–25.

—— and Derrida, J. (2003) 'Nach dem Krieg: Die Wiedergeburt Europas', *Frankfurter Allgemeine Zeitung*, 31 May. (Appeared simultaneously in French as 'Europe: plaidoyer pour une politique étrangère commune', *Libération*, 30 May–1 June).

Hobbes, T. (1969 [1651]) *Leviathan*. Harmondsworth: Penguin Classics.

Hurd, E. S. (2001) 'Towards a Postsecular Alternative: Secularism and Political Islam in Historical and Relational Context', paper presented at the Middle East History and Theory Conference, The University of Chicago, May 2001.

—— (2004) 'The International Politics of Secularism: U.S. Foreign Policy and the Islamic Republic of Iran', *Alternatives*, 29(2): 115–38.

Juergensmeyer, M. (1993) *The New Cold War? Religious Nationalism Confronts the Secular State*. Berkeley, CA: University of California Press.

—— (2000) *Terror in the Mind of God: The Global Rise of Religious Violence*. Berkeley, CA: University of California Press.

—— (2004) 'Religious Terror and the Secular State', *Harvard International Review*, Winter.

Keppel, G. (1995) *The Revenge of God: The Resurgence of Islam, Christianity and Judaism in the Modern World*. London: Polity Press.

Kjølberg, A. (2003) *Når Religionen Blir Truet: Årsaker til og konsekvenser av islamistiske gruppers sikkerhetisering av religion*. Oslo: Forsvarets Forskningsinstitutt, FFI-rapport 2003/00330.

bin Laden, Osama (2005) *Messages to the World: The Statements of Osama bin Laden*, ed. B. Lawrence. London: Verso.

—— al-Zawahiri, A., Abu-Yasir Rifa'i Ahmad Taha, Mir Hamzah, S. and Rahman, F. (1998) *Second Declaration of Holy War: Jihad Against Jews and Crusaders*, Washingtonpost.com: Reprinted as 'Jihad Against Jews and Crusaders: World Islamic Front Statement' in Y. Alexander and M. S. Swetnam, *Usama bin Laden's al-Quaida: Profile of a Terrorist Network*. Ardsley: Transnational Publishers, 2001, Appendix 1 B; and in bin Laden 2005, pp. 58–62.

Laustsen, C. B. and Wæver, O. (2000) 'In Defence of Religion: Sacred Referent Objects for Securitization', *Millennium: Journal of International Studies*, 29(3): 705–39.

Madsen, B. B. and Ottosen, S. S. (2003) 'A Place for Religion? A Discourse Analysis of the Hindu Nationalist Staging of the Sacred City of Ayodhya'. MA thesis, Department of Political Science, University of Copenhagen.

Marty, M. E. and Appleby, R. S. (eds) (1995) *Fundamentalisms Comprehended*, Volume 5 of 'The Fundamentalism Project', sponsored by The American Academy of Arts and Sciences. Chicago: University of Chicago Press.

McCutcheon, R. T. (2003) 'The Category "Religion" and the Politics of Tolerance', *Religion and the Social Order*, 10: 139–62.

Mouritsen, Per (2006) 'The Particular Universalism of a Nordic Civic Nation: Common Values, State Religion and Islam in Danish Political Culture', in T. Modood, R. Zapata-Barrero and A. Triandafyllidou (eds), *Multiculturalism, Muslims and Citizenship*. London: Routledge, pp. 70–93.

Pew (2005) 'American Character Gets Mixed Reviews. U.S. IMAGE UP SLIGHTLY, BUT STILL NEGATIVE', *16-Nation Pew Global Attitudes Survey*, 23 June 23. http://pewglobal.org/reports/pdf/247.pdf.

Qutb, S. (2000) '"The America I Have Seen": In the Scale of Human Values' (1949), reprinted in Kamal Abdel-Malek, ed., *America in an Arab Mirror: Images of America in Arabic Travel Literature: An Anthology* (New York: Palgrave, 2000), pp. 9–28.

Riesebrodt, M. (1993) *Pious Passion: The Emergence of Fundamentalism in the United States and Iran*. Berkeley, CA and London: University of California Press.

Rorty, R. (1989) *Contingency, Irony, and Solidarity*. Cambridge: Cambridge University Press.

Ruthven, M. (2002) *A Fury for God: The Islamist Attack on America*. London: Granta Books.

Scheuer, M. (2002) – see Anonymous.

—— (2005 [2004]) *Imperial Hubris: Why the West Is Losing the War on Terror*. Washington: Potomac Books (with new epilogue).

Sheikh, M. K. (2005) 'Fear for Faith – Religion and Security Politics in Radical Islamism'. MA Thesis, Institute of Political Science, University of Copenhagen.

—— and Wæver, O. (2005) 'Lines in Water and Sand: Comparative Secularism as Analytical Tool for Conflict Containment', paper presented at the March 2005 International Studies Association Convention in Hawaii, USA. Revised version forthcoming in A. B. Tickner and O. Wæver (eds), *Inflections of the International: Geocultural Epistemologies, Volume II*.

Smith, W. C. (1991 [1962]) *The Meaning and End of Religion*. Augsburg: Fortress Publishers.

Wallis, J. (2005) *God's Politics: Why the Right Gets It Wrong and the Left Doesn't Get It*. San Francisco: Harper.

Wren, K. (2001) 'Cultural Racism: Something Rotten in the State of Denmark?', *Social and Cultural Geography*, 2(2): 141–62.

Wæver, O. (1995) 'Securitization and Desecuritization', in R. D. Lipschutz (ed.), *On Security*. New York: Columbia University Press, pp. 46–86.

—— (2006) 'Aviser og religioner i en globaliseret verden – dannelse og diplomati i Danmark', in L. Christoffersen (ed.), *Gudebilleder – Ytringsfrihed og religion i en globaliseret verden*. Copenhagen: Tiderne Skifter, pp. 181–208.

—— (forthcoming) 'What's Religion Got to Do with it? Terrorism, War on Terror and Global Security'. Keynote lecture at the Nordic Conference on the Sociology of Religion, under revision for *Nordic Journal of Religion and Society*.

—— Buzan, B. and de Wilde, J. (2007) *The Politics of Security: a Comprehensive Framework of Analysis*. Boulder: Lynne Rienner Publishers (follow-on edition to Buzan et al. 1998).

—— Buzan, B. and de Wilde, J. (forthcoming) *Politics of Security: A Comprehensive Framework of Analysis*. Boulder, CO: Lynne Rienner.

11
Nomadism and the Ghetto

Bülent Diken and Carsten Bagge Laustsen

> History is always written from the sedentary point of view and in the name of a unitary State apparatus, at least a possible one, even when the topic is nomads. What is lacking is a nomadology.
> (Deleuze and Guattari, 1987: 23)

Classical social theory and philosophy have focused predominantly on the life-forms of the settled. Indeed, both *Gesellschaft* and *Gemeinschaft*, the two basic concepts of social theory, express sedentary life-forms. So it is not surprising that the nomadic – that which is in movement – has been systematically excluded from the narrations of 'society' and 'community'. The basic antagonism that characterizes the constitution of 'the social' is, therefore, nomadic movement versus fixed territories, transgression versus the law, flow versus borders. The 'other' of society is, in other words, not 'community' but the nomad.

From this perspective, the history of civilization is a history of the ways in which the settled have tried to neutralize, territorialize and control nomadic movements, to slow them down. Who is the nomad, then? The nomad, in Deleuze and Guattari's definition, is that which escapes the law of the settled and its limitations. Above all, the nomad is defined by speed and deterritorialization: as deviation from norms, the law, territoriality and community.

The plight of the nomad – particularly in the figure of the modern migrant – shows us the real constitutive underside of the contemporary obsession with the creation or maintenance of a settled community of citizens, sharing a fixed set of accepted virtues, identities and culture. On the one hand, the nomad is seen to jeopardize the status, and to necessitate at all cost the consolidation of stable communities through processes of control. On the other hand, the nomad migrant also serves as the scapegoat other which helps us maintain the illusion of a fixed identity of the modern city.

The 'revenge of the nomads'

Foucault's *Discipline and Punish* (1977) describes the neutralization or normalization of the nomad with an emphasis on panoptic enclosure. The panopticon is a universal, virtual diagram of disciplinary enclosure that can be actualized in a diverse set of concrete contexts or institutions (see Bentham, 1995: 31–4). Thus Foucault describes disciplinary power as an 'anti-nomadic technique' that endeavours to 'fix' mobilities (1977: 215, 218). In Foucault's genealogy the premodern society was characterized by a technique of government, whose basic form was sovereignty. The sovereign demanded total obedience from his subjects and his most significant instrument of power was the threat of corporeal violence and, in extreme cases, death. Modernity, in contrast, was characterized by the use of disciplinary techniques for governing populations: as such, discipline needs independent subjects who can move through the institutions of civil society such as work, education, consumption. Significantly, these institutions were characterized by mutual delimitation: prisons, schools, hospitals, factories and the family constituted social spaces of enclosure, and one moved from one institution to another, often in a successive order: nursery, school, military service, labour market, marriage, and so on (Deleuze, 1995). This idea of territorial enclosure was seen by Foucault – and later by Deleuze – as the most significant characteristic of the disciplinary society.

Thus, in disciplinary society, the panopticon had become a symbol of engagement. Being 'a model of mutual involvement and confrontation between the two sides of the power relationship', the panopticon required the constant co-presence of power-holders and those subject to power (Bauman, 2000: 10). Consequently, both the disciplinary power and the disciplined subjects were territorially bound together within panoptic institutions, which made surveillance and control possible.

This is, however, changing. The distinction between societies of discipline and societies of control, in which power is nomadic, is illuminating. Deleuze claims that capitalism is no longer characterized by panoptic, place-bound discipline forcing people to overtake given subject positions, but by a permanent movement, in which the subject is always in a state of becoming. 'Control', he says, 'is short-term and rapidly shifting, but at the same time continuous and unbounded, whereas discipline was long-term, infinite and discontinuous' (Deleuze, 1995: 181). If the geography of discipline works in terms of fixed points or positions, control operates in terms of mobility, speed, flexibility, anonymity and contingent identities, in terms of 'the whatever' (Hardt, 1998: 32). The symptom of control society is the collapse of the institutional walls. But it is not the case that discipline ends with the deterritorialization of institutions. Rather, discipline, now freer than ever from territorial constraints, has become more immanent to the social field (Hardt and Negri, 2000). In control society subjectivity is 'produced simultaneously by numerous institutions in different combinations and doses'; hence social space tends to lose its delimitation: a person 'is factory worker outside the factory, student outside the school, inmate outside prison, insane outside the asylum – all at the same time. It belongs to no identity and all of them – outside the institutions but even more intensely ruled by their disciplinary logics' (Hardt and Negri, 2000: 331–2). In short, the territory of 'control society' is a nomadic territory.

It is precisely in this context that Bauman's definition of globalization as the 'revenge of the nomads' is interesting (2000: 12). This relates to a major change in relation to the development or nature of modernity and capitalism. We are experiencing today a new phase of modernity, 'liquid modernity', which is replacing 'solid modernity'. Solid modernity was itself characterized by a thorough disembedding. But, as Bauman argues, this took place only with a view to 're-embedding'; the panopticon was, above all, a tool for re-imbedding the melted solids. Disembedding through solid modernity had taken place predominantly to replace the inherited, defective solids, 'traditions' and other pre-modern social structures, with new, even more permanent solids (2000: 3). In other words, the logic of solid modernity was a simultaneous disembedding and re-embedding of social structures. In contrast, the logic of liquid modernity is disembedding without re-imbedding, deterritorialization without territorialization.

> Throughout the solid stage of the modern era, nomadic habits remained out of favour. Citizenship went hand in hand with settlement, and the absence of 'fixed address' and 'statelessness' meant exclusion. . . . While this still applies to the homeless and shifty 'underclass', which is subject to the old techniques of panoptical control (techniques largely abandoned as the prime vehicle of integrating and disciplining the bulk of the population), the era of unconditional superiority of sedentarism over nomadism and the domination of the settled over the mobile is on the whole grinding fast to a halt. We are witnessing the revenge of nomadism over the principle of territoriality

and settlement. In the fluid stage of modernity, the settled majority is ruled by the nomadic and exterritorial elite (Bauman, 2000: 13)

In a society dominated by nomads the threat is to be left, to remain fixed to the ground. Holders of power and those who are subordinate are no longer tied at the same point; common ground no longer exists. If in 'solid' modernity the panopticon had become a symbol of engagement, today's society nomadic power does away with engagement, that is, with the necessity of discipline. Instruments such as volatility, liquidity and speed make power free to move at short notice, while the walls of the institutions of the civil society are crumbling. Disengagement is no longer the outer limit of power relations, and uncertainty does not lead to conflict; they have both become effective strategies of power. Conflict requires relations; yet one side of the mutual (panoptic) relation opted out. Even worse, you cannot strike against an ex-territorial power that plays on absence rather than presence. Therefore the new game of domination is between the quicker and the slower, not between the bigger and the slower (2000: 188).

Bauman argues that contemporary power is able to 'travel light' (2000: 150–1). Domination belongs to those who can avoid uncertainty and externalize it onto others whose choices are constrained. It is about being in a position to flee. In liquid modernity, 'hit and run' is the logic that makes people obey, a logic that increases the security for the mobile elite, while insecurity increases for those who are immobile or who become immobilized. In a nutshell, we are today 'condemned to nomadism, at the very moment that we think we can make displacement the most effective means of subversion' (Virilio and Lotringer, 1997: 74). Significantly in this context, speed liberates global power from politics; whereas power belongs to the space of flows, politics remains 'hopelessly local' (Bauman, 1999: 19; see also Castells, 1996: 376–428). Power has become ex-territorial, yet politics remains territorial. In short, power is the power to disappear: a power that can sail away from the agora, from parliaments and beyond citizens' democratic control, disappearing into virtual space; a power whose strategic principle is 'escape, avoidance and disengagement, and [its] ideal condition is invisibility. . . . And so public space is increasingly empty of public issues' (Bauman, 2000: 40).

It is in this context that Bauman refers to Virilio's claim that speed is the 'end of geography' (see Bauman, 1998: 12). In the contemporary world real geography is to a large extent cancelled by the deterritorialized logic of flows (Virilio, 2000: 8; Castells, 1996). Power works according to the principle of mobility: the fast consume the slow (see Bauman, 2000: 188). Ours is a 'nomad capitalism' (Williams, 1989: 124); it justifies itself and advertises its products with reference to mobility – and a new capitalist discourse based on metaphors of mobility is emerging in business organizations, promoting the notion of a 'constant adaptive movement' and flexible organizational forms that can 'go with the flow' (Thrift, 1997: 38–9).

In a globalized world, characterized by the increasing mobility of both people and objects, mobility is 'a major, perhaps the paramount, factor of social stratification and the hierarchy of domination' (Bauman, 2000: 150–1). Hence the losers of mobility (and globalization) are those who are 'moved' in spite of their will or those who cannot move at all. As Lash and Urry express it, 'the new . . . underclass do not circulate but move. And they tend, with the occasional trip back to the country of origin, to stay' (Lash and Urry, 1994: 30). What characterizes this new 'underclass' inhabiting the 'periphery' is a stark deficit of social and physical mobility and, consequently, a deficit of reflexivity.

Hence there are emerging in today's mobile world society two distinct and contradictory topologies: the 'space of flows' and the 'space of places': a deterritorialized 'network society', in which power circulates through networks and flows, on the one hand, and politics and identity that remain territorial and immobile, on the other. They tend to exist in different time/spaces; 'they live by each other, but do not relate to each other' (Castells, 1996: 476). Together, the two kinds of spaces constitute a 'schizophrenic structure'. The space of flows operates according to a reticular logic, in which a 'network' is defined as a set of interrelated points and 'flow' (of subjects and objects) as that which moves between those points (see Castells, 1996: 376–428). Castells emphasizes that the distance between the nodal points of a network equals zero (e.g. it takes 'no time' to send an email to a distant wired place), whereas the distance between the network and that which is excluded from the network is infinite. That is, what is decisive in network society is inclusion in or exclusion from networking – in a nutshell, access.

The worst-case scenario is no longer one solely of exploitation or other forms of vertical inequality, but simply being redundant in relation to different networks and therefore the indifference of networks in relation to those who are made redundant. The redundant are reduced to territorially bounded life-forms. Whereas the network is globally connected and locally disconnected, a 'space of place', in contrast, is locally connected but globally disconnected. The 'place' in this sense signifies that which is excluded from the net, that which cannot flow. Mobility, though, is a relational concept: there is thus a schizophrenic relation at work between the deterritorialization of the elite and (re)territorialization of the locals (Castells, 1996).

The ambivalence of migration

What makes migration interesting in this context is, above all, its ambivalence in relation to globalization. While the situation of the migrants can be perceived to be rigid and fixed from the point of view of globalization, migrants are often perceived to be nomadic from the point of view of national politics. Let us elaborate: Udo Voight, the leader of the National Democratic Party in Germany, said once that attacks on foreigners are 'a responsibility of the established parties who continue to allow *uncontrolled flows of foreigners*' (*The Observer*, 6 August 2000, emphasis added). Here 'foreigners' obviously stand in for the mobile evil whose 'flows' destabilize the supposedly stable society. They, the 'nomads', enjoy in excessive, 'uncontrolled' ways, and the source of their enjoyment is of course *our* enjoyment, our welfare, which they steal from us. Is not the most popular image of welfare today something stolen or chronically under threat, something 'we' are determined to defend in 'fortress Europe'? The migrants are, so to speak, fighting on two fronts: against the nomadic elite and flows on the one hand, and against the settled locals and the 'solid' borders on the other.

Migration stimulates flows of people and thus it is part of globalization. At the same time the groups of migrants in the West are among those who are 'hit' hardest by globalization. This takes place against the background of deindustrialization and informationalization in the post-industrial society. When many unskilled jobs disappeared in the 1980s and 1990s many migrants became redundant as labour power with the consequence of a deficit of 'economic capital'. At the same time, their 'social capital', that is, their social networks and mobility, is limited. Their 'cultural capital' is characterized by a stark deficit in the form of lack of educational skills. And finally their 'symbolic capital', that is, their value and prestige in others' eyes, is the most problematic aspect in the light of ever-increasing racism and discrimination. The rather negative overall composition of different forms of deficit and the difficulties related to 'translating' different forms of capital into one another (e.g. translating education into a job) place the migrant at the bottom of the social hierarchy. As a result, the migrants are today one of the least mobile groups. Their physical as well as social mobility are limited. With the exception of summer holidays to 'home' countries, migrants do not move much. The majority stay in their ghettoes, which are increasingly emptied as better-off residents and important institutions move out.

Migrants are, in other words, among those who experience globalization as a moment of anxiety. Seen from their point of view, the flexibilized world of the networks is a world characterized by Bauman's '*Unsicherheit*' or Bourdieu's '*precarization*' (see Bauman, 2000: 135). Globalization is unavoidable and yet something against which they are powerless. *Unsicherheit* manifests itself in three forms: *uncertainty* related to social processes; *insecurity* related to lack of control over events; and *unsafety* related to the body. In face of these interrelated fears, which are all consequences of globalization, political institutions cannot do much, according to Bauman. A public space, an *agora*, where private fears can be translated into public, collective issues, does not really exist any more (Bauman, 1999: 6). While it is increasingly necessary to reinvent politics, the existing political institutions seem to concentrate on a single aspect of *Unsicherheit*:

> In a fast globalizing world, where a large part of power, and the most seminal part, is taken out of politics . . . institutions cannot do much to offer security or certainty. What they can do and what they more often than not are doing is to shift the scattered and diffusive anxiety to one ingredient of *Unsicherheit* alone – that of safety, the only field in which something can be done and seen to be done. (Bauman, 1999: 5)

Significantly, this search for *Sicherheit* goes hand in hand with scapegoating. Herein remains the most significant link between globalization, migration and national politics today. In this context it is telling that the ghetto itself is perceived to be a local phenomenon, as the spatial cause of social problems, which, in reality, result from globalization. The urban development in recent decades has been characterized by globalization. In such a system the single localities compete for participation in global communication and information networks. Consequently, a locality is 'ghettoized' if it cannot access such networks.

In the ghetto the discrepancy between globalization and local planning attempts is illustrated in an almost ironic way. Even though the ghetto is by and large a 'wild zone' regarding communication and information networks, many migrant families have relatively intense transnational relations, also compared to other population groups. Migrants hybridize cultures in their daily practice and increasingly develop transnational loyalties and interests.

There are thus practices and processes in the 'ghetto' that can only be perceived as anomalies if one does not consider new forms of socialities based on mobility. Today, network mobility is reshaping the relationship between physical and social proximity. The classical idea of community presupposes a sociality that requires both physical and social proximity,

yet increasing mobility enables social relationships in spite of geographical distance (Urry, 2000). Trying to deal with new mobile cultures in
terms of a rigid 'local district planning', the dominant form of planning
in the context of migration has important consequences: instead of perceiving the mobile aspects of the ghetto as resources in an age of globalization, such territorial policies often operate in terms of stereotypes and
therefore perceive hybridization and differentiation as a problem. Thus
migrants' transnational loyalties only signify a lack of assimilation or
integration, or even worse: a lack of will to assimilate/integrate. The relationship between 'us' and 'them', the network city and the ghetto, is,
however, more complex than it appears to be. Indeed, as we argue in the
following, 'we' cannot live *with* the ghetto, hence we see it as an anomaly,
but we cannot live *without* the ghetto and its migrant residents either.

The city and the ghetto

The city has a significantly fluid aspect: it behaves, in spite of numerous
attempts at planning, codifying or disciplining, as a flow, a flow of people
and things. It remains heterogeneous and ambivalent, which is why it is
both fascinating and anxiety-provoking. Therefore it seems as if we can
neither live with nor without flows. Capital and labour must circulate,
knowledge and signs must be mobilized more and more, tourists must be
attracted to heritage sites, and so on. Thus a lot is impossible *without* flows.
But we have at the same time problems *with* flows and are determined to
neutralize them. The politics of migration is perhaps the best example in
this context. It is a flow which provokes anxiety and symbolizes more than
anything else a movement – the ambivalent and the hybrid – because it
transgresses limits and 'contaminates' that which is imagined to be pure.
  Seen within the perspective of ambivalence, planning is often an
attempt at segregating the desired and undesired flows from one
another, a war waged against undesired flows. Planning is about clear-
cut borders to be able to 'tame' and channel the flows in desired directions. Consequently, the 'planned city' is first and foremost a reflection
of segregated structures and zones constructed by experts. On the map it
consists of differentiated zones, solid spatial units, each with its own
colour. These zones and units together constitute the topographical
whole called the 'city'. A centre, which guarantees clear-cut borders and
structures, which can avoid ambivalence and heterogeneity, is what the
'planned city' seeks above all.
  But in spite of the ambition of an unambivalent, easy-to-represent
'city', the order of the city remains fragile. What is excluded in rigid

representations returns as anomaly. While order itself produces ambivalence as its own excess – by codifying the (un)desired flows – there is always a remainder which escapes the legislator's panoptic gaze. As Deleuze and Guattari (1987: 207) are keen to emphasize, no power relation can be totally stabilized; something always escapes. Hence power centres (and cities) should be defined primarily by what escapes them. Whereas power seeks to territorialize the city as a conglomerate of more or less stable regions, there are always deterritorialized flows that transgress and destabilize them. Official technologies of governing the city (municipal planning) and the 'flows' of urban dwellers are thus antithetical: if the former associates to 'order', the latter associates to pure disorder and to spaces occupied by nomads.

What can be said about the identity of the 'city' in this context? Historically, the city has been imagined as an enclosed space surrounded by 'walls' demarcating the limits of inclusion and exclusion. Enclosure establishes a distinction between the polis and (the state of) nature. Yet the transition from the nature (the real) to the polis (the symbolic) is not clear and it is here we must look for the pre-ideological kernel of fantasies that sustain urban reality: 'in the fact that there is no reality without the spectre, that the circle of reality can be closed only by means of an uncanny spectral supplement' (Žižek, 1994: 21). Urban reality is not a thing in itself, but is always structured through symbolic mechanisms, and because this symbolization always ultimately fails, leaving part of reality non-symbolized, the unsymbolized Real 'returns in the guise of spectral apparitions' (Žižek, 1994: 21). Urban reality presents itself via its failed symbolization and it can never be a Whole. It is precisely this (w)hole in the 'urban' that is foreclosed through urban fantasies, and it is precisely through these fantasies that the Real returns in the form of an abject or object of desire, constructing a scheme in which the lack in the urban 'reality' (the symbolic order) can be filled and the city can be experienced as an imaginary whole with fixed coordinates.

In this, the logic of fantasy is necessarily nostalgic, and typically the wholeness of the city is depicted as lost or destroyed, stolen. The best examples are those discourses focused on the 'original' city. Neoclassicism and 'New Urbanism', for instance, look for the stability and order of a 'lost' city: the contemporary city lacks something, which modernism has destroyed, and that sublime 'something' is what, if not lost, would have given the city its identity. The question is of course whether the pre-modern city really had that order. The same retroactive mechanism was, ironically, also persistent in the pre-modern city, albeit in different forms. According to Sennett, for instance, when Venice entered its crisis in the eleventh century, its politicians created the scapegoat, the Jew, the phantasmatic identity which supposedly contaminated the morals of the city and led to social and economic crises. The fantasy created was: if the hole (in the symbolic incarnated by the Jew) did not exist, Venice would have been a whole city.

> The making of the Ghetto occurred at a crucial moment for Venice. The city leaders had lost a great advantage in trade, and suffered a crushing military defeat, a few years before. They blamed these losses largely on the state of the city's morals . . . from this moral campaign to reform the city came the plan for the Ghetto. By segregating those who were different, by no longer having to touch and see them, the city fathers hoped peace and dignity would return to their city. (Sennett, 1994: 216)

In other words, the symptom, the scapegoat, held Venice together; thanks to the Jew and the Jewish ghetto Venetians could imagine their city as a non-antagonistic unity. Likewise, the 'ghetto' as a fantasy space, symbolizes what is beyond the ambitions of planning, or what is the other of urban normality. It is the space that blocks the realization of urban development and integration; a 'contingent' space that hinders the urban order that would have been if the ghetto did not exist. What this fantasy hides is of course the 'ghetto', which is actively created as a 'necessary' effect and affect of urban development, as an excess of the urban order itself. What fantasy hides is, in other words, that 'we' ourselves have created that. The ghetto as a fantasy space thus serves as an image of a chaotic space, an archaic state of nature, beyond 'our' space and time, thus beyond our responsibility: the space of secret enjoyment (idolized networks, sexual perversions, etc.) or of the absence of law (crime, repression, etc.).

The ghetto is an anti-thesis, it is what we fantasize the city is not, and precisely that is why the ghetto not only interrupts but also participates actively in the construction of the urban reality. Thanks to the ghetto, we can imagine a non-antagonistic, non-chaotic city in harmony: as a fantasy space the ghetto gives the city an identity. Thus a radical position in the ghetto debate is to say that the ghetto does not exist: the city is always already antagonistic, the city is an antagonism that can only be united through fantasy. The ghetto is the symptom of the postulated identity of the city. And if the symptom dissolves, the imaginary unity of the city cannot be sustained. The city is always already antagonistic. The city *is* an antagonism, which can be overseen only through the fantasy.

Disneyland

Baudrillard (1988) claimed once that Disneyland was built to create the illusion of an illusion. With Disneyland it became possible to imagine that the outside of Disneyland was real. But in reality the outside, the rest of the US itself, is a Disneyland – a simulacrum. So to speak, Disneyland is the 'real' US. The migrants have the same function: they are an instance of hyper-realization, which creates the illusion that the 'rest' is genuine and harmonious. This simulation of the ethnic identity paradoxically illustrates the lack of an origin; the construction of the migrant identity basically functions to stop the flow, to give a fluctuating desire a direction, or, to territorialize a culture without coordinates.

The phantasmatic construction of the migrant creates the illusion that a stable identity really exists. National identity sought in this way is, paradoxically, always already a lost identity. The national essence is always a simulacrum, a construction, which hides the fact that there is no organic, substantial unity in identity, that it only exists in fantasy. What makes it possible to define what is 'specifically' national, and hence to avoid the traumatic confrontation with the fact that national identity (Englishness, Danishness, and so on), does not exist (without reference to the symptom, e.g. the migrant). We seek to hide our lack (of identity) by constructing the migrant as the one who has stolen what could have been the kernel of our identity from us.

> Why does the Other remain Other? What is the cause of our hatred of him? . . . It is hatred of the enjoyment in the Other. This would be the most general formula of the modern racism we are witnessing today: a hatred of the particular way the Other enjoys. . . . the Other as he who essentially steals my own enjoyment. (Jacques-Alain Miller, quoted in Žižek, 1993: 203)

It goes without saying that the nomadic character of identity can be denied in the same way. The projection of the lack onto the migrants/ strangers is an attempt to deny our own decentring, an attempt at fixating a desire, whose primary form is a flow. We define our own normality in relation to the strangers' transgression of its limits. Our 'normality' is thus juxtaposed to the 'perversion' the migrant symbolizes. In short, in the confrontation between 'us' and 'them' there is something decisive at work. This lack has nothing to do with the migrants (e.g. their 'lack of will to integrate'), but rather it relates to a fundamental lack in identity. A lack which can only be localized in 'our' will to identity, in our desire for a centre that holds. And it is precisely this lack we desperately try to mask and cultivate through the fantasies on migrants.

We imagine that migrants have a special secret, something sublime, which we ourselves lack. But the point is, of course, that the migrants have no secret. It is therefore not primarily necessary to 'uncover' truths or untruths in the migration debate and to show, for instance, how they 'really are'. Thus, again, the most radical response to essentialism prevailing in the discourse of migration is to say that the migrants do not exist: they do not have a secret, homogeneous identity or culture corresponding to *our* fantasies about *them* – which is also the very reason we are afraid of them. Thus, as Slavoj Žižek nicely puts it, Freud's answer to the threat of Fascist anti-Semitism was to endeavour to prove that Moses, the founding father of the Jewish identity, was Egyptian, that is, the Jews were not the chosen people and their identity was 'decentred' in its origins.

> Notwithstanding the historic (in)accuracy of this thesis, what really matters is its discursive strategy: to demonstrate that Jews were already in themselves 'decentered', that their 'originality' is a bricolage. The difficulty does not reside in Jews but in the transference of the anti-Semite who thinks that Jews 'really possess it', *agalma*, the secret of their power: the anti-Semite is the one who 'believes in the Jew', so the only way effectively to undermine anti-Semitism is to contend that *Jews do not possess 'it'*. (Žižek, 1993: 220–1)

Let us, at this point, emphasize that fantasies bring with them a fixation of identities (of both 'them' and 'us'), which does not easily dissolve through 'rational' debate or enlightenment. On the contrary, such debate often contributes to the sedimentation and further fixation of cultural identities. Therefore, what is necessary is a re-evaluation and analysis of the basic assumptions and taken-for-granted aspects of the debate rather than debating migrants, integration and so on further, the most radical position in the debate being, again, to say that the 'migrants do not exist'.

But even though the migrant does not exist, there exist many problems within the field of migration. One could, for instance, focus on how the economic system could become more receptive to migrant labour that is in many cases considered to be redundant or excluded. Or one could put the political system under focus and investigate the possibilities of political participation – after all, many migrants in Europe do no not have the right to vote in national elections, which determine their life-chances. And what about education? Why is it the case in many European countries that more and more migrants acquire education and at the same time more and more of them are unemployed?

The problem is that today an underclass is being created which is simultaneously excluded from several systems and networks, an underclass, characterized by an overall deficit in their composition of economic, social, cultural and, above all, symbolic capital. Which is exactly what is not raised in the 'culturalist' discussions on migration. Instead of discussing structural issues related to the functioning of the contemporary systems and networks, the 'culture' of migrants is elevated to the cause of being excluded from these systems and networks. Which is also why it might be strategically necessary to refer to the migrant even though s/he does not exist.

How can we then relate to the other if not within a culturalist discourse? There is no easy way out here in so far as an ethics of this encounter on the one hand must acknowledge that the other is different, and on other must erase this difference in order to welcome the other as one amongst equals. The other does exist: there are plenty of problems related to migration and foreigners. But the culturalist framework in which these problems are dealt with force us to claim the exact opposite: that the migrant does not exist. Perhaps a way out of this dilemma is not to dissolve it but to turn it around. Instead of addressing the migration question one can use this question to question oneself and one's way of relating to the other. In this sense the migrant question becomes the question of the question, the question which questions me, or simply put the question of ethics.

Hospitality

> Ethics is the question of care for the other, a question of welcoming the other, of hosting him or her. But hospitality is not an ethics amongst others. One is mistaken if one sets out to cultivate *an* ethics of hospitality. Insofar as it has to do with the *ethos*, that is, the residence, one's home, the familiar place of dwelling, inasmuch as it is a manner of being there, the manner in which we relate to ourselves and to others, to others as our own or as foreigners, ethics is hospitality; ethics is so thoroughly coextensive with the experience of hospitality. (Derrida, 2001: 16–17)

This ethics is a matter of enabling openings and recognition (Dikeç, 2002: 229). Opening towards and recognition of the other. Ethics is thus a question of relationships, of relating differently, without following the path of sovereignty and abandonment. The subject is, to paraphrase

Levinas, simultaneously host and hostage. Subject *for* the other, the one who welcomes him, the one who resides over the home, but also subject *of* the one who is exposed to the other and put into question by the other's very being. The other (the refugee, the stranger or just simply the neighbour) is the one who begs for hospitality in a language which is not his own. And herein consists an unavoidable act of violence. In determining the other as stranger, the conditionality of family, nation, state and citizenship is already presupposed (Derrida, 2000b: 8). Thus the other is subjected to the laws of the visiting country, the rules of hospitality. The foreigner must accept that his host is the master (Derrida, 2000a: 15). Hence the tension, the double bind, inscribed at the heart of hospitality: hospitality is a right, a duty and an obligation, but at the same time is conditioned by the host, who opens his home. The law of hospitality is the law of the household, the law of place: house, hotel, hospital, hospice, family, city, nation, language. It is a law of space, which delimits the place and time of hospitality, which thus turns to be a conditioned gift (Derrida, 2000b: 4).

The border crossed is between 'the familial and the non-familial, between the foreign and the non-foreign, the citizen and the non-citizen, but first of all between the private and the public, private and public law, etc.' (Derrida, 2000a: 49). What marks this border between inside and outside, familiar and foreign, is the door, an opening towards the other and towards infinity (Derrida, 1999: 26). There can be no habitable home without openings, without doors and windows that allow passage to the outside. No society without nomads and nomadism. On the other hand, if there is a door, there will no longer be unconditional hospitality. Sovereignty is exactly the ability to close the door, to abandon a subject. If there is a door there will also be a key and someone holding this key. Hence the distinction between visitation (with key) and invitation (without key), between entering (lacking a key) and coming (having one's own key), and between conditional and unconditional hospitality, a distinction between hospitality as it exposes itself to the visit, to the visitation, and the hospitality that adorns and prepares itself in invitation (Derrida, 2000a: 61; 2000b: 14; 2002b: 362).

As Bauman (1995: 18) argues using Lévi-Strauss's concepts, there are two predominant strategies of dealing with the stranger. One is anthropophagic and aims at assimilating the stranger's strangerhood; the other is anthropoemic and aims at banishing, excluding the stranger. Eating up versus vomiting. The question never raised by either strategy is being *for*, what we can do for the stranger. Rather, today the figure of the stranger arouses fear, hospitality has become subject to the possession of passports, bank statements and invitation letters. Further, the pretext of combating 'bogus refugees' or economic migrants constantly denigrates the status of the strangers as something unwanted. Indeed, hospitality has become a crime, as is the case when people hide foreigners whose applications of asylum have been rejected. 'What becomes of a country, one must wonder, what becomes of a culture, what becomes of a language when it admits of a "crime of hospitality," when hospitality can become, in the eyes of the law and its representatives, a criminal offense?' (Derrida, 2002a: 133).

Hospitality is self-contradictory and can only destroy itself, it is a concept defined by its very impossibility, by a non-dialectizable antinomy. It deconstructs the very idea of being at home and as such of the self and its other (Derrida, 2002b: 364). On the one hand the unconditional imperative principle of radical hospitality, a hyperbolic principle, which defies all laws and identities, and on the other all the innumerable conditions (see Derrida, 2000a: 77). There is a plight to question the authority of the logos and ethnos. But the tension is not only one between the host and the other exposed to the welcoming gesture. The host has to keep within the laws of hospitality and transgress them, and so does the guest. Hospitality must never simply be a duty, a law. One must welcome without the 'must' (Derrida, 2002b: 361).

What is significant in terms of ethics is the demand for developing hospitality into a culture of hospitality, to 'multiply the signs of anticipation, construct and institute what one calls the structure of welcoming, a welcoming apparatus' (Derrida, 2002b: 360–1). Even in keeping within the law of unconditional hospitality one needs laws to make it effective and to avoid the risk of becoming an abstract, utopian and illusory idea (Derrida, 2000a: 79). Ethics, and thus hospitality, is not just a matter of the two, of the self and the other. There is, as Levinas stressed, always 'a third'. One cannot give all to the other, for there will always come another. A sort of mediation is thus necessary and in this respect the third is the beginning of justice as law. The exterior of the third will however always disturb the relation of the two. There can be no ethics without perjury (Derrida, 1999: 29–33). The other is the birth of the question, not just of ethics, but also of the subject itself. The other brings the subject into question. Ethics is thus not just a question of the other, but also a self-questioning. Ethics, in short, urges a reversal: the one who invites becomes the invited; the one who gives receives. Ethics demands a constant process of engagement and role exchange; a constant becoming, a becoming in question.

Why are there so many becomings of man, but no becoming-man? First because man is a majoritarian par excellence, whereas becomings are minoritarian; all becoming is a becoming-minoritarian. When we say majority, we are referring not to a greater relative quantity but to the determination of a state or standard in relation to which larger quantities, as well as the smallest, can be said to be minoritarian: white-man, adult-male, etc. Majority implies a state of domination, not the reverse . . . It is important not to confuse 'minoritarian', as a becoming or process, with a 'minority' as an aggregate or a state. Jews, Gypsies, etc., may constitute minorities under certain conditions, but that in itself does not make them becomings. One reterritorializes, or allows oneself to be reterritorialized, on a minority as a state; but in a becoming, one is deterritorialized. Even blacks, as the Black Panthers said, must become-black. Even women must become-women. Even Jews must become-Jewish . . . As Faulkner said, to avoid ending up a fascist there was no other choice than to become-black. (Deleuze and Guattari, 1987: 291–2)

References

Baudrillard, J. (1988) *America*. London: Verso.
Bauman, Z. (1995) *Life in Fragments*. Oxford: Blackwell.
_____ (1998) *Globalization. The Human Consequences*. New York: Columbia University Press.
_____ (1999) *In Search of Politics*. Cambridge: Polity Press and Blackwell.
_____ (2000) *Liquid Modernity*. Cambridge: Polity Press.
Bentham, J. (1995) *The Panopticon Writings*. London: Verso.
Castells, M. (1996) *The Information Age. Volume I: The Rise of Network Society*. Oxford: Blackwell.
_____ (1998) *The Information Age. Volume III: End of Millennium*. Oxford: Blackwell.
Deleuze, G. (1995) *Negotiations*. New York: Columbia University Press.
_____ and Guattari, F. (1987) *A Thousand Plateaus. Capitalism and Schizophrenia II*. Minneapolis and London: University of Minnesota Press.
Derrida, J. (1999) *Adieu to Emmanuel Levinas*. Stanford, CA: Stanford University Press.
_____ (2000a) *Of Hospitality. Anne Dufourmantelle invites Jacques Derrida to Respond*. Stanford, CA: Stanford University Press.
_____ (2000b) 'Hospitality', *Angelaki*, 5(3): 3–18.
_____ (2001) *Cosmopolitanism and Forgiveness*. London: Routledge.
_____ (2002a) *Negotiations*. Stanford, CA: Stanford University Press.
_____ (2002b) *Acts of Religion*. London: Routledge.
Dikeç, M. (2002) 'Pera Peras Poros. Longings for Spaces of Hospitality', *Theory, Culture & Society*, 19(1–2): 227–47.
Foucault, M. (1977) *Discipline and Punish*. London: Penguin Books.
Hardt, M. (1998) 'The Withering of Civil Society', in E. Kaufman and K. J. Heller (eds), *Deleuze and Guattari. New Mappings in Politics, Philosophy, and Culture*. Minneapolis. MN: University of Minnesota Press.

_____ and Negri, A. (2000) *Empire*. London: Cambridge University Press.

Lash, S. and Urry, J. (1994) *Economies of Signs and Space*. London: Sage.

Sennett, R. (1994) *Flesh and Stone*. London: Faber and Faber.

Thrift, N. (1997) 'The Rise of Soft Capitalism'. *Cultural Values*, 1(1): 29–57.

Urry, John (2000) *Sociology Beyond Societies. Mobilities for the Twenty-First Century*. London: Routledge.

Virilio, P. (2000) 'The Kosovo War Took Place in Orbital Space'. John Armitage's interview with Paul Virilio, *CTHEORY, Theory, Technology and Culture*, 23(3), Article 89.

_____ and S. Lotringer (1997) *Pure War*. Semiotex(e). New York: Columbia University Press.

Williams, R. (1989) *Resources of Hope*. London: Verso.

Žižek, S. (1993) *Tarrying With the Negative. Kant, Hegel, and the Critique of Ideology*. Durham, NC: Duke University Press.

_____ (1994) 'Introduction. The Spectre of Ideology', in S. Žižek (ed.), *Mapping Ideology*. London: Verso, pp. 1–33.

Index